To John
   For B
Wonderful friend - for
giving so much of your
life to the cause of
philanthropy, and for
being an important part
the positive evolution of
key organizations in
this field. I'm very proud
of you.

                    Jack 12/23/93

Modern American Philanthropy

Other Titles in the Nonprofit Law, Finance, and Management Series

Charity, Advocacy, and the Law by Bruce R. Hopkins

Financial and Accounting Guide for Not-for-Profit Organizations, Fourth Edition by Malvern J. Gross, Jr., William Warshauer, Jr., and Richard F. Larkin

Fund-Raising: Evaluating and Managing the Fund Development Process by James M. Greenfield

A Guide to Real Estate Development for Nonprofit Organizations by Bennett L. Hecht

The Law of Fund-Raising by Bruce R. Hopkins

The Law of Tax-Exempt Organizations, Sixth Edition by Bruce R. Hopkins

A Legal Guide to Starting and Managing a Nonprofit Organization, Second Edition by Bruce R. Hopkins

Modern American Philanthropy: A Personal Account by John J. Schwartz

The Nonprofit Counsel by Bruce R. Hopkins

Nonprofit Litigation: A Practical Guide with Forms and Checklists by Steve Bachmann

The Nonprofit Management Handbook: Operating Policies and Procedures by Tracy Daniel Connors

Partnerships and Joint Ventures Involving Nonprofit Organizations by Michael I. Sanders

Tax Planning and Compliance for Tax-Exempt Organizations: Forms, Checklists, Procedures, Second Edition by Jody Blazek

The Tax Law of Charitable Giving by Bruce R. Hopkins

The United Way Scandal: An Insider's Account of What Went Wrong and Why by John S. Glaser

Modern American Philanthropy
A Personal Account

John J. Schwartz

John Wiley & Sons Inc.
New York • Chichester • Brisbane • Toronto • Singapore

This text is printed on acid-free paper.

Copyright © 1994 by John Wiley & Sons, Inc.

All rights reserved. Published simultaneously in Canada.

Reproduction or translation of any part of this work beyond that permitted by Section 107 or 108 of the 1976 United States Copyright Act without the permission of the copyright owner is unlawful. Requests for permission or further information should be addressed to the Permissions Department, John Wiley & Sons, Inc., 605 Third Avenue, New York, NY 10158-0012.

This publication is designed to provide accurate and authoritative information in regard to the subject matter covered. It is sold with the understanding that the publisher is not engaged in rendering legal, accounting, or other professional services. If legal advice or other expert assistance is required, the services of a competent professional person should be sought.

Library of Congress Cataloging in Publication Data
Schwartz, John J., 1919–
    Anatomy of American philanthropy : a personal account / John J. Schwartz.
      p. cm. — (Nonprofit law, finance, and management series)
    Includes Index.
    ISBN 0-471-59283-8
    1. Charities—United States—History—20th century. I. Title. II. Series.
HV91.S296   1993
361.7'0973—dc20   93-5464

Printed in the United States of America
10 9 8 7 6 5 4 3 2 1

DEDICATION

I dedicate this book to two special individuals. First, John W. Gardner, founding Chairman of Common Cause and INDEPENDENT SECTOR. John's wisdom and leadership qualities guided the path to many improvements in the effectiveness and general understanding of American philanthropy. With persistence, care and creativity, he inspired actions that brought out the best in many of us. We and philanthropy owe him an eternal debt of gratitude.

And secondly, Katharine S. "Katy" Schwartz, my only blind date, who became my wife a month after Pearl Harbor. For 51 years she has watched over me with love and loyalty. Her patient support and encouragement enhanced my life and my career. Without her this book could not have been written.

ACKNOWLEDGMENTS

As a neophyte, I needed help to attempt this book. From the early planning stages on, Marla J. Bobowick, acquisitions editor of John Wiley & Sons, Inc., guided me with professional counsel, caring, gentle prodding, friendship, and encouragement. Rose Kernan, as development editor, helped immeasurably to make it better organized and more coherent. And, they both did their best to refine my stumbling prose and busted syntax—a job that took admirable dedication. Thank you for being good friends and making my job doable.

I will always be grateful to Glenn Alan Cheney, Professor of Writing at Fairfield University, whose classes helped me to gain a better sense of creative nonfiction and the confidence to keep trying. And last, my thanks to all in the Georgetown Group, a writers workshop that often cut my efforts into little pieces, but conducted their tough critiques with respect and affection. (The hardest part was to obey the rules and keep absolutely quiet for 45 minutes during the critiques.) They helped to give me a better perspective on this book which I have always wanted to write.

PREFACE

The Problems And Promise Of Philanthropy

It's not easy to understand. Even though Americans contributed $124.3 billion to charities in 1992—a 16-fold increase since 1955—few people seem to know what philanthropy really is. In part, this may be because we have yet to develop a good definition of all it entails. Philanthropy's five main components are donors, donees, volunteers, enablers (fund-raising professionals), and, most importantly, the voluntary spirit. The total value of these things is greater than the sum of their parts.

A total of 89.5 percent of all charitable giving still comes from individuals. This figure reveals that the philanthropic process has made a tremendous impact on our society. But despite this progress, the unsettling fact remains that philanthropy is in a crisis. During the 1989 celebration of the sesquicentennial of John D. Rockefeller's birth, David Rockefeller clearly stated the problem:

> The world is at a critical juncture. Democratic values are spreading; voluntary associations are filling the vacuum created by the ideological and political failure of government; the possibilities for new forms of cooperation and partnership among business, foundations, and government are very promising. But philanthropy is unable, at the moment, to respond adequately to these challenges. The spirit of philanthropy is alive and well and growing, but the substance of philanthropy is inadequate to the tasks before it.

The gap between needs and resources increases daily. The current economic climate, combined with such critical issues as AIDS, the homeless, escalating medical costs, inadequate education facilities, and the drug crisis, make it impossible for philanthropy's limited resources to resolve society's pressing and growing needs. Government participation seems bent more on regulation than on funding its share; in addition, the public has grown more skeptical, questioning the stewardship, effectiveness, and the credentials of nonprofit board members, especially in the wake of the 1992 scandal of excesses perpetuated by the president of the United Way of America.

Philanthropy's programs need more effort, more participation, and more support in order to meet society's growing needs. Consequently, as we approach the 21st century, society's growing problems must be addressed. The key difficulties faced by those of us in the field are outlined below.

THERE NEEDS TO BE MORE GIVING

George A. Brakeley Jr. founder of Brakeley, John Price Jones Co., Inc., one of the leading fund-raising counseling firms, wrote about "The Uninvited Billions." His thesis: Most Americans can and should give much more to philanthropic programs than they do. But to achieve this they must be better cultivated by nonprofit organizations and, of paramount importance, they must be asked. Harold J. "Si" Seymour said it best:

> No campaign ever fails because too many people say no. They fail when not enough people are asked.[1]

More must be done to improve the public's understanding of and respect for both the philanthropic process and fund-raising.

GOOD LEADERS ARE SCARCE

To help philanthropy become more effective, we need to enlist, train, and involve the next generation of leaders now. We need to inculcate in the younger generation the wisdom and experience of the older generation. The inadequate representation of minorities in the nonprofit sector needs serious attention. To solve this problem, philanthropic studies should be incorporated in *all* levels of education. We need to demonstrate that not only are there viable professional careers in this

---

1. Seymour, Harold J. *Designs For Fund-Raising,* McGraw-Hill Book Company (1966).

field, but that a career in the nonprofit sector invokes a sense of fulfillment, a feeling of making a difference, and an opportunity for both professional and personal growth.

PARTNERSHIP WITH GOVERNMENT

Philanthropy's relationships not only with state and federal legislators, but with those who have so much influence in setting their agendas (i.e., the administrative staffs) leave much to be desired. We are a pluralistic society. As such, programs which help society are best accomplished through a partnership between the private sector and government. A major program to educate government leaders is needed to emphasize the importance of philanthropy and to show that improving its effectiveness can't be done with punitive legislation and reduced tax incentives.

DEALING WITH PAROCHIALISM

John W. Gardner, founding chair of Common Cause and INDEPENDENT SECTOR, states, "We must do all we can to reduce parochialism." Unless we can open up more communications between donors and donees and the variety of nonprofit organizations for causes such as health care, education, the arts, advocacy, environment, minority and church groups, human services, and international philanthropy; the tendency for each group to protect only its own unique considerations will continue to inhibit progress. We must recognize that all nonprofits share philanthropy's concerns and working together is the only effective way to deal with them.

BOARD AND EXECUTIVE RESPONSIBILITIES

As highlighted by the 1992 United Way controversies about excessive executive salaries and benefits, measures are urgently needed to bring nonprofit boards face to face with their responsibilities. At least, these should include a genuine enthusiasm for the mission of the organization, the necessary time and energy to perform board duties, and accountability and support for policies of efficient management. Everyone in the field of philanthropy should have both a strong set of ethics and a pride in their unselfish and altruistic motives. (Those who don't rarely stay in the field very long.)

The mission of any philanthropic organization is primary to the cause and should never become secondary to personal gains. Philanthropy, by its very nature, has great integrity, although it has not yet become a rallying point or an official criterion. Setting and adopting a universal code of ethics will help to prove the commitment of the field, unite its disparate and conflicting elements, and diminish current public skepticism.

The salaries and benefits of executives of major nonprofit organizations are made possible by contributed funds. This is a point which must never be forgotten. While these individuals in today's competitive market must be well paid, they should never aspire to the pay level of executives in similar positions in the for-profit sector. To ensure this principle, there should be standards and ranges set for executive salaries and benefits.

INTERNATIONAL PHILANTHROPY

Philanthropy in America is much more advanced than in most other countries, especially those in the Third World. We need to join forces to share and disseminate our rich experience and proven techniques which have been developed over the past century. Our learned knowledge should be exported to help make international philanthropy and voluntarism more effective.

THE STRENGTH OF VOLUNTARISM

The voluntary spirit must continue to dominate. This has become even more important in the midst of a growth trend toward the adoption of promotion techniques used by the for-profit business community. Telemarketing and sophisticated direct-mail solicitations help nonprofit organizations expand their donor bases, but they are impersonal and do little to involve donors with the cause. Nor do these methods raise nearly as much money as volunteers soliciting on a face-to-face basis.

Cause-related marketing during the 1980s raised millions for the U.S. Olympic Committee and over $36 million for the Statue of Liberty campaign. In such an arrangement, the corporate partner can charge all costs as business expenses, expand its market and improve its public image. The charity receives funds without much effort, but such partnerships are invariably limited only to well-known national charities. At a time when corporate giving is stagnant, this process can invite skepticism by corporate board members (who often are only interested in profits) on why there should even be a corporate giving program. We must remind ourselves that cause-related marketing is *not* philanthropy. Nor is it a substitute for the philanthropic process. Without people to represent your cause, results will be limited and temporal.

Si Seymour said it so well:

> Every cause . . . needs people more than money. For when the people are with you and are giving your cause their attention, interest, confidence, advocacy and service, financial support should just about take care of itself. Whereas without them—in the right quality and quantity, in the right places, and the right states of mind and spirit—you might as well go and get lost.[2]

WHAT OF PHILANTHROPY'S FUTURE?

The field is becoming progressively more challenging, complicated, and competitive. This can best be met by increasing the level of professionalism of nonprofit executives, fund-raising managers, and program officers of foundations and corporations. A single universal certification process for fund-raising managers is one step deserving consideration.

On a more positive note, there are some encouraging developments in philanthropy. At last, academia has begun to take it seriously. Donors and donees communicate with each other, share seminars and even cooperate in discussions on the apportioning of scarce resources. There is training and coordination between the various sectors of philanthropy on fund-raising, board responsibilities, and management. Several sets of ethical standards are established and respected. Many courses in and out of academia are available and the number of qualified young persons entering the field is growing.

This book is an effort to examine how this measurable improvement has come about. We must ask ourselves how long has it been this way, and does this mean that philanthropy is thriving so well that it will become effective enough to meet society's expanding needs? If so, what of its future?

---

2. *Ibid.*, p. ix

The many changes in American philanthropy since World War II need to be documented. Recounting the important events and identifying the influential people who aided in a remarkable, on-going evolution will help to increase the public understanding of this complex field. Over the past 48 years my job and volunteer assignments have involved me in many activities that have helped to change and improve American philanthropy. In the pursuit of these tasks, I have experienced trials of patience, some pain, and a good measure of pleasure and pride. Working with people whose vision and leadership made things happen has been a constant inspiration. Now, using my lifetime experiences, I will relate how philanthropy has evolved and identify some key lessons which can be used as guidelines for planning a productive future.

This book is in two sections. The first section covers the years of 1946 to 1966, during which I served as a fund-raising director for five nonprofit organizations and two professional fund-raising firms. My experiences will help to show the encouraging growth of professionalism and public acceptance of the fund-raising profession. Key fund-raising tips are indicated wherever appropriate.

The second section covers the period of 1966 to 1990, when a major portion of my time and duties were focused on working with the leadership of key national nonprofit organizations. The main agenda for this period was to strengthen the relationships and the cooperative efforts within the entire philanthropic field. The shared concerns were identified, studied, and recognition of the need to join forces to strengthen the philanthropic process gained substantial ground. Philanthropy's critical issues are recorded at the appropriate points.

John J. Schwartz
Westport, Connecticut

CONTENTS

Prologue	The Maturing of American Philanthropy: A Personal Account	xix

SECTION 1: 1946–1966
Fund-Raising Management Becomes More Professional

Chapter 1	After World War II—The Rebuilding	3
	The Metropolitan Museum of Art	4
	The Legendary John Price Jones	6
	The Medical and Surgical Relief Committee	8
	Community Service Society	10
	Grove City College	12
	Lessons Learned	16
Chapter 2	The Fabulous Fifties—Reaching for the American Dream	18
	Norwalk Hospital, Connecticut	20
	The Traveler's Aid Society	23
	The Community Service Society	27
	The Near East Foundation	31
	Lessons Learned	37
Chapter 3	The Sixties—The Increasing Competition and the Challenge to Improve Professionalism	39
	Early Fund-Raising Associations	40
	G. A. Brakeley & Co., Inc.	42
	The International Schools Foundation	43
	Syracuse University	44
	The Foreign Policy Association	48
	The American Cancer Society	51
	The American Association of Fund-Raising Counsel, Inc.	54
	Lessons Learned	55

SECTION 2: 1966–1992
American Philanthropy Gets Its Act Together

Chapter 4	The Sixties Continued—Fund-Raising Influences All of Philanthropy	59

	The American Association of Fund-Raising Counsel (AAFRC)	60
	The 1967 East West Conference	68
	Branching Out: The 501(c)(3) Group	71
	The National Council on Philanthropy	73
	Giving USA and AAFRC Public Relations	73
	1968 East-West Conference	74
	The Peterson Commission (The Commission on Foundations and Private Philanthropy)	75
	The Tax-Reform Act of 1969	79
	Lessons Learned	81
Chapter 5	The Early Seventies—A Time of Burgeoning Efforts to Bring Together Most Elements of Philanthropy	83
	The 1970 AAFRC East-West Conference	85
	Personnel Changes at the AAFRC	86
	Ford Foundation Seminar for Educational Interns 1969–1972	87
	Institute for Educational Management, Harvard Business School	89
	The Campaign for Philanthropy, 1971	91
	The Effect of Taxes on Charitable Giving, 1971–1973	94
	The 1973 Tax Reform Act	95
	The National Institute of Continuing Education (NICE)	96
	Lessons Learned	97
Chapter 6	Philanthropy Enters a New Threshold	98
	The Evolution of the Filer Commission	98
	The Role of John D. Rockefeller III	99
	Funding the Filer Commission	101
	The Donee Group	106
	Lessons Learned—Major Recommendations of the Filer Commission	110
Chapter 7	Post-Filer Commission Activities—A Gathering of Forces	114
	National Council of Philanthropy Conference, 1975	116
	Prospectus for a Private Commission on Philanthropy, 1976	117
	Coalition of National Voluntary Organizations, 1976	118

CONTENTS

	Tax Reform Proposals, 1977	121
	Congressional Efforts to Regulate Charities, 1977–1978	123
	AAFRC State Legislation Monitoring Program, 1976–1979	125
	New Efforts to Get Philanthropy's Act Together	126
	White House Conference on Voluntarism, September 1979	132
	Charter Meeting of INDEPENDENT SECTOR, March 1980	133
	J. C. Geever, Inc.	133
	Lessons Learned	134
Chapter 8	Entering the Eighties—Improving Compatibility and Growing Professionalism	136
	The National Charities Information Bureau (NCIB)	139
	The National Center for Charitable Statistics, 1980	140
	The National Society of Fund-Raising Executives (NSFRE)	142
	INDEPENDENT SECTOR: The Early Years, 1980–1984	143
	The National Institute of Independent Colleges and Universities (NIICU), 1979–1981	144
	United Way Outstanding Agency Professional Award, 1982	146
	501(c)(3) Group, 1980–1982	147
	Ditcheley Foundation Conference on Private Giving, 1982	148
	Giving USA: 1983 Annual Report	151
	CIAO	153
	Richard W. Lyman Becomes Chair of INDEPENDENT SECTOR	153
	A Day With John Gardner, 1984	154
	The State Model Law Project, 1984–1986	155
	Lessons Learned	157
Chapter 9	Last Half of the Eighties—Nonprofits Learn to Collaborate, Reduce Duplication and Enhance Programs	159
	AAFRC Trust for Philanthropy, 1985	161
	AAFRC 50th Anniversary, 1985	163
	Interphil Conference, 1985	165
	Indiana University Center on Philanthropy, 1986	168

	Personnel Changes	172
	Retirement Dinner for AAFRC's President, 1987	173
	The World Fund-Raising Council, 1988	175
	National Philanthropy Day, 1988–1990	177
	The New Climate for Fund-Raising Counsel	179
	AARP Andrus Foundation, 1986–1990	182
	Lessons Learned	183
Chapter 10	Is American Philanthropy Ready for the 21st Century?	185
	American Association of Fund-Raising Counsel, Inc. (AAFRC)	186
	Association for Healthcare Philanthropy (AHP)	187
	Council for Advancement and Support of Education (CASE)	189
	Council on Foundations	190
	The Foundation Center	191
	INDEPENDENT SECTOR (IS)	192
	National Society of Fund-Raising Executives (NSFRE)	194
	Lessons Learned	196
Epilogue		197
Appendix A	Peterson Commission	201
Appendix B	National Council on Philanthropy	202
Appendix C	Filer Comission	204
Appendix D	Coalition of National Voluntary Organizations	206
Appendix E	501(c)(3) Group	207
Appendix F	INDEPENDENT SECTOR Organizing Committee	209
Appendix G	INDEPENDENT SECTOR Charter Board	211

PROLOGUE

The Maturing Of American Philanthropy: A Personal Account

Flying at 8,000 feet, we could feel and see the sunrise early in the day. The change from faint streaks of light arching across the dark sky to a blazing blue canopy took only minutes. Baby cumulus clouds, their tops reflecting a dazzling glare, covered one-fifth of the brightening sky.

We were half-way to the target from our base on Guam. It was a mission we dreaded because we had to cringe our way through some of the most accurate flak bursts the Japanese could muster. It was a 13-hour flight—a long time sitting enveloped in the thundering roar of four Pratt and Whitney engines. Our ears usually rang for twelve hours after landing. My right ear still rings, 48 years later.

It was June 1945. Our plane was on auto-pilot. The crew was napping or day dreaming. As navigator, I shot a celestial fix, had a cigarette, and let my mind spin with whatever thoughts surfaced. My fear was intense. Once again our lives were at risk. Being shot at compels you to readjust your values. None of us were immune to the havoc caused by our raids. We couldn't help but reflect on what was on the other end of our bombs. Enemy or not, they were human. I found myself thinking of home, my wife Katy, and my future. And, if I survived this war, how could I compensate for being a part of so much destruction?

In 1939, I had gone to work for Standard Oil Company of New Jersey, Inc., with the impressive-sounding title of "Executive Trainee." As the firm was moving its headquarters, my first important and humbling assignment was five round trips a day on the subway from 26 Broadway to 30 Rockefeller Plaza. But this career was cut short by the darkening war clouds which persuaded me to join the Seventh Regiment of New York's National Guard. We were federalized a year before Pearl Harbor and I instantly became an ex-civilian.

In February 1941, our Regiment, now the 207th Coast Artillery, reached its station at Camp Stewart, Georgia. One of my first assignments was driving, after dark, into the Georgia swamp, in order to set up and man our searchlights to track the planes from Savannah Air Base while they simulated air attacks. From that very first night, standing in that swamp flailing fruitlessly at the myriads of mosquitoes while following the piercing rays of our light as it hit the glistening silver wings of our planes, I knew I was on the wrong end of that searchlight.

When an Air Force recruiting trailer came to camp that summer, I was first in line. I received my wings as a navigator in February 1943, instructed navigation for another year, and joined my crew in the spring of 1944.

If you were a direct part of the fighting, you felt its effects. By 1945, the war had changed my human values in many ways. My first taste of the business world was hardly inspiring. I no longer cared to fit into the common mold of financial success. I took small comfort in the fact that Standard Oil was committed to rehiring all their employees returning from service. When peace came, there would be many efforts to rebuild devastated societies. I wanted a job that would help make a difference in the rebuilding. And, after five years of the tight restrictions of Army regimentation, I knew that I would have more individual freedom working in the private sector than in government work.

Soon after VJ Day, we flew our tired bomber from Okinawa to Mather Field, California. I began my quest for a job in December 1945. Before long, five possibilities turned up: a chauffeur, a trainee at Anaconda Copper, a trainee at Merrill Lynch, my old job at Standard Oil, and a navigator with American Overseas Airlines. The latter called me on a Friday asking me to navigate a passenger plane to Paris the following Monday. When I pointed out that I'd never navigated across the Atlantic, they said my air-time over the Pacific was enough. I didn't agree.

Then I hit pay dirt. At a dinner with mutual friends, I sat next to Wolcott Street, Vice-President of John Price Jones Company, Inc., a leading fund-raising counselling firm. After dessert, some fine wine, and a discussion about the war, he asked me, "Jack, have you figured out what kind of job you hope to find?"

"Well, I haven't any interest in the business world. If possible, I'd

PROLOGUE

like to join an organization that's doing something to improve society and to work with people whose goals go beyond the next paycheck."

"I'm in charge of publicity for the Metropolitan Museum of Art's 75th Anniversary Campaign and I need an assistant to train and lighten my work load. Would you be willing to start at the bottom for low pay?"

"Would I? Oh yes, yes indeed," I said.

What a stimulating way to enter the field of philanthropy. I was placed in a group of experienced fund-raising professionals who guided and motivated me. The Museum was rich in scholars, art, sculpture, drawings, decorative arts, photography and even arms and armor. Each day, as I climbed the two flights of massive stone stairs into that dramatic entrance with its marble floors and soaring ceiling, I hoped that some of this cultural feast would rub off on me. Being a peripheral part of a such a firm with an impressive client list (Columbia University, the YMCA, American Cancer Society, Harvard College, The United Negro College Fund, and the Salvation Army) eventually steered me into a wonderful, lifelong career. This not only compensated for my concerns from my war experiences, but gave me more personal and professional rewards than I had dreamed possible.

SECTION I: 1946–1966

Fund-Raising Management Becomes More Professional

Immediately after World War II, fund-raising programs for nonprofit organizations depended on the lessons learned in a different time—the Twenties and Thirties. While these lessons were durable, the war's trauma had changed the attitudes and priorities of our society. More professional skills were needed to organize and implement successful fund-raising campaigns.

This section reviews some campaigns over this twenty-year period and highlights key fund-raising tips. It also traces:

1. The development of improved fund-raising techniques.
2. The establishment of new nonprofit organizations with programs designed to enable those in the field to share concerns, experiences; and to develop programs to increase professionalism, as well as to improve the public's understanding of philanthropy's benefits to society.

CHAPTER 1

After World War II— The Rebuilding

The winter of 1945 and 1946 brought peace at last. Within months, millions of military men and women became civilians again. All sought just rewards for their services: jobs, new homes and careers, a chance to raise a family, and, most of all, the conditions necessary to enjoy the world they had been missing. The initial euphoria wore off quickly, replaced by the growing realization that the war had stretched our resources well beyond current needs and rapidly growing demands. The life they had dreamt about, enhanced by prewar memories, would require much time, and substantial rebuilding.

Like individuals, nonprofit organizations needed to make up for the funds lost during the war years. Many colleges, universities, museums, health and social service agencies, and public service organizations launched fund-raising campaigns, creating tense competition for scarce philanthropic dollars. Not all would succeed. Most people were too preoccupied with adjusting to the postwar society. I, on the other hand, became entrenched in a new mission as a result of the war. I began my career in philanthropy at the Metropolitan Museum of Art. It was just the beginning of what was to be a rewarding life.

From 1946 to 1950, my assignments and responsibilities on the staff of the fund-raising counseling firm, John Price Jones Co., Inc., included:

| Publicity Assistant, Metropolitan Museum of Art | March to December 1946 | My introduction to a capital fund-raising campaign guided by the professionalism of the John Price Jones Co., Inc. |

Campaign Director, The Medical and Surgical Relief Committee	January to December 1947	Worked with top leadership, wrote and conducted the campaign plan, and worked under the supervision of the legendary John Price Jones.
Director of Commerce and Industry, Community Service Society Campaign.	1948 to early 1949	A major fund-raising campaign using top New York City corporate leaders to raise funds for the oldest and largest social agencies.
Director of Grove City College's Capital Campaign	1949 to Late Summer 1950	A major program for a college in a small provincial town in Pennsylvania challenged my professional experience and capacity to relate to a very different subculture.

THE METROPOLITAN MUSEUM OF ART

I began my career in philanthropy with the Metropolitan Museum of Art. The museum's 75th Anniversary Campaign had a far from modest goal of $7,500,000. Gaining public attention and interest were essential to raising this kind of money. The Museum's fund-raising counsel, John Price Jones Co., Inc., made a strong public relations program a top priority.

In February 1946, I joined the campaign staff as a trainee and "gofer." I was assigned to review the Museum's many exhibits and treasures to identify those that might provide story material for campaign publicity. To aid in this mission, I interviewed most of the curators to determine those who might be enthusiastic about possible public recognition of their cultural specialties. One objective discussed was to set up an "Avenue of the Arts" in Fifth Avenue's prestigious department stores such as Bergdorf Goodman, Bonwit Teller, Lord and Taylor, and Saks Fifth Avenue. The Museum agreed to release art objects to be displayed in these stores' windows.

Two curators were especially memorable. One, Emanuel Winternitz, was in charge of a collection of ancient and medieval musical instruments unequaled anywhere outside of Europe. From this pedestal, he reigned over everyone despite his small stature and guttural slavic accent. He would throw back his head, focus on you with his

AFTER WORLD WAR II—THE REBUILDING

sharp brown eyes set in a bony face with a bold Roman nose and say, "Veee cannot do thees. Ve cannot do anyting vitout meee."

The second was Dr. Ambrose Lansing, Curator of Egyptian Art. He was tall, patrician, topped by a shock of white hair matched by a flowing moustache and beard. He thrived on public attention. Though British, he was Egyptian in heart and spirit. At times, he would pause in his marathon of extolling the glories of Egyptian history and culture to roll a cigarette, using, of course, Egyptian tobacco. With his enthusiasm and knowledge of a fascinating era, he was a public relations dream.

They both were a "trip." Yet their strong desire for public attention set a good example for strengthening the campaign's publicity program. Their actions stimulated the interest of other curators, making most of them very cooperative in providing rare and beautiful art objects for the Fifth Avenue stores' window displays. This resulted in an encouraging increase in the interest and support of many affluent New Yorkers.

After spending a lot of time with these fascinating characters, it wasn't easy to concentrate on essential but mundane duties, such as staff and client luncheons, and planning sessions. Yet, as a newcomer, I was grateful for this opportunity to observe and begin to acquire some understanding of the complexities of a capital fund-raising campaign.

> **KEY FUND-RAISING TIP #1**
>
> *The importance of influential and committed leadership was brought home again and again. The extent of their participation was reflected in all aspects of the campaign.*

Thomas J. Watson, founder of IBM, was the campaign chair. Although the governor, the mayor, top government leadership, and a distinguished array of volunteers supported this campaign, in the end it fell short of its goal. By the close of 1946, only $4,000,000 had been raised. The John Price Jones Co. Inc., had assigned its top and most experienced professionals to conduct interviews, and develop the original campaign plan that took most contingencies into account. However, the one thing that was not anticipated turned out to be of crucial importance, namely the economic state of the union immediately after the peace was won. Most participants agreed, in hindsight, that the campaign would have had a much better chance of success if it had been conducted a year later.

> **KEY FUND-RAISING TIP #2**
>
> *A complete and accurate fund-raising study must take into account all factors which will affect results, including the current economic climate and social attitudes.*

THE LEGENDARY JOHN PRICE JONES

In the early fall of 1946, I was summoned to the headquarters of The John Price Jones Co., Inc., at 150 Nassau Street for my next assignment. These were the former offices of the *New York Sun* where Mr. Jones had once been a reporter. The old offices had remained unchanged since their newspaper days. A large T-shaped area, called the "bullpen," housed a few beat-up mahogany tables serving as temporary desks. Worn, ragged, and patched carpet runners followed the shape of the room. Encircling everything were tiny glass-enclosed offices, equipped with old desk-sized tables, two stiff chairs and typewriter stands. These luxurious suites, of course, were for the officers. Although functional, everyone felt the surroundings were much shabbier than necessary, especially considering the roaring business the firm was then enjoying. Mr. Jones adhered strongly to the precept that when potential clients visit the home office, shabby and modest surroundings were evidence of frugal management. This is an interesting contrast to some of today's philanthropy management standards now under so much scrutiny because of the United Way scandal.

John Price Jones, then 69, was truly a legend in his own time. In 1969, five years after his death at 87, the firm celebrated its 50th Anniversary. Robert F. Duncan, associated with Jones and the firm from its founding in 1919 until 1950, used this occasion to write a moving and complete memoir of this interesting and remarkable man. As Duncan noted, "John Price Jones was a complex individual, a man of great contradictions difficult to describe."

His beginnings were humble. Born August 12, 1877, in Latrobe, Pennsylvania, he was the son of a coal mine foreman. After working his way through Phillips Exeter Academy and Harvard College, he became a newspaper reporter. During World War I, he conducted the publicity program for the sale of Liberty Bonds. In 1918, Thomas W. Lamont, Harvard class of 1892, recruited Jones to raise $15,000,000 for the Harvard Endowment Campaign. Jones was successful in raising

$13,790,000 by the fall of 1919, which enabled him to start his own firm, the John Price Jones Co. Inc.

Duncan notes:

> Paradoxically, he [Jones] was inarticulate, but surrounded himself with men who were capable of grasping his ideas and interpreting them . . . . Perhaps his greatest contribution was in adapting the newly developed techniques of publicity and advertising to the selling, not of goods and services, but of socially valuable ideas . . . . He took an idea, applied promotional and organization techniques that he and his staff devised, and, with the aid of selected community leaders, saw those ideas grow into national crusades . . . . He systematized the knowledge of raising philanthropic money.

After 31 years of working together, Jones reminded Duncan of the reply made by an elderly matron on her 50th wedding anniversary party. Her niece asked her, "Aunt Mary, in all your 50 years with Uncle Henry, didn't you ever consider divorce?" With a sharp stamp of her right foot, the aunt replied, "divorce, never; murder frequently."

Mr. Jones (none of us would dare call him anything less) was only five feet, four inches tall, slightly stooped, with straight well-groomed graying hair, pince-nez glasses, brown eyes that could pierce armor plate, and a thin, determined mouth that mumbled rather than shaped words. Staff, when meeting with him on any matter, automatically scheduled a postmortem session to see if a consensus could be reached on both what he said, and what he really wanted from the last meeting.

He was absolutely hipless. As he wandered around the bullpen, we would wonder how much longer his belt could keep his trousers from falling down over his ankles. Word must have reached him, for, one day, he arrived with a belt *and* suspenders. We all cheered.

As near as I could tell, Mr. Jones accepted me as one of the trainees crowding the bullpen. After I'd been with the firm a few months, he passed by my table, read what I was writing and said, "Jack I never would've hired you if I'd known you'd never gone to college."

"Are you going to fire me?" I asked. "No, I guess not," he said over his shoulder as he walked away. "But you better get damned good, fast."

We fondly called Jones the "benevolent tyrant" behind his back. Even so, we were aware of his tremendous stature in our field. Without any doubt, he contributed more to the evolution of American philanthropy and the critical role played by the fund-raising profession, than any man of his time.

Research and statistics were among Mr. Jones' passions. My first bullpen chore was to dig out statistics on the nature of successful solicitations, gift tables, and prospect lists. I also spent many hours reviewing client campaign plans for former clients. These were then called *Surveys, Analyses, and Plans*. Today, these studies are known as *Feasibility or Development Planning Studies*. They were produced by conducting 60 to 90 confidential interviews with persons representing potential leadership or major donors, key staff, and those who could give a professional opinion on both the worth of, and the need for the programs the campaign hoped to finance. These interviews were analyzed professionally by counsel, which then presented a plan that recommended; a campaign time schedule, a feasible goal, the organization necessary to conduct the campaign, the role of the client's staff, volunteer leadership and professional counsel, a campaign budget, and a plan of action to achieve the goal.

MEDICAL AND SURGICAL RELIEF COMMITTEE

Early in World War II, the Medical and Surgical Relief Committee began soliciting and collecting medical gifts-in-kind from pharmaceutical firms to distribute to war-devastated countries. The end of the war, if anything, heightened the merit of this program. There was great need to increase the number of gifts of medical supplies from drug firms and to raise more money for staff support and distribution. At this point, however, funds were very low.

Admiral William F. Halsey, U.S.N. (retired) was the Committee's President. He came to Mr. Jones seeking very inexpensive advice. So Mr. Jones gave me the assignment and agreed to directly supervise my work. This gave me a rare learning experience unmatched by anything else I've experienced over the years. I learned to *almost* understand some of what Mr. Jones wanted. I also had the privilege of working with famous and accomplished people.

Serving on the Committee board with Admiral Halsey were the Chairman, Edwin R. Stettinius, former Secretary of State; and such dignitaries as Dr. George Gallup, Malcolm Muir, two of the Admiral's wartime fleet staff; Robert Montgomery (the actor), and Dr. Carnes Weeks, his surgeon.

Early in the campaign, I attended a small dinner reception for a few of the Committee's Trustees at the brownstone residence of Dr. Carnes "Piggy" Weeks. He was dubbed "Piggy" because of his remarkable collection of piggy banks in all sizes and colors resting on every horizontal surface in view. We started with drinks in a gracious room, seated in soft red leather chairs surrounded by mahogany walls and bookcases. The floor was covered with colorful Persian carpets brightened by the intermittent flashes of a roaring fire in a white brick fireplace. My initial tension eased as I watched and listened to Admiral Halsey. He was a charming and almost gentle man, with leathery skin attesting to many years spent on the open seas, and blazing blue eyes surrounded by laugh wrinkles. He rotated his attention around the room. When it rested on me, he said how pleased he was that Mr. Jones had made me available to the campaign, and then asked, "Mr. Schwartz, were you in the war?"

"Yes sir," I replied. "I was a navigator with the Seventh Air Force."

"Oh, were you on Okinawa?"

"Yes."

"Ah, you were in the group that bombed and missed the Battleship Haruna."

" 'Fraid so," I replied.

"Well, thanks for leaving it for my guys."

The Battle ship Haruna was famous because it was the target of Captain Colin Kelly in the Philippine Sea on the first day of the war. Kelly crashed and was killed trying to dive bomb it. By the summer of 1945, it was the sole surviving major ship in the Japanese Navy, moored in the Inland Sea between Kyushu and Honshu. It was finally laid to rest by planes from Halsey's fleet.

I was moved by the friendly backing and confidence the board had given me. Of even more importance at this stage of my new career was the opportunity to apply the principles of fund-raising counseling that I had been taught. This cause was important and capable of generating enthusiasm. For the first time, I was the voice of a firm noted for its experience and professionalism. Writing a persuasive solicitation pamphlet for a mission so dramatic, enhanced by the vivid memories of war, was almost easy.

KEY FUND-RAISING TIP #3

There is no adequate substitute for this caliber of leadership, a leadership that is both committed to the cause, and willing to solicit its peers and key corporations. These individuals made it possible for the Committee to double its funds and increase its gifts-in-kind threefold after 10 months.

COMMUNITY SERVICE SOCIETY

At the finish of the Medical and Surgical Relief Committee campaign, I had a short stay in the bullpen. A few weeks later, I was told to report to Albert C. "Gummie" Gumbrecht, a JPJ vice president assigned to direct a campaign for a new client, the Community Service Society.

Community Service Society was a cause easy to relate to. It was founded in 1939 through a merger of two of New York's oldest charities—the AICP (Association to Improve the Conditions of the Poor) and COS (Charities Organization Society). Ably led by its general director, Stanley P. Davies (a rare mix of sociologist and good executive), its army of social workers dealt with countless social problems of this complex city overcrowded with ethnic differences, juvenile delinquency, family turmoil, the homeless, violence, and crime.

Entering CSS' solemn and functional offices at 23rd Street and Lexington Avenue, the traditional, inherited values guiding the programs were made apparent by the gray rug runners, beige walls, wooden, mostly pine furniture, and modest offices. As one the leading New York charities, it attracted top leadership. Walter S. Gifford, President of General Electric was Chairman and Bayard Pope, President of Marine Midland Bank was President. The board had 74 members whose names read like a Who's Who of New York society. Today, CSS' board has full representation by all the ethnic groups it serves.

CCS was traditional in both appearances and their fund-raising methods. Claire M. Tousley, director of public information, and Emily Logue, list supervisor, used a method they called "double dic."

KEY FUND-RAISING TIP #4

Once a month, CSS would review last year's donors whose gift anniversaries were coming up. Claire, who knew everyone, would dictate personal renewal letters. This process had limited results. Rarely did any one increase the size of their last gift and virtually no new money was raised because most efforts were confined to this narrow base.

This campaign became my first experience in organizing a *commerce and industry effort*, known as a C&I. In order to be successful at C&I, you must begin by enlisting a prominent business executive as the chair. Then by using the chair's influence, chairmen of a wide variety of industries are enlisted to write solicitation letters to other executives and firms in their commercial field. I was able to use this process again and again in my future New York campaigns.

> **KEY FUND-RAISING TIP #5**
>
> *C&Is made it possible for "Mr. Big" to solicit "Mr. Not-Quite so-Big," an ideal combination.*

In 1948, New York City was booming. But this boom also created growing social unrest. The demands for CSS' services soon far exceeded its resources, so they engaged the John Price Jones Co. Inc. to set up a campaign to increase their annual fund in order to raise more money from more people. From CSS' headquarters, Gumbrecht directed the campaign, concentrating on the organization of a Special Gifts Committee. This committee enlisted key board members and their friends to personally solicit affluent business and society leaders in their respected circles of influence. For most members of the board, this was the first time that they did much beyond attending a few meetings and lending their names. Gumbrecht also helped plan approaches to key corporations and foundations, emphasizing the urgent need to expand the kind of services only CSS, with its experienced and trained staff, was equipped to provide.

My assignment was to spend each morning with the general campaign chairman, S. Spencer Scott, President of Harcourt Brace. Scott looked like the chief executive of a publishing firm with his tall, slim well-tailored figure, blond hair, and sharp blue eyes. He was intelligent and very self-assured. He opened our first visit with, "Mr. Schwartz, just what do you expect of me?"

"With your help, we hope to organize from 30 to 40 Commerce and Industry Divisions, each with a top executive as chairman who could write an appeal letter to his peers using his letterhead. This has been a proven way to raise new money. The key is to enlist top leadership," I replied.

"Just how do we do that?" he asked.

"You are a well-known and important executive. Your name on an enlistment request would get attention," I said. "Your most difficult task will be to make a follow-up telephone call to all those who don't respond after 10 days. I will provide the candidates, draft the enlistment letters for your approval, and mail them out on your stationery over your signature."

"Well, that sounds like real work. We better meet for at least an hour every morning to stay ahead of this chore. I'll expect you to give me all the necessary information every morning."

We soon developed a warm rapport and dug into the task of enlisting C&I chairmen from such diverse fields as retailing, the garment industry, public relations, advertising, book publishing, banks, brokerage houses, utilities, and the manufacturing industry. I drafted an enlistment letter and Scott polished it injecting his own style. One week after each letter was mailed, Scott followed up with a personal phone call. As head of Harcourt Brace, his calls always got through.

The process worked. Top executives soon filled the chairman spots. My job was to call on each of them in order to enlist their help in building a prospective donor list (Scott had made clear that this was part of their assignment). The prospective donors would be other executives from their respective fields to whom we would send an appeal letter over their signature on their corporate letterhead. Two weeks later, a follow-up letter would sent.

Thousands of new dollars were raised in this way, broadening the contributors base, and helping the campaign exceed its goal. It also laid the foundation for the future. (In most cases, 70 percent of all donors, if thanked graciously and asked again, will renew the following year.)

I also had the opportunity to get to know Stanley Davies, General Director, Claire Tousley, Director of Public Information, and Frank Hertel, Assistant General Director of CSS. This proved to be very important to me seven years later when I was approached to join CCS as Director of Development.

GROVE CITY COLLEGE

In the winter of 1949, following the success of the CSS campaign, I was asked to fulfill a commitment I'd made when I was hired, namely to take an out-of-town assignment. Since everyone in my field had to go to the client, any reluctance to live away from home for a campaign period could retard your career. My next post was a far cry from urban New York.

Grove City College was a small (1,400 enrollment) Presbyterian school located on the western edge of Pennsylvania, halfway between Pittsburgh and Erie. The town of Grove City had 6,000 people and 13 churches. J. Howard Pew, head of Sun Oil Company in Philadelphia, was campaign chairman. The campaign goal was $3,000,000, a tremendous sum in those days for such a small school.

> **KEY FUND-RAISING TIP #6**
>
> *Mr. Pew took some of the sting out of the campaign by agreeing to match up to $1,500,000 of money raised from other sources. Without doubt, this initial contribution from a prominent corporation was the key to a successful campaign.*

Also assigned from John Price Jones, was Donald T. Sheehan, a colleague who became a lasting friend of mine before this campaign was over. Sheehan was as Irish-looking as his name, tall and sturdy, with kindly brown eyes, black hair with sideburns shot with grey, a strong nose and chin, and a warm smile. A public relations expert, he had been a Lieutenant-Colonel in World War II.

We arrived the same day, both by train into Pittsburgh—he from Washington, and me from New York. We then had a seven-hour bus ride to our new temporary home in provincial, highly religious, and abstemious western Pennsylvania.

The next day, we were met and warmly greeted by the College's President, Dr. Weir C. Ketler. Ketler called Gus Forquer, chairman of the local Rotary Club suggesting that he introduce us to the local businessmen at their Rotary luncheon that day. Forquer complied with obvious reluctance since he was also chairman of the local Red Cross Drive and wasn't happy at all about our presence. At the luncheon, with a smug smirk on his face, he introduced Sheehan who was much more dignified looking than I was, as "Mr. Donald Sheehan from Washington" and me as "Jack Schwartz from Wall Street, New York City." This was not an auspicious beginning.

The College, perched on top of the hill rising from the town, had a beautiful and spacious campus with ample room for the expansions planned if the campaign succeeded. Dr. Ketler made a cottage right across from the Administration Building available to Sheehan, his lovely wife, Betty and their six-year-old son, Mac. I found a room in an old house at the edge of the campus, owned by a pleasant, elderly, and very religious couple.

Sheehan and I, as veterans of the Army Air Force, liked to have at least one cocktail before dinner, but Grove City was in a dry county. It had no liquor stores, bars, or restaurants that served drinks. We were very much aware of the need to relate to the local people and their customs and we knew that we'd have to work toward obtaining their acceptance and respect, so we developed a ritual each evening. Betty would pull down the living room shades (from the entrance stairs of the Administration Building one could look right in on us) and we would enjoy our reception hour. The JPJ (John Price Jones) writer of the Case Statement was Ed Reed, a sophisticated, fully confirmed New Yorker. Duly warned by us, when Reed made his first visit to Grove City, he stayed in character by taking a taxi from the bus station (a four-minute walk) and politely refused Sheehan's offer of a cocktail. Instead, he asked for a chilled glass and ceremoniously poured a martini from a thermos in his briefcase he had carried from New York. He said, "I wasn't about to rely on the primitive resources around here."

The Campaign Headquarters set up on the campus became very busy almost immediately and demanded our full attention. Not so for the weekends and evenings. The town shut down completely at dusk and the only thing open on Sundays were the 13 churches. My landlord was a good example of how religious those people were. He wouldn't water his lawn before midnight on Sunday or read the Sunday paper before Monday. The College tennis courts and the local movie house were also closed. On more than one Sunday, I attended church twice because there simply wasn't anything else to do.

Don and Betty had a warm sympathy for my loneliness. I had dinner with them many nights and on weekends we'd drive for two or three hours seeking a good Sunday dinner. We found several good restaurants over the course of a few months in small towns which served, without exception, home-style meals of gigantic proportions. These plus my tendency to follow the eating habits of the students (lots of cheeseburgers and milkshakes) prompted Katy to say when I got back home 10 months later, "Good you got out of there just in time, you're getting downright fat." Sheehan, with his family, finished his stint after five months leaving me very much on my own.

I was allowed to fly home every fourth weekend. Each trip, I took more notice of how different life was in the big city. New York seemed so frantic with too many self-centered people in contrast to the casual pace and abiding respect for family, church worship, and community shown by my new friends in Grove City.

In many ways, I enjoyed my stay. With $1,500,000 in matching funds pledged by Mr. Pew, many local merchants and Western Pennsylvania industries were very approachable and responsive. There were no other colleges in the vicinity to compete with us for local funds.

> **KEY FUND-RAISING TIP #7**
>
> *We concentrated on individuals, alumni, and companies capable of giving generously and matching these prospects with the most influential solicitor from the board and campaign committee.*

This activity was aided considerably by the beautiful mission statement written by Ed Reed, our urban friend. Reed's brochure skillfully articulated that this campaign was a very important cause for the community, the faculty, the students, and the future of the younger generation.

The spirit on the campus was inspirational. Nearly 20 percent of the enrollment was comprised of veterans under the GI Bill. While in service, most of them had to put up with someone superior in rank with too little intelligence and too much arrogance—a hard way to learn the importance of self-improvement. They now had a more mature approach to their studies and took their educational opportunities seriously. This rubbed off on their younger less-experienced classmates, which lifted the level of education for everyone. Also, there was great satisfaction in completing a successful campaign—more than $3,000,000 was raised and nearly 10 percent came from the small town itself.

It took about six minutes to walk down Grove City's main street. Stepping from the bus station at one end, you would pass by a food counter, a general store, a book store, a haberdashery, a women's wear store, a movie house, a restaurant, a drug store, a hardware store, and finally the railroad station at the other end of town. Every day, I strolled through town as if running for mayor during those 10 months. Before I left, I would allow up to 30 minutes for the same walk.

I remember being asked by one faculty member at lunch, "Jack, are you really from New York? You don't act like it."

> **KEY FUND-RAISING TIP #8**
>
> *I had become a familiar and nonthreatening person and developed several close relationships. I began to see more clearly how vital it is to adjust to the local situation and relate to people for who they are, without regard to their cultural differences. Without this focus, your ability to guide the campaign and fulfill its objectives is seriously handicapped.*

LESSONS LEARNED

- From the end of the War through the Fifties, the techniques for raising funds for nonprofit organizations established in the decades before the War by John Price Jones and the principal heads of other fund-raising firms; (i.e., Carlton Ketchum, Dr. Arnaud Marts, Charles Sumner Ward, and others) were re-tested. They still worked, and needed little adjustment for societal changes.
- To succeed, a campaign must have five elements:
  1. A compelling case.
  2. Top and committed leadership.
  3. Enthusiastic volunteers.
  4. A cultivated constituency.
  5. A campaign plan.

- The plan must include a feasible goal, quotas, a time schedule, defined roles for all the players, and staff support.
- Counsel needs to constantly remember that this is a "people business" and that all the client bases we are to help are, in essence, subcultures. Relating to them well is critical. If they do not respect you both as a person and a counsel worth listening to, you cannot be very effective. It's important to be patient, especially in the first few weeks. You must allow some time for the new people you're working with to gain both respect for your word and confidence in your advice.
- And, you must gear the campaign to the often unique style of your client. There is a tremendous difference between a campaign for a small college and one for a museum in large city.
- By 1950, the understanding and appreciation of the entire philanthropic process and the concept of philanthropy was a long way off. It was summed up in too many peoples' minds as "charity," usually confused with welfare programs. Often giving was at the smallest amount a person could get away with gracefully and was almost entirely dependent upon who did the asking with little concern about the worth of the cause.
- Too many (in some cases, virtually all) members of nonprofit boards were enlisted on the basis the value of their names, not their commitment to the cause. Instead, they should have been enlisted with the advanced understanding that they would actively participate in the organization's fund-raising programs.

- With examples of successful campaigns increasing, more non-profit organizations were expanding their fund-raising programs. This quickly brought to the surface intensified competition both for leadership and funds, as well as the lack of enough qualified fund-raising professionals.

CHAPTER 2

The Fabulous Fifties—Reaching For The American Dream

By 1950, memories of World War II and the economic and the social debris it left behind had nearly faded. Although peace was soon to be sullied again by the Korean War, for the moment, American society turned its attention to molding the life depicted by the booming art of the Madison Avenue hyperbole. Their ads featured glistening new cars, shining suburban homes, exciting breakthroughs in household products, and colorful styles. The inevitably clean-cut happy smiling faces of these images seemed to say, "our society can now provide you with a piece of the American Dream."

In this climate of confidence, most nonprofit organizations began to plan ahead with more surety. They realized that if they documented a genuine need to expand their programs and developed realistic plans to reach out to their constituencies, they could obtain a larger share of the potential untapped, but growing philanthropic support. Also, the steady corporate and economic growth helped to encourage nonprofit board members to accept the demanding responsibility of beginning major fund-raising efforts.

The four positions I held in this decade broadened my experiences in many ways:

Assistant Campaign Director, Norwalk Hospital, Connecticut—My last campaign for JPJ	1950	A major capital campaign requiring the organization of seven communities, building and training staff, and learning this is a seven-day-a-week job.

Director of Public Relations and Fund-Raising, Traveler's Aid Society of New York	1951 to 1955	My first position as a staff fundraiser without the backing of professional counsel. It taught how to me make my own plans and guide staff and leadership for a successful campaign. This position also gave me the chance to learn and relate to the agency's programs and personnel.
Director of Fund-Raising, Community Service Society	1955 to 1957	A challenging task to direct all the fund-raising efforts for the largest and oldest social service agency, and build its annual support to meet growing social needs in New York City.
Director of Development, Near East Foundation	1957 to 1960	I learned much about the partnership of our government and the private sector in trying to meet the needs of Third World countries.

In the urban centers, where so many of philanthropy's top leaders lived and worked, business executives and affluent society leaders often considered philanthropy a hobby and referred to it as "charity"—something they did more for appearances' sake than out of real conviction for a cause. Benefits soared. Receptions, theater previews, dinner dances all provided a wonderful way to be seen by the right people, have a good time with peers and make a modest gift to a well-known charity. The net proceeds to a charity were the total amount donated after all expenses were deducted. Usually the costs, including expensive promotion efforts, reached 75 percent and higher. Yes, nonprofit organizations received attention. But most affluent donors felt they had fulfilled all obligations by their ticket purchase and quickly turned to other interests.

Competition stimulated most community organizations such as hospitals, social agencies, colleges and universities, churches and museums, to become more skilled at building larger constituencies. They recognized the value of applying more resources to develop programs that involved improved relations with new volunteers and the old faithful.

NORWALK HOSPITAL, CONNECTICUT

The campaign for Norwalk Hospital in affluent Fairfield County, Connecticut was a good example of the new competitive trends. A feasibility study by John Price Jones Co. recommended an 18-week campaign to raise $750,000 beginning in June 1950. The hospital's trustees, in accepting the study's findings, automatically committed themselves to rolling up their sleeves and going to work. Back in those days, this was a very ambitious goal. It would require the successful participation of local businesses, foundations, the hospital and medical staffs, and all the communities served by the hospital—Norwalk, New Canaan, Ridgefield, Weston, and Wilton. Always looming in the background was the excellent service provided to the same communities by Stamford Hospital.

James B. "PT" Powell-Tuck, Vice President of John Price Jones Co., Inc. (JPJ) was the campaign director. PT, an Englishman who served in the British Navy, was now an American citizen. A short impressive man, who used a quiet well-modulated British accent to immediately establish a powerful self-confident presence, would confront his staff with the dark eyes of a fox about to pounce. He left you with little choice but to humbly succumb and jump to do whatever he requested. After a particularly bad session, staff would mumble, "He never got over being an officer in the British Navy." At our first staff meeting PT turned to me and said, "Jack, since you've lived around here, you're going to concentrate on organizing all the communities served by the hospital except Norwalk, which I'll handle."

I replied, "Great, this won't be easy, but it can become fun."

To do this well, I knew I had to mine every bit of my campaign experience. While I was prepared to work hard, I found that not only was I very much on my own, but had to keep a steady and sharp eye on the administration of the campaign headquarters. When PT wanted anything, he wanted it "now." I had to keep in mind that I was second in command, there to act as the buffer between the director and the staff. I was responsible for keeping the staff performance both effective and smooth flowing. The hired staff were locals and new to this kind of operation. It took time to train them. My attitude, performance, and relations with the volunteers and staff were under constant scrutiny.

Learning to relate to PT's moods and demands was a very important growth experience for me. To do a good job, it was essential that I earn his respect. This required patience and fortitude as well as an open mind in order to learn how to respect him.

THE FABULOUS FIFTIES—REACHING FOR THE AMERICAN DREAM

> **KEY FUND-RAISING TIP #9**
>
> *No campaign will run very well or smoothly with a staff disrupted by personality or character clashes. Responsible fund-raising managers must respect and cooperate with each other.*

One day, I realized that PT had a good sense of humor. Our campaign office, an old three-story building once a nurses' residence, sat on the top of a rise behind the hospital's main building. The entrance porch was approximately 20 steps above street level. We all worked six days a week in those days. One Saturday afternoon, we were finally ready to begin enjoying what was left of the weekend. Katy came to pick me up. PT was also leaving and had climbed down to nearly the bottom step just when she was starting to climb up. He is only about five feet, six inches, Katy is five feet ten. As they began a cordial conversation, PT was on the step above her. She promptly climbed up to join him. He immediately retreated one step to keep his head above hers. Each time PT stepped up, my ever-mischievous wife also climbed to the next step to remain taller. He finally said, "Damn it Katy, please show more respect for my position."

For the community organizing, I began my task by enlisting the help of the hospital president, Currier Lang, and several board members first in order to identify several key leaders in each community. I needed their view as to what would be the best strategy to enlist these leaders.

In most cases, the board member who knew the candidate agreed to ask that person to host a campaign dinner party for their local and influential friends. At these dinners, PT and Lang would give a very effective presentation of the value of the hospital's programs and services and the need to expand them to meet growing community demands.

> **KEY FUND-RAISING TIP #10**
>
> *Our strategy, which usually worked, was to convince the host or hostess to agree in advance of the dinner to chair the community effort and dramatically present Mr. Lang with a pace-setting gift at the appropriate moment in the evening.*

With only one exception, the chairs of the six communities were capable women. This confirmed a very valuable and not-to-be-forgotten lesson.

> **KEY FUND-RAISING TIP #11**
>
> *Women, with a natural intuition that fosters people skills, are great fund-raisers. When women are enthused about a cause they can persuade even the most reluctant prospects to dig deeper for a more generous gift than they originally intended to give. Always look for committed women volunteers. Women can be critical to a campaign's success.*

It would have been much better if we also had some professional women involved. In reflecting on those Dark Ages 43 years ago, I note with sadness that most, if not all, the staff positions then available for women were list supervisors, secretaries, and clerks. We have come a long way since then. At least half of today's fund-raising professionals are women and they continue to make up a large part of the volunteer force.

Beside directing the campaign, PT did a superb job of bringing in gifts from local corporations and foundations. He organized the hospital staff and physicians into an active campaign with impressive results.

> **FUND-RAISING TIP #12**
>
> *Volunteers and potential contributors always produce better results when there is strong evidence of generous support from the institution's staff and board.*

To top prospects, we emphasized that the hospital would welcome three-year pledges which helped to increase the size of many gifts. The tax benefits were also emphasized. Under the tax laws of 1950 and 1951, a couple with no dependents could reduce their taxable income by 75 to 79 percent of their total hospital contribution, thus making each gift a much smaller sacrifice.

Fund-raising quotas were set for each community. The process of reaching these goals generated a competitive spirit between the communities which served to enhance the campaign results. After the campaign closed, this spirit prevailed and became a lasting factor in later fund-raising efforts.

During late fall of 1950, the campaign attained its goal. I remember the letter from PT, dated December 4th, with warmth and appreciation:

> Now that you have completed your assignment here I want to thank you for a job well done. This was no easy task and the fact the outside communities did so well compared to previous building efforts is due *greatly* to your efforts. As you know, you made many friends who all thought, as I do, that you carried out your assignment with real credit.

PT's dedication, perfectionism, energy, and strong personality created results we all respected and eventually grew proud of. He decided not to go back to JPJ but stayed in Connecticut and continued to counsel the hospital on its fund-raising for many successful years.

THE TRAVELER'S AID SOCIETY

In October 1950, Katy and I returned to our New York apartment on East 61st street. I began a calmer life of researching and writing fund-raising materials in the bullpen while waiting for my next JPJ assignment.

During late fall of 1950, at a mutual friend's party, I met David W. Haynes, the general director of the Traveler's Aid Society of New York. Haynes filled the room with his imposing presence. Tall and balding, in a slightly rumpled suit, he projected wisdom, respect and a genuine interest in other's welfare. He was full of questions about my career and surprised me with his knowledge of the nuances of fund-raising. I liked him immediately and we became good friends that evening. Just as my wife and I were leaving, he asked, "Jack, our director of development after three successful years, is taking a new position in advertising. Would you be interested? If so, I'd like to put your name in the hat to be interviewed by the search committee."

"Gee," I replied. "Thanks, but I haven't even thought of changing jobs at this point. Let me have a few days to think about it and get back to you."

My hesitation was prompted by some self-doubt and several considerations. Was I ready to get out on my own? Could I give up my strong loyalty to my firm? Would I miss working with a fascinating variety of clients? And, could I ignore the strong feeling I should change jobs only after I had more experience and confidence?

> **FUND-RAISING TIP #13**
>
> *A good fund-raising consultant should be viewed as the "dance-master" of the campaign. In my previous assignments, I always had to be prepared to deal with typical campaign problems: Leadership recruitment and/or second rate leaders, pace-setting gifts that come in short, lagging volunteer enlistments, missed deadlines, uninvolved boards of directors, and waning enthusiasm. All could hurt results. Until now, whenever one of these problem surfaced, I could always turn to one of the firm's vice presidents who was just a telephone call away. The firm's resources provided solutions when necessary.*

Whenever a difficulty arose that was beyond my capacity to solve, I could always get fast help from a vice president from the firm. We would schedule a conference and, if necessary, call on the combined experience of the firm's top staff to develop a plan to help solve the problem. Trying to get along in the future solely on my own knowledge and experience was an intimidating thought.

Yet, here was a rare opportunity to go out on my own and test my mettle. I called Haynes the next day, "I'd like to put my name in the hat. Would you please send literature about the Traveler's Aid's program and background on the members of the search committee?" Over the next three weeks, I was interviewed by six members of the Society's board. I was impressed by their enthusiasm and commitment to the Society's program, a good portent for effective campaign leadership, an essential asset for developing a successful campaign. Haynes called me, "You have done well but the search committee is still interviewing other candidates."

Waiting another four weeks for word seemed an eternity, for I had become very interested in the job. It was especially hard because I had to try to show a genuine interest in my JPJ activities. Finally, on November 15, 1950, I received the good news. I was appointed director of public relations and fund-raising for the Traveler's Aid Society of New York as of December 1, 1950. It was a whole new life. Instead of being a constant itinerant, I had a permanent office, my own secretary, a full-time staff of six looking to me for direction, and a honeymoon period to find my way.

The Society was established in 1905. As a member of the United Services Organization (USO), it had helped thousands of service men and their families as well as hungry, lost, and confused travelers from the United States and abroad. With the outbreak of the Korean War, it was very much in the public eye. Its distinctive globe lamp set on a seven-foot column identified the Traveler's Aid booths in New York's Grand Central and Pennsylvania stations and a newly opened one in the Port Authority bus terminal. Because of annual fund-raising campaigns for the past few years, it had both a current cultivated constituency and an army of volunteers. Its well-established campaign organization included a women's committee, a group to solicit apartment houses in affluent locations, a special gifts committee, and an annual fall dinner dance in the Persian Room of the Plaza Hotel. Despite all this, their fund-raising results had been on a plateau for the past several years.

The 1951 goal was $340,000 ($314,900 was raised in 1950). October had been cleared with the Greater New York Fund (United Way's local chapter) as the traditional campaign month. We had more than 10 months to organize and conduct our solicitations.

Since 10 months was plenty of time, I had a beautiful chance to learn more about the Society. I began visiting the station's booths and interviewing the Society's social workers and volunteers who dealt directly with troubled travelers. As I got to know some of them better and observed their warmth, compassion, and the caring service they provided, I became more enthusiastic about this program. I also realized that this was the first time in my career that I had both the time and opportunity to study and understand an agency's program in real depth. This, I know, helped me to do a much better job.

Most of the previous year's campaign leaders and volunteers could be re-enlisted. The women's committee was very well staffed by the experienced and most capable Charlotte MacDonald. She was a true professional. The society women loved and respected her which further strengthened my conviction that philanthropy and/or fund-raising is an ideal field for women. This committee's main responsibility was to organize the fall benefit at the Plaza. This was an entirely new arena for me and I was grateful many times for Charlotte's know-how.

My first campaign priority was the formation of a commerce and industry effort similar to my successful one at the Community Service Society three years prior. With the other committees already in good hands, I prevailed on the Campaign Chairman, Baldwin Maul, Vice President of the Marine Midland Trust, to work with me on enlisting chairs for 125 fields of businesses. Called the business and professional committee, we both realized that its success could go a long way toward increasing last year's results.

Haynes and the board accepted my campaign budget which included funds to hire two staff members for the last six months of the year. Their responsibility was to work with each committee chairman to build a prospect list for his field, draft a solicitation letter to go out on the chairman's stationery, track its results and send a follow-up appeal to those who didn't respond after two weeks. Thanks to this staff back-up, each of the chairmen completed their task before the end of the year. A staff publicity man, Roger Hawkins, wrote an excellent campaign brochure emphasizing the increasing number of requests for assistance by travelers at our terminal booths. It also stressed our services to thousands of servicemen who had been passing through New York and requesting all kinds of help since the Korean War began.

The fall reception and dinner dance in the Persian Room of the Plaza Hotel was most impressive. After the costs of promotion, food, and drink, the Society netted over $25,000. New York high society was resplendent in black ties and evening gowns created by top couturiers. The attendees, almost without exception, were wealthy, prominent, and capable of giving generous gifts which, in many cases, could equal the entire benefit proceeds to our campaign.

KEY FUND-RAISING TIP #14

In my first year, I saw that these guests were not solicited after the benefit. Most considered their purchase of a benefit ticket and their presence more than sufficient. Frustrated, I made next year's priority to approach these prospects on a special gifts basis. Potential donors were assigned to one of our top volunteers and solicited personally.

Although we fell $20,000 short of our goal in 1951, we still raised more money than ever before. More importantly, we targeted areas for improvement that would continue to build on our strengths—an experienced staff, better campaign structure, and good leadership. While not euphoric, I was excited about my new responsibilities, which were helping me grow both personally and professionally.

For nearly four more years, I continued to refine the campaign process, build and train a competent staff, improve results that eliminated the deficit, gain a better understanding of New York's problems and the value of social workers in alleviating them, and acquire self-confidence in my dealings with top leadership and my administrative abilities. But, I also faced a growing problem.

THE FABULOUS FIFTIES—REACHING FOR THE AMERICAN DREAM

> **KEY FUND-RAISING TIP #15**
>
> *To do the best job as a fund-raising director, you must maintain your enthusiasm for, and be stimulated by, your organization's programs and mission. Both volunteers and staff look to you for motivation and guidance.*

Putting together an annual fund-raising campaign several years in a row becomes redundant. You begin to feel static and lose interest. I was primed for change. This condition is endemic to the field and causes a larger turnover than most of us like to see.

THE COMMUNITY SERVICE SOCIETY

In the early spring of 1955, I received a call from Sallie Bright, director of public relations of the Community Service Society. "Jack, Clair Tousely, the longtime fund-raiser for CSS is retiring and suggested you as someone who knows both fund-raising and the CSS program. We're establishing a new position of Director of Fund-Raising. Would you be interested?"

"Thank you, I think I would, but only after I discuss this with Haynes." Haynes, now my mentor and close friend said, "Jack, CSS is not only the largest and best-managed social agency around, it sets an example for the rest of us. I'd hate to lose you but I won't stand in the way of your career advancement. It would be foolish of you not to look into this."

CSS' budget was three times the size of Traveler's Aid. From my work on its 1948 fund-raising campaign, I was acquainted with most of its executive staff and its city-wide programs. I didn't want to leave what had become a most satisfying and comfortable job, yet I knew I would grow in this new position.

CSS' search committee was chaired by J. Richardson Dilworth then a partner in the investment firm of Kuhn, Loeb & Co. In 1958 he became president and senior financial advisor to the Rockefeller Brothers Inc. I will always remember our first meeting. His warm, book-lined office with a mahogany stand-up desk, made me feel I was in a classic 19th century office. Still in his thirties, he seemed more mature because he spoke with such clarity and intelligence about CSS' needs. As a CSS' board member he remembered favorably my role in the 1948 campaign. Also, I found out later, Stanley Davies, the general director, had given

Dilworth a strong recommendation. Although I still had to meet with the other committee members, Sallie Bright reported to Davies after this interview, "Dick Dilworth has already hired Jack Schwartz."

On May 1, 1955, I became the Director of Fund-Raising for CSS, the largest nonsectarian family and health agency in the United States. Its annual budget was $3,500,000. Dilworth prevailed on the board to set the campaign goal at $1,000,000, more than $250,000 greater than they had raised in the past, and he agreed to chair the effort.

Chartered in 1848, CSS, under the superb administration of general director Stanley Davies, served some 20,000 families a year in Manhattan, the Bronx, and Queens. CSS received no state or federal funds. All its services were made possible by contributions. I remembered from the 1948 campaign that CSS had an impressive board of 72 distinguished business and society leaders, the ideal foundation from which to pull the chairs of the campaign committees. The growing social turmoil in New York's poor sections increased the need for the special skills of CSS' social work staff and more was required.

As general chairman, Dilworth was forceful and persuasive, enlisting several who had only lent their names to previous fund-raising efforts. Kersting & Brown Co., a professional fund-raising counseling firm, had been engaged to oversee an expansion of the fund-raising program. For the first time, I was supplied not only with a mentor and troubleshooter, Carlton Cameron, a K&B vice president, but with a board-approved campaign plan. I enjoyed this turn around very much. October 1st was set as the opening day of the campaign. Drawing heavily on the board members, the campaign was divided between two major units—the women's and the men's committees. The women's committee had the following sections:

- Foundations;
- General solicitation;
- Manhattan district;
- Bronx district;
- Special projects;
- Special gifts, and
- Apartment house canvassing.

The sections of the men's committee included:

- Special gifts;
- Manhattan general solicitation;

- Uptown Manhattan district;
- Downtown Manhattan district;
- Bronx district;
- Queens district; and
- Business and professional.

I expanded the fund-raising staff to include directors of the women's and men's committees. I had no choice but to be in the spotlight, and along with my fund-raising department, would have to take any blame or credit for success. Even though this campaign had all of the same elements of those I had run before, I had to reach into every crevice and corner of my accumulated experience. The campaign results were cause to celebrate. We exceeded our $1,000,000 goal early in January 1956 and Dilworth hosted a beautiful party at the Yale club for the volunteers, board members who worked on the campaign, and the staff. He also enlisted Gilbert Clee, a partner of McKinsey and Co. and chair of the business and professional committee to be general chairman of the next campaign.

The first campaign was history, and the time to get ready for the next campaign was immediately. We were ready to gear up early for the 1956 Family Fund.

KEY FUND-RAISING TIP #16

Learning from experience, we took care to reenlist the most effective volunteers giving some of them more responsibility, keeping the same committees, and concentrating on building a better special gifts effort. To address the latter, first we identified the 1955 donors capable of increasing their gifts and assigned them to the special gifts committee regardless of how we first obtained their gift. The best way of all to maximize a gift is to have the donor personally solicited by a peer.

So, we began intensive efforts to enlist enough volunteers from their peers to serve on a select special gifts committee. These volunteers accepted assignments from three to five donors and agreed to solicit them personally in the fall.

That winter, I hired Alfred Moran as full-time director of the men's committee. Although inexperienced, he was full of energy, fresh ideas, and a very quick learner. Having previously worked for the YMCA before he was drafted for the Korean War, he also had an extensive interest in social work. Under his guidance, the men's committee was much better organized than in 1955. After working for CSS for several years, he became the highly effective executive director of Planned Parenthood of New York until his retirement in 1989.

We increased our 1956 goal to $1,100,000, and once again proudly announced in early 1957 that we had exceeded it by several thousand dollars. We were now blessed with many committed volunteers and an impressive group of new donors whose response would continue to increase through more personal approaches next year. I had received important help over the last two years from Carlton Cameron of Kersting & Brown (I enjoyed being on the other side of the client-counsel coin) but our organization was now so well put together, their services were no longer justifiable. This was ultimate testimony that they had done their job well.

At this point, I began to feel both uncertain and restless about my career. I felt confident that I'd done a good job for CSS. I felt comfortable with most of the executive staff and key board members. Yet, both past experiences and general nature had made me pretty pragmatic.

Being on the staff of Traveler's Aid Society and CSS taught me that not only do social workers enjoy philosophizing, some tend to get bogged down by the consideration of all possible options before taking any direct action, no matter how overdue. Every Friday afternoon, Ms. Bright would conduct a staff meeting to review the week's activities and set action plans for the next week. Characteristically, I would start attacking my tasks the following Monday morning and usually report completion of my assignments at the next staff meeting. Not so with most of the others. They spent hours reviewing options and would ask the assembled staff, "Before we make this move, do you think it will work and what other steps might we take?"

After the successful completion of the second campaign, I began to skip these staff meetings, pleading a full schedule. The fact was that I never would be able to change my ways enough to truly relate to the social workers' way of dealing with issues. After two years, a growing disenchantment made me start thinking about the next step. I did not let this stand in the way of doing all I could to plan the new campaign but my ear was to the ground for sounds of new possibilities.

THE FABULOUS FIFTIES—REACHING FOR THE AMERICAN DREAM

NEAR EAST FOUNDATION

Ironically, Carlton Cameron invited me for lunch that spring primarily, I thought, to be brought up to date on the next campaign. As we talked, he mentioned his excitement over a planning study K&B was doing for the Near East Foundation.

"What is that?" I asked.

Carl answered, "It's an outgrowth of the old Near East Relief, formed during the first World War to 'feed the starving Armenians.'" He described how the Foundation's technical assistance programs in the Near East were designed to teach people in rural sections of developing countries how to help themselves to overcome poverty, disease, ancient inhibiting superstitions and ignorance. When Truman went to Congress for funds for the Point Four Program, he cited the Near East Foundation programs in Lebanon, Iran, Greece, Jordan, and Syria as examples of what American technicians can accomplish in cooperation with host governments.

My interest soared. "What does the study recommend?" I asked.

He explained that, "because of Russian efforts to use benefits of technical assistance to manipulate the politics of oil production and distribution, the time was overdue to strengthen programs like NEF. They need an expanded fund-raising program and a full-time director of development as soon as possible." He added, "I think you would be perfect for them."

"Boy, I'd sure like to look into it, but it's a far cry from raising funds for New York City social work."

He reminded me of a point that had come up in previous conversations: The skills required for a good fund-raising manager are very portable. He added that the essential ingredients are that you must be a "quick study," understand the cause well, and generate enthusiasm for that cause whatever it may be.

The next week, I had an interview with the Foundation's president, Dr. John S. Badeau. He rose to his full six feet, two inches to shake my hand as I entered a huge office that looked like a library, with three walls of bookcases, a high ceiling, and a floor covered with oriental rugs. Never, before or since, have I met a more fascinating man. Badeau, then in his early fifties, was overweight, dressed in clothes almost, but not quite, shabby, waving an aromatic cigar in his left hand. The cigar's fumes permeated the room almost, but not quite, as much as the spell he created of an awe-inspiring intellect, skillfully polished by a remarkable eloquence. No one's attention would wander while he spoke—and speak he did about the beauty and importance of the Foundation's program, and the need to be more responsive to the desperate needs for our technical skills by so many developing countries:

> Our programs currently being conducted in Lebanon, Jordan, Syria, and, until recently, Greece, are designed to give people a better life—not just economic, but with hope, dignity and respect. We do this by raising the level of rural development and understanding by people in villages from the fifteenth to the nineteenth century. We enter a country by invitation only with assurances of host government participation. NEF technicians conduct demonstration projects in agricultural improvement, home welfare, rural sanitation, adult literacy, and village leadership training. Our aim always is to do ourselves out of a job. Today we need more money to respond to increasing opportunities. And if you are interested, with your background and experience, we have a lot to sell to corporations working overseas, host governments, the Federal Government's Aid program, and more than 15,000 individuals who have supported us for years. If you join us, you will have an early opportunity to go overseas and see these remarkable programs firsthand.

I left his office hooked and exhilarated. I hadn't the slightest doubt about accepting Badeau's offer but I first had to face the difficult step of sharing my feelings with CSS' general director, kindly, avuncular Stanley Davies, who had been such a warm supporter of all my fundraising activities. Like Haynes two years earlier, Davies said he didn't want me to leave but congratulated me on this exciting way to broaden my experience. He also asked if I could recommend a successor. Without hesitation I suggested, "Al Moran, despite his short experience, has learned all the essentials of CSS' campaign, has been in on every step this year, knows most of the leadership, and also knows how to take charge." After a cursory search, Davies and the key CSS leadership appointed Moran as the successor.

On April 15, 1957, I was appointed Director of Development of the Near East Foundation. We all have high points in our careers, and my next three years with this Foundation was truly one of mine. This program transcended political considerations and represented the true spirit of philanthropy. It was best exemplified by an old adage Badeau liked to cite, "Man is brother to man, whether you like it or not."

The Foundation's previous fund-raising efforts had concentrated on direct mail to 15,000 current and lapsed donors many of whom were growing old. Little or no effort had been made to expand this group. There were several construction and oil corporations doing business in some of these countries and some had responded to modest grant requests. In 1957, the host government's support in personnel, equipment, local currency, and dollars was $1,452,000. An additional $291,000 had to be raised from American contributors to fund the Foundation's share of ongoing programs.

The NEF board had some strong leadership from the chairman Cleveland E. Dodge, of the Phelps Dodge family; George C. McGee, former U.S. Ambassador to Egypt; and Harley C. Stevens of Standard Oil. All could and were willing to open doors to major corporations, but they would not take any action until they were shown a plan and good reasons to do so. NEF needed an immediate campaign plan to inspire action from the available leadership. Also missing was any plan to take advantage of this beautiful office space—a magnificent five-story mansion on 54 East 64th Street, lording over an elegant neighborhood. Badeau's office, I later discovered, was, in fact, the library of the former mansion. It was an ideal site to stir the interest of New York society women once a benefit program was introduced.

My next steps were easily defined. Badeau and Dodge were very willing to present my campaign plan to the board. Even with Dodge's help, we were unable to find a highly placed executive who was qualified to chair the campaign. Dodge graciously stepped in. As chairman of the Foundation's board, he regularly agreed to do the tasks that would normally be asked of the campaign chairman, like signing enlistment letters, presiding over campaign planning sessions, and making follow-up telephone calls. This prompted him to ask me, "Jack, whether I like it or not, I'm doing all the things a campaign chairman would do, aren't I?"

"Yes," I responded, "and every day I thank my lucky stars."

KEY FUND-RAISING TIP #17

But, not having a top leader committed to the responsibility of chairing the effort slowed us down. The results of the campaign surely could have been greater because a well-qualified chairman attracts other good leadership.

There was growing evidence of the need for expansion of private support of aid programs. New requests from governments in the Near East and Africa were being stimulated by the increasing awareness of the success of our ongoing programs, plus the willingness of the U.S. aid program to provide matching funds. We began to build a committee from officers of construction and oil firms who enabled us to break new ground in obtaining grants. We also targeted several major foundations with proposals for three-year grants to start new programs that would become, in that time, nearly self-sufficient.

Reaching out to the socially prominent wives of several board members, we established a women's committee with two objectives: First, to enlist a group of volunteers who would accept assignments to solicit, face-to-face, a carefully screened set of affluent individuals in Manhattan who had given to NEF in very modest amounts over the last few years, and second, to plan a theater, dinner dance, or Broadway show premiere benefit for next fall. While the process was slow at first, an impressive group of young society women began to meet regularly at NEF's headquarters (which they all thought were great) to take on solicitation approaches and scan the landscape for a movie or theater opening appropriate for a benefit.

Word was getting around. Several began, slowly but surely, to identify NEF as their charity. To celebrate the opening of the fall campaign, the women's committee organized a cocktail reception at headquarters featuring a firsthand report by Badeau on his recent trip to the Near East. While there, he had personal audiences with Colonel Nasser of Egypt, King Hussein of Jordan, and President Al-Kuwatli of Syria. Barclay Acheson, was the Foundation's executive director in its early days when its religious base was both strong and dominate. At the reception, as cocktails were being served, his sister and cofounder of Readers Digest, Mrs. Lila Acheson Wallace, whispered to me out of the corner of her mouth, "At this moment, Barclay is probably rolling over in his grave, but with a big smile. Alcoholic beverages here? Wow." This well-attended and elegant party helped to instill pride in the women's committee, which began to pay off in the 1958 campaign.

Before joining NEF as president in 1955, Badeau, a former missionary, had served as President of the American University of Cairo for over 20 years. He was the acknowledged expert on the political and social trends of the Middle East. Every year he made a trip to inspect the Foundation's programs, and while there, he had audiences with the top political leaders. Requests to hear his reports on these visits poured in from universities, civic groups, and local chapters of the Council of Foreign Relations and the Foreign Policy Association. I was responsible for arranging speaking tours to dozens of cities. Each fall, he and I would go on the road for three or four weeks. In the many hours and days we lived together on trains, airplanes and in hotels I had the wonderful opportunity to observe and learn from this remarkable man who was also a marvelous teacher. I would take extensive notes while in the audience of his many speeches and became, vicariously, quite well-acquainted with the current political and social conditions of these countries.

Dr. Badeau was a very large man of six feet, two inches, and carried at least 240 pounds. He still had most of his brown, slightly graying hair. He wore loose jackets, always with a disarranged tie, and looked much like the typical academic or former minister that he once had been. Nevertheless, he was an accomplished speaker, and the audiences loved him.

It was my privilege to watch him prepare for his lectures, and he taught me some lasting lessons about public speaking. Even when he had three speaking engagements in the same day, he *never* gave the same speech. He would sit at a typewriter in his hotel room before each appearance and with awesome two-fingered speed, roughly draft what he planned to say, making sure it had the essential facts but was tailored to the next audience. Then he referred to this draft as he typed a complete outline on file cards including the date, the audience, the title, an opening anecdote to warm the audience, another story at the middle of his speech ("to bring back the wandering minds," he would tell me), and a closing story ("hopefully to leave them laughing"). He kept these cards in his speech file, an irreplaceable record to use when he was invited back, as he often was. This meticulous method gave his presentation a distinctive flow that avoided the stiffness most people show when they are reading a speech and encouraged him to be much more extemporaneous.

One memorable day in February 1958, Badeau called me into his office and said, "Jack, your first campaign went well and you seem to be geared up for this fall. This spring would be a good time to make a tour of our programs, don't you think?"

"I admire your splendid judgment," I responded. "Seriously, I can't wait, and I'm confident this will be a great boost for my job."

"Well, one thing you'd better be ready for: after you return you'll begin to relieve me of some of the speaking engagements that take so much of my time." This is the first indication that Badeau was grooming me to be one of the Foundation's spokesmen. I was both flattered and pleased.

My visit started in early June of 1958. My first stop was Amman, the capitol of Jordan where I was given a guided tour by a Lebanese, Hannah Khouri, one of our senior technicians. Khouri showed me the results of our work in several small villages which all now had good sanitation systems, irrigated crop rotation, home welfare for the women and an atmosphere of self-sufficiency. It was moving to view, first hand, the programs that I'd been raising funds for but had never seen before. This experience deepened my interest and zeal for this work.

Other stops included Jericho on the Dead Sea, and Jerusalem. Visiting the holy city was an unforgettable experience. I was captured by the ancient beauty of the Church of the Holy Sepulcher with the tomb of Jesus and the spiritual aura of the Dome of the Rock sitting on top of its own hill on the Eastern edge of the city. Wandering through the segregated Jewish, Muslim, and Christian quarters, and their places of worship makes you realize that no where else in the world are there comparable symbols and evidence of civilization's traditions and roots.

After Jericho and Jerusalem, I went on to Iran where Bill Fuller, our country director, guided me from Shiraz, four hundred miles south of Teheran, to Rasht at the northern border on the Caspian sea. In those days, the Shah was turning over Crown Lands to the peasants, a far cry from the tyrannical rule of later years. Everywhere we stopped we were welcomed. The natives were well aware of the benefits they had gained through the Foundation's programs. In hindsight, it is unfortunate that this enlightened approach could not have prevailed longer in Iran for everyone's sake.

On my way home, I met Dr. Badeau back in Amman, just north of the Dead Sea surrounded by rising hills. Two Arab refugee camps looked down on the city. One morning, he gave me a tour of them. Shabby tents were surrounded by dusty paths. Few women were visible and the men were mostly elderly and sour-looking. Small bands of lively young boys were playing and laughing until they spotted us and promptly sulked away out of sight. Badeau said to me, "God help us when these children grow up!"

Hannah Khouri drove Dr. Badeau and me to Damascus the next day to view two programs the Foundation had completed on the desert plane surrounding the capitol of Syria. Later Badeau and I entered the paved, columned walk that is the entrance to the Grand Mosque of Damascus. Badeau, as usual, was dressed in a Harry Truman brightflowered shirt, chinos, two straps for his camera and exposure meter crossing his chest like bandoleers, a straw hat with its brim turned up all around, and the inevitable big cigar—the quintessential American tourist.

He spotted the head Mullah of the Mosque at the other end of the courtyard and strode toward him. As we approached the Mullah, I saw in his face a look of disdain and eagerness to find a quick exit. But, he smiled as soon as Badeau began to talk to him in fluent Arabic, albeit with an Egyptian accent. The Mullah's face relaxed as Badeau's strong voice began with the lilting sounds and rolling Rs that characterize Arabic speech. Badeau used to say that Arabic is the most expressive language and the hardest to learn. Their conversation became instantly friendly and lasted for more than 15 minutes. Badeau reported that the Mullah had heard of NEF and his role with it, but somehow had expected him to look differently. Indeed.

When I returned, I was quite ready to respond to public speaking opportunities on behalf of the Foundation. My enthusiasm was really heightened after my tour. Adding to this, the teachings of Dr. Badeau helped me to enjoy sharing my feelings about the tremendous value of using American technicians and resources to show people in less fortunate countries how to help themselves build better lives.

I composed every talk as he taught me. I had never learned to type, so I scrawled a draft of my speech in advance (after doing careful homework) and transposed this draft as an outline on three by five inch index cards. These cards recorded the date, site, sponsoring organization, an opening anecdote or story, a mid speech audience-awakener and a closing story. Today, I have a set of cards for every speech I've made since 1958. They are a priceless resource for tracking my engagements, planning the next presentation, and avoiding redundancy.

As the decade of the 1950s came to a close, I completed the third annual campaign for NEF. Each one bettered the results of the preceding year. The foundations programs were expanding into Africa and Korea, which provided new fund-raising prospects. The fact that Russia was pressing to do more technical assistance in these areas strengthened our case to the American people. Our women's committee expanded and matured. Several foundations were responding to three-year proposals. The progress of fund-raising, along with the added zest of being called on to help various audiences understand the importance and values of the Foundation's programs, made my job both pleasant and rewarding.

LESSONS LEARNED

- The essential skills needed to be a successful fund-raiser, once learned, are very portable as long as you can generate honest, intellectual and emotional enthusiasm for the mission of your organization.
- The redundancy of several successive annual campaigns can

become trying and make you seek new ways to rebuild enthusiasm.
- Dealing with a variety of organizations and causes is one of the main attractions of working for a professional fund-raising counsel.
- There is no acceptable substitute for top, committed leadership.
- Good planning demands that you do all you can to ensure that the largest potential contributors be assigned to the most effective volunteers and are solicited first, because their gifts should set the standards for all others.
- More and more nonprofit organizations were setting up indigenous fund-raising departments creating growing professionalism and competition.
- Several new organizations were beginning to appear that would become, within the next few years, important to the professional growth in this field.

CHAPTER 3

The Sixties—Increasing Competition and the Challenge to Improve Professionalism

American philanthropy received $11.5 billion in 1960 from individuals, foundations, and corporations, sustaining an annual growth of over 9 percent. Yet, this munificence did not begin to match the increasing pace of demands for the services of nonprofit organizations, or allow for the financial needs of newly established organizations whose numbers were expanding rapidly. Most professionals agreed that the full potential of American generosity had barely been tapped. This created more fund-raising appeals and intensified competition.

In the early Sixties, my volunteer and professional assignments became more daunting:

Vice President G.A., Brakeley Co., Inc. Main clients were the International Schools Foundation and Syracuse University	1960 to 1962	I had the excitement of serving a completely different set of clients with the disadvantage of being away from home for extended periods.
I joined the boards of the National Society of Fund Raisers (NSFR) and the Association of Fund-Raising Directors (AFRD)	1960 to 1965	The influence and activities of these two organizations began to reach more into the field to develop early steps toward making fund-raising a profession.

Director of Development, the Foreign Policy Association	1962 to 1964	This was another venture in seeking support for foreign affairs, working with leaders devoted to public service. FPA's programs were designed to make Americans better informed in dealing with the pressing problems of the world.
Assistant Vice President for Crusade, the American Cancer Society	1964 to 1966	I was charged with increasing the fund-raisng capacity of the largest (the "Tiffany") of the national health agencies.
Executive Director, Executive Vice President of the American Association of Fund-Raising Counsel (AAFRC)	1966 to 1969	The AAFRC provided the platform to expand my activities beyond just fund-raising into the larger field of philanthropy as well as acting as a catalyst for bringing component parts of the field closer together.

The atmosphere of this decade was more competitive. No nonprofit organization could survive, much less flourish, without access to fund-raising professionals, experienced staff or outside counsel. There was an increasing number of individuals who, by choice or circumstance, had become professional fund-raisers. Shared concerns and common interests began to bring them together to foster organizations that would open the lines of communication within this field and give them a chance to compare notes. Grantors also started to devote some time and resources to examine the philanthropic scene in order to improve the effectiveness of their funding.

EARLY FUND-RAISING ASSOCIATIONS

Several fund-raising organizations already were in existence. The American Association of Fund-Raising Counsel (AAFRC), founded in 1935, had operated without paid staff or headquarters until 1955. Then they set up an office and hired David M. Church, John Price Jones Co.

THE SIXTIES—INCREASING COMPETITION 41

Inc., Vice President for Public Relations, as executive director. The AAFRC had 25 professional fund-raising counseling firms as members. The firms' clients were major churches, colleges and universities, museums, social agencies, and national organizations like the American Red Cross and the YMCA.

One of Mr. Church's most important and lasting accomplishments was to initiate publication of the annual statistical review of American philanthropy, *Giving USA*, which is still the most authoritative voice on American giving today.

While the AAFRC provided a good forum for firm's officers and staff, it was not open to the new breed of individual fund-raisers who were permanent members of the staff of nonprofit organizations. In New York City, this latter group had formed its own organization before World War II called the Association of Fund-Raising Directors (AFRD). Many of its members were women, who served as office managers and list supervisors. It had yet to attract significant numbers of development officers from the larger charities. The "old boy's network" was still in flower.

The National Society of Fund-Raisers (NSFR), the predecessor of the National Society of Fund-Raising Executives (NSFRE), was chartered in 1960. Several of the original organizers envisioned it as a sort of "trade union" to provide employee benefits such as health insurance and improved salary levels, as well as to promote greater public acceptance and appreciation of the fund-raising field. Church, as a former JPJ vice president and head of the AAFRC, was established as one of the top leaders in the field. He, and others, were concerned about this approach. They felt that to be effective, the NSFR should not only seek more recognition of the work of fund-raisers but become a forum for the exchange of experiences and discussions of successful fund-raising techniques. They considered plans to provide training facilities and to reach out to younger people in the field.

Dr. Abel Hanson, president of Columbia University Teachers College and a well-known educator, was an ideal person to lead the Society beyond areas of self-interest. Thanks to a grant of $13,000 from the AAFRC, he organized the first regular course on fund-raising at Teachers College. Dr. Hanson accepted Church's invitation to be the founding president of the NSFR.

During this period, many alliances within the fields of education and foundations were strengthening. The Foundation Center and the Council on Foundations had come of age. Wilma Shields Rich, executive director on the Council of Foundations, and F. Emerson Andrews, president of the Foundation Center, expanded their programs designed to open more communications, increase accountability, and gather and disseminate more data about the giving pattern and programs of foundations. The American College Public Relations Society (ACPRA) and the American Alumni Council (AAC), forerunners of the Council for Advancement and Support of Education (CASE), intensified recruitment efforts, and gathered more public relations and development directors from leading universities. Their programs included regional and national conferences on constituency cultivation (alumni and potential applicants) and improving the professionalism of fund-raising for higher education.

Thus, early in this decade, the forces gathered that would have a far-reaching affect on the growing professionalism of management of fund-raising and fund-giving.

G. A. BRAKELEY & CO., INC.

George A. Brakeley, Jr. joined the John Price Jones Co., Inc. right after he graduated from the University of Pennsylvania in 1939. I had heard much about his abilities and distinctive personality. When I was a trainee in the JPJ bullpen in the fall of 1946, he was a campaign director, fully occupied with directing the New York City Cancer Society campaign. One memorable day, he dropped in to our headquarters. I sensed his presence standing along side me as I was concentrating on drafting a memo.

"Are you Jack Schwartz?" he asked.

"Yes,"

"I understand you're a veteran. I'm George Brakeley, and I was in CBI (China-Burma-India theater). I served as a captain."

"I served as a captain too, but on Okinawa," I replied. This began a friendship that still prevails 47 years later. He left JPJ in 1953 to set up his own firm in Canada. In 1956, he acquired Stanford University as a client and established the G. A. Brakeley Company, Incorporated in San Francisco. In 1958, he opened his New York Company, G.A. Brakeley Co., Inc.

In the winter of 1960, Brakeley asked me to meet him for lunch at the University Club. Since I hadn't seen him in several years, I assumed

THE SIXTIES—INCREASING COMPETITION

he just wanted to catch up. Arthur C. Frantzreb, executive vice president of Brakeley's firm joined us. After small talk, they started to quiz me about my work with NEF and how well I had established relations with persons involved in international affairs. They were interested in new business and felt that this field had strong possibilities. They asked me if I would be interested in joining the firm as vice president. My immediate and positive reaction surprised me because, for the first time, it hit me that as much as I loved working for NEF, the nature of my position could not provide much future career growth. Here was a tempting offer from a young and exciting professional fund-raising counseling firm headed by a much-respected friend. It offered me growth opportunities and a chance to apply 15 years of experience. After giving NEF proper notice and taking a short, but much-needed vacation, I joined the Brakeley company in July 1960.

One of the major attractions of my position with NEF had been the pleasure of working with and learning from Dr. Badeau. Saying goodbye to him wasn't easy, although he was most gracious about my responding to a new and greater opportunity. Ironically, less than two months after I joined the Brakeley Company, Dr. Badeau was appointed by President Kennedy as the first American Ambassador to the newly formed United Arab Republic—Syria and Egypt. If I had still been with the Foundation, without Badeau, I would probably moved on very soon anyway.

THE INTERNATIONAL SCHOOLS FOUNDATION

The Brakeley Company had just moved its offices to 400 Park Avenue, so once again I found myself in elegant quarters. For the first time in 10 years I was involved in seeking new business and working with a *variety* of clients. One of my first clients was the International Schools Foundation. ISF, headquartered in Washington was started in 1955 under the guidance of several persons with first-hand experience in launching overseas schools in Geneva, Rome, and the United Nations in New York. As American corporations were extending their overseas operations, other schools were being established in Asia, the Middle East and Africa. Initial funds came from Samuel Horowitz, a Cleveland industrialist, and John D. Rockefeller III. In its first full year of operation ISF helped place teachers and administrators in schools throughout 15 fifteen countries.

> **KEY FUND-RAISING TIP #18**
>
> *In recent years, the Ford Foundation led a growing trend to make a matching grant to a nonprofit organization whose fund-raising goal was for proven needs. This inevitably made the nonprofit's staff and leadership work harder to raise qualifying funds. The amount raised by colleges and universities receiving such matching grants was triple that which the same schools had raised in previous campaigns. Always give obtaining a matching grant lots of effort. It can really pay off.*

In 1959, the Ford Foundation made a $250,000 grant to ISF provided the Foundation could match it with another $187,000 from other sources—roughly three dollars for every two dollars raised. We completed a feasibility study and a mission statement for ISF with fund-raising goals of $118,400 in 1961, $138,400 in 1962, and $156,100 in 1963 for a total of $412,900. These funds would enable the Foundation to set up several new schools and provide additional teachers and administrators for schools already established. Several foundations and corporations responded with grants, including the Rockefeller and New World Foundations, the Carnegie Corporation, Standard Vacuum Company, and *The New York Times* Foundation.

SYRACUSE UNIVERSITY

Although my next major assignment was much closer to home, eventually it turned out to be a rough commute. Syracuse University engaged the Brakeley Company to do a feasibility study in order to plan a capital campaign. Chancellor William P. Tolley selected the Brakeley company, George Brakeley, and Arthur C. Frantzreb from several competitors because, as he said, "I want a firm with young and energetic personnel. We have such a strong desire to make our University a leading institution, our fund-raising program must be planned with imagination and skill."

Frantzreb and Fred P. Hubbard set up nearly 100 interviews with board members, deans, key alumni, parents, educators, foundations, corporations within the Northern State area and past supporters. These interviews, conducted on a confidential basis, were to determine how the University was regarded as an institution, how well it was meeting the current demands for improved educational facilities, and whether it could anticipate financial support if it launched a well-planned campaign with documented needs. Chancellor Tolley made it clear that the prime objective was to raise the funds necessary to make all of the University's departments at least as strong as, if not stronger than, that other school across the state (i.e., Cornell University).

Both Frantzreb and Hubbard opened their confidential interviews with the University department deans and heads with the same question, "What additional facilities, research, and personnel does your department need to make it competitive to your counterpart at Cornell?" One evening until very late, they both sat at an old fashion adding machine located in the alumni office, an ancient house on the campus, and totaled the cost of meeting all the demands of the deans and department heads. The adding machine after ticking away several hours, showed that their needs, plus other board-set priorities such as new classrooms, student residences, distinguished scholarships and increased endowment totalled an awesome (for 1960) $167,000,000. Our interviews with potential large donors to this campaign, had convinced us that a feasible goal would be $75,000,000, no larger, and it would take 10 years to raise. The long-term goal would be $144,000,000. Needless to say, our conclusion to set the campaign goal at $75,000,000 shocked and disappointed the chancellor and other university leaders.

KEY FUND-RAISING TIP #19
This campaign study was an outstanding example of the worth of the study process. Its careful, professional, and documented review of the client's fund-raising potential persuaded the board, even though reluctantly, to accept its findings including the size of the goal even though it meant they had to scale down much of their "wish list." In doing so, they avoided the disaster of launching a campaign with an unrealistic goal that would have surely failed.

A new review of the University's entire needs was undertaken by the board and executive staff. After many sessions and with a great deal of pain, they deferred or eliminated needs of lesser importance until the projected costs were reduced to a total of $75,000,000.

Frantzreb recalls that during the interviews, Samuel I. Newhouse, the newspaper publisher whose two sons had attended the university, expressed his desire to see a new communications center established that would prepare students for the pending communications explosion caused by increased TV broadcasting.

Beginning in February 1961, I moved up to Syracuse as the campaign director along with Andrew Jackson as associate director. Immediately, we began to work closely with Newell Rossman, the university's vice president for development. Jackson and I each found an apartment and began to adjust to a very different setting than the rapid pace of New York. Syracuse, at that time, was mostly residential with a modest downtown which closed down after 6:30 p.m. In the middle of the snow belt, we saw more heavy snow falls than we would have liked, but this city was so used to it we soon became hardened to the cold and inconvenience. Syracuse was the only place I recall seeing sidewalks being plowed as regularly as roads. These heavy snows and lack of evening activities made Jackson and I wonder how everyone spent their evenings. One answer presented itself as we walked downtown on James Street the next summer: It seemed as if every third woman was pregnant.

We set up a campaign office downtown. Our first priority was to systemize the university's alumni and supporter files and identify and research the top potential prospects.

KEY FUND-RAISING TIP #20

To maximize giving from the top group, it was necessary to set up schedules and controls to make sure teams consisting of only the most influential volunteers and the appropriate staff from the University (many times the chancellor or at least a dean) meet with these prospects. It often took not one but several visits before the prospect decided to make a generous gift.

For these key solicitations we worked with Rossman and Chancellor Tolley to identify the top volunteers both from the board and those to whom the board could open doors.

The mission statement was Jackson's prime responsibility and, with the important help of Rossman, they did an excellent job. It was not only persuasive, but it was attractively designed as well. It contained all the essential elements necessary to guide the solicitor in coaxing the prospect. It delineated and documented the university's needs and described special projects and their costs. It also emphasized the high caliber of the campaign leadership.

THE SIXTIES—INCREASING COMPETITION

> **KEY FUND-RAISING TIP #21**
>
> *Large potential donors like to associate their names with a particular project. The campaign was given a fabulous boost by a pledge of $15,000,000 by Mr. Newhouse to build in his name, the School of Public Communication.*

Every third Friday afternoon, Jackson and I would take a Mohawk Airline plane from Syracuse to the White Plains Airport for a weekend with our families. The following Monday, we would meet at White Plains and do our best not to look or seem too glum at the prospect of being away for three more weeks. But now more than ever, the need was growing for improved educational facilities all over the country.

> **KEY FUND-RAISING TIP #22**
>
> *This campaign gave us a lot of professional satisfaction and surely would lead to other accounts. It had impressive leadership, an exciting set of pace-setting gifts that predicted a successful result, and was an excellent model for other universities to follow.*

I spent nearly a year at Syracuse. Like my earlier experience on the Grove City College campaign in Western Pennsylvania, I was confronted with attitudes, work habits, and regional culture that were different than any I had previously experienced. Acknowledging these differences helped me to become more persistent, patient, and take the necessary time to build good relationships and gain respect from persons with whom at first I had little in common. It was important to keep my mind and actions focused on the mission of the program. I also learned that this kind of life away from my home, friends, and family was not for me.

> **KEY FUND-RAISING TIP #23**
>
> *Working for a professional fund-raising firm, more often than not, necessitates extended periods of time on the road, living with the client and being detached from the administrative activities of the firm. You can do a much more effective job if you remember to be patient in building client respect. Also, be ready to adjust to what is often a different subculture than you're used to.*

By November 1961, we had completed our contract with the university. According to the stated objective and professional plan, their campaign organization was up and running, the pace-setting gifts phase was launched with good initial results, and the excellent development department no longer needed our services. We had accomplished what good counsel should, we had done ourselves out of a job.

Right after the holidays, I sat down with Brakeley to review my concerns about further assignments which required extended periods away from home. Our relationship was close and warm. He understood my position and regretfully accepted my resignation to be effective in 60 days. So in January 1962, for the first time since World War II, I began a job search.

THE FOREIGN POLICY ASSOCIATION

Thanks to my experiences with the Near East Foundation, my interests in foreign affairs had not abated. I applied to the Peace Corps and was invited to meet with the director, Sargeant Shriver. I had an exciting two days in their Washington headquarters, first closeted with Shriver for several hours, and then called back the next day to attend their staff meeting. I was being considered for the director of relations with nonprofit organizations. After a painful two-week wait, I had had no word whatsoever.

Propitiously, the Foreign Policy Association (FPA) was searching for a new director of development, and I knew several members of its board. I made an appointment with the president, Dr. John W. Nason, and spent an enjoyable hour discussing FPA's needs and plans. Nason was a distinguished educator, well-versed in foreign affairs and showed real aptitude and capacity for being an effective fund-raiser with key corporations and foundations. FPA's 57 board members included notable businessmen, former ambassadors, several leading and active society women, and educators, many of whom had been involved with the United Nations and/or U.S. government foreign relations. They included distinguished lawyers, educators, the Presidents of such companies as Kennecott Copper, IBM World Trade, Encyclopaedia Britannica, Standard Oil Company (NJ), and Federated Department Stores.

Five board members interviewed me. Following each interview, I became progressively more interested in FPA. The Peace Corps posi-

THE SIXTIES—INCREASING COMPETITION

tion was awarded to a man with more qualifications than I could muster. So as of March 26, 1962, I became Director of Finance and Development for FPA. The only cloud on the horizon was that Nason was leaving FPA to become president of his alma mater, Carlton College. As an aside, Nason and I were both on the program in November 1984 in Nashville. We had a warm reunion at this conference of the Boy Scouts of America. He has written a great deal about the stewardship role of nonprofit board members. His views are very respected and are referred to today as many nonprofit organizations are re-examining the role of boards in wake of the United Way of America scandal.

FPA's new president was Samuel P. Hayes, former Director of Research and Economic Development at the University of Michigan, who had spent several years in the State Department. He gave me a very free hand and supported my recommendations. My staff was excellent, particularly Cyril Brosnan who went on to become a Vice President of Empire Blue Cross/Blue Shield in New York.

I found FPA exciting. I was pleasantly surprised to discover the large number of prominent Americans keenly interested in foreign affairs. The extent of their participation with the programs of the United Nations, the Council of Foreign Relations, and FPA was impressive. For the first time, I could observe the UN in action. Despite its bureaucracy so typical of an organization composed of so many cultures, it generated an aura of genuine concern about the serious world problems on its agenda.

One of FPA's main programs was called "Great Decisions." As an annual nationwide review of eight critical foreign policy problems facing the American people, it provided a fact sheet on each issue designed to create discussions that would encourage citizen groups across the country to formulate their own views on policy alternatives. Comparing world problems today with the eight critical issues of 1962 produces real *deja vu*. They were:

Vietnam—Win, lose or draw?
Red China—Third greatest power?
Brazil—Which way for half a continent?
Nigeria—Democracy in a new climate?
Iran—Middle East pivot?
Berlin—Test of allied unity?
United Nations—Independent force?
United States—New directions in foreign policy?

FPA worked with national organizations concerned with any aspect of world affairs and served as a clearing house for thousands of organizations in this field. It established a world affairs center for briefings and conferences.

These programs attracted not only national attention, but the interest and support of leading corporations and foundations, enabling it to achieve its an annual goal of more than $1,000,000. My main priority was to expand the already effective business and commerce committee, and identify special projects that appealed to foundations for multiyear grants. We also had an active women's committee stimulated by a good number of professional women that foreign relations seemed to lure and foster with more opportunities than most other fields in those days. The Associates Program, a group of business leaders who paid for membership, held monthly luncheons featuring a key person in world affairs. FPA's offices were at 345 East 46th street, right across from the United Nations. This proximity provided many opportunities to interchange programs and conferences. To be part of this exciting and cogent organization stimulated both my job awareness and my deep interest in world affairs.

I commuted daily from Westport to New York except for occasional travel. Soon I became quite involved with the New York efforts of other fund-raisers to improve the communications and professionalism of the field. I joined the board of the embryonic national organization, the National Society of Fund-Raisers (NSFR) in 1962, and was elected president of the New York group of the Association of Fund-Raising Directors (AFRD) in 1963. NSFR held its first national conference, October 10, 1963 at the Motel on the Mountain, Suffern, NY, and we had 90 members in attendance. Jess Speidel, who worked for the American Cancer Society as Vice President for Crusade (as their fund-raising campaign was called) succeeded Abel Hanson as President of NSFR in 1962.

Speidel also commuted from Westport and we began playing bridge together on the train. We had many discussions on the need to bring organizations together and agreed that a good start would be to make AFRD the first chapter of NSFR. My AFRD board agreed to this and on July 15, 1964, a letter signed by Speidel as NSFR president and myself as AFRD president went out to the joint membership announcing the formation of AFRD as NSFR's first national chapter. Within six months chapters of the NSFR were formed in Philadelphia and Washington, D.C. This is a far cry from NSFRE today with its 143 chapters and over 14,000 members, but a strong beginning nevertheless.

THE SIXTIES—INCREASING COMPETITION

We began to conduct monthly luncheon meetings featuring a good range of leaders including local college presidents, senior fund-raising directors and heads of major nonprofit organizations.

> **FUND-RAISING TIP #24**
>
> *Out of this evolved a steady growth of understanding of successful fund-raising techniques, and a new awareness that most of the problems encountered as a fund-raising executive were shared by all, regardless of the respective missions of our organizations.*

The biggest challenge I faced was the fact that the high-caliber of leadership, and the almost exalted level of the program activities of the Council of Foreign Relations, made it a tough competitor for fund-raising in the field of foreign relations. Even though their programs didn't compete (CFR focused more on diplomatic relations while FPA's main thrust was public education), CFR had established an entree to many leading corporations and foundations that we simply could not match.

> **KEY FUND-RAISING TIP #25**
>
> *We built greater support though through expansion of the business and commerce committees, increased effort in special gifts and carefully planned approaches to several corporations and foundations.*

I felt resolved to continue in this position for the foreseeable future.

THE AMERICAN CANCER SOCIETY

Speidel, my bridge partner and peer, had been in fund-raising for many years. Tall and slim, his grey hair was cropped short to matched a grey bushy mustache. He had the wonderful experience of having had, as his counsel in building the Crusade (campaign) Department, the distinguished Harold J. (Si) Seymour, author of the "classic" *Designs for Fund-Raising*. To give Seymour's book its fully deserved credit is beyond my capacity with words. However, I will always be grateful to Edgar M. Gemmel, a senior officer with Princeton University. He captured a good measure of the book's spirit and effectiveness in his memo of December 1966:

> I do *not* urge dipping into the Seymour book. I urge wallowing in it. The hippopotami on the Victoria Nile waddle in and submerge themselves until only their eyes, and I presume eyebrows (I was too timid to get close enough to see exactly) float above the surface like two black tennis balls.... Seymour's prose presents such a beckoning through the woods that the innocent reader may be beguiled by the easy slope of the chapter ... that he mounts a shiny velocipede for the trip.... In a few minutes he pulls up happily at the end of the chapter, not even breathing hard.

Speidel mentioned one day that he had persuaded his boss, Lane W. Adams, Executive Vice President of American Cancer Society, to hire an assistant in order to broaden the fund-raising efforts for ACS. He said, "I would like you to meet Adams because your background is exactly what he and I are looking for."

"I have no interest in changing jobs, right now, Jess, but I'd like to meet Adams just because he has such a fine reputation as a good executive."

Speidel impressed me with his broad view of the future of philanthropy. As we had gotten to know each other better, we shared common goals for action needed to bring the key organizations of this field closer together. The "Tiffany" of the health agencies, the American Cancer Society, showed the way for others. I became aware that it had the same problems which plagued large national organizations. They were:

- No one policy could gain society-wide acceptance;
- There was intense competition between its divisions;
- Its divisions had varied and sometimes conflicting agendas springing from the differences in subcultures lodged in areas ranging from Mississippi to Massachusetts to California; and
- It had an oversized cumbersome national board of directors.

But what a compelling cause! It's a rare person indeed who hasn't some kind of direct personal encounter with this dreaded disease.

Over a long lunch, Adams and Speidel questioned me about everything from my limited formal education to how my experience could be applied to their expanding national fund-raising efforts. Speidel called me when we both had returned to our respective offices to say,

"Adams likes the cut of your jib and wants me to make you an offer." And make an offer they did at a salary 20 percent higher than what I was earning at FPA. This, combined with the prestige of the ACS and my many common interests with Speidel, led me to accept the position even though I was reluctant to leave FPA. I gave Hayes six weeks notice and joined ACS as Assistant Vice President for Crusade on August 3, 1964. In his enlistment letter of May 28, 1964, Speidel outlined my duties,

> Besides being the person who is responsible, next to myself, for the overall progress of the Crusade nationally, your principal duties will be in the multiple fields of gifts which require special handling (both corporate and individual); intensive work with foundations; maintaining and bettering our legacy and memorial program; and staffing the special committees of the Crusade Committee having to do with these facets of our work.

I've never worked for any organization that inspired such deep loyalty and enthusiasm. Formed before World War II, its mission of research, education and service made it a unique private organization to coordinate national efforts in order to better understand and seek eventual solutions for this devastating disease. It had one division for each state as well as seperate divisions for large cities like New York and Chicago. The national headquarters, through the national board, set standards of governance and performance for all the divisions. Every year, each division had to document its performance in order to qualify for a renewed charter for the following year.

Most divisions had fairly successful fund-raising departments but there never were enough trained fund-raisers to meet the growing needs. Seymour, as ACS counsel, guided Speidel in setting up an annual "Crusade Clinic" to teach fund-raising techniques to newer staff members selected by the division executive directors. They were held each October in centrally located Cincinnati for 40 to 50 young staff members from all over the country. My first clinic was in Cincinnati in October 1964. I was brand new to staff, but Speidel put me in charge of the opening program. My subject was "An Overview of Philanthropy." Edwin Bergstrom and Victor Swanson were fellow members of the national Crusade Department. They, with Speidel, stood in the back of the meeting room as I addressed the clinic students.

I had barely begun when Speidel, flanked by smirking Swanson and Bergstrom, held up a large cardboard sign with large letters announcing, "Your fly is open." My cool dribbled away in seconds. I turned and literally jumped to the rear of the blackboard just behind me. I checked myself. Everything was OK. My cool returned and the humor hit me. Emerging from behind the blackboard, I looked at the sea of questioning faces and gestured to the still smiling Speidel. "Jess, please come up here and bring that sign with you." When he reached the front of the class, I said, "Folks here is how they treat a new staff member." Jess flashed the sign. The laughter bounced off the four walls. Perhaps, the formality and decorum of the clinic suffered a little, but everyone felt warmer and more relaxed from that moment on.

The ACS Crusade Department provided the means to help divisions and regions within a state to improve their fund-raising techniques. In addition to the annual Crusade clinics, we organized special gifts round tables for local staff and volunteers. These demonstrated the importance of carefully researching the interests and past giving performance of potential large donors and assigning the most effective volunteer to solicit them. I conducted numerous fund-raising planning studies for regions, and did a fair amount of trouble shooting for regions with lagging fund-raising results. Everywhere, the staff showed both dedication, willingness to learn, and work hard. Nevertheless, the intense rivalry between divisions for recognition, funds, and national political power kept us aware of the characteristics so typical of a vital national organization.

THE AMERICAN ASSOCIATION OF FUND-RAISING COUNSEL, INC.

David M. Church retired as Executive Director of the American Association of Fund-Raising Counsel in 1964. Eldridge Hiller, former Vice President of the Council for Financial Aid to Education, succeeded him. In the spring of 1966, Hiller resigned and a search committee was formed under the chairmanship of Erwin D. (Tut) Tuthill. Tut was both President of the AAFRC and the John Price Jones Co. I had worked with him when he was a JPJ vice president in the late Forties and knew him pretty well. In June 1966, I got a call from my old friend and colleague from the Grove City College days, Donald Sheehan, now vice president for public relations at the University of Pennsylvania.

"Jack, you know Tut pretty well," he said. "Would you mind calling and telling him that I'm interested in the AAFRC job?"

"Be glad to Don, though I'm surprised that you would even consider working for that conservative gang."

THE SIXTIES—INCREASING COMPETITION

On the phone, Tut was most friendly, said he'd be happy to put Sheehan's name in the hat and asked, "How about you Jack? Would you be interested?"

"Thanks Tut for the thought, but no," I replied. "I'm very happy at ACS."

Two weeks later, Tut called and said, "Jack, several of the members have told me they'd like to talk to you about this position and the search committee has set up a meeting at the University Club in early August. David Church is staffing the effort and the Presidents of seven firms will be there. You'll get a chance to see several old friends if you'll join us." Obviously there was no way I could turn down such an invitation. I was curious about their plans for the future and I had nothing to lose so I agreed to meet with them.

LESSONS LEARNED

- Being on the staff of a professional fund-raising counseling firm provides you with broader experience with an ever-changing variety of clients, but you must be willing to be away from home for extended periods.
- The perception of the organizers of NSFR made the organization a pioneer in providing training and forums to increase the professionalism of fund-raising management. It also established an early goal of building public confidence in fund-raising practices.
- Most all the national headquarters of nonprofit organizations such as the American Cancer Society fight a constant battle to control competition between the regions, to be able to speak with one voice, set policies acceptable to all regional representation, establish common goals, and share professional resources.
- The fundamental steps to set up a fund-raising program never vary, even for an organization with the caliber of leadership and esoteric program such as the Foreign Policy Association. But a exciting program like this can make the fund-raising manager enthusiastic and more effective.
- In the early Sixties, grantors and grantees became aware of the broader dimensions of the philanthropic process and, at least, began to try to communicate better with each other.

- The platform of AAFRC provided many opportunities to become involved with other key nonprofit organizations. The AAFRC's Fair Practice Code set a standard of ethical practices that other organizations began to emulate. The fund-raising profession started to gain more respect and recognition within the entire field.

SECTION II: 1966–1992

American Philanthropy Gets Its Act Together

During the past 25 years, there has been a considerable gain in the capacity of the philanthropic process. Through trial and error, the many components of this complex field have learned to share concerns and combine resources to improve the effectiveness of American philanthropy.

This section traces the development and results of several major research projects and the work of the Peterson and Filer Commissions. These efforts expanded our knowledge and understanding of the field. It also reviews the efforts of the federal and state governments to regulate the activities of charities and the success the nonprofit field has had in joining forces to fend off legislation harmful to charitable giving.

Finally, this section reports on the evolution of national nonprofit organizations that are now equipped to identify and deal effectively with philanthropy's critical issues.

CHAPTER 4

The Sixties Continued—Fund-Raising Influences All of Philanthropy

Many in the field of philanthropy accepted fund-raising as a "necessary evil," never understanding how much the role of fund-raising effects all aspects of the field. It is an intrinsic part of the philanthropic process. During the late Sixties, there were a number of events which improved the public understanding and attitudes about both the fund-raising profession and the importance of philanthropy to our society. Because of my new position with the Association of Fund-Raising Counsel, Inc. I joined the membership or the boards of several organizations and was active involved with several new developments. Among them were:

The AAFRC East-West Conference on Philanthropy, Chicago	February 1966	While this was the third such conference, this one brought together an unprecedented number of key nonprofit organizations.
The Preparation by the 501(C)(3) Group for the 1969 Tax-Reform	1968 to 1969	Studying the effect of proposed tax measures on charitable giving, prepared us for our testimony before the House Ways Committee.
The National Conference on Philanthropy	1966 to 1969	Serving on the NCOP board allowed more participation in planning conferences for both grantors and grantees.

AAFRC East-West Conference in New York City, over 700 persons attended	May 1968	This was another step toward bringing key nonprofit organizations together to share common concerns. Benjamin J. Buttenweiser, Chairman of Columbia University's $200 million campaign, gave the keynote speech and all the faculty were top officers of AAFRC firms.
The Commission on Foundations and Private Philanthropy (the Peterson Commission)	1969 to 1970	This was an overdue study of the problems and goals of American philanthropy. Its results pointed the way for further action and increased understanding of philanthropy's problems.
The 1969 Tax Reform Act	1969	This effected future congressional tax reforms and planted the seeds for more coordinated efforts in the future by key nonprofit organizations.

THE AMERICAN ASSOCIATION OF FUND-RAISING COUNSEL, INC.

In 1935, the American Association of Fund-Raising Counsel, Inc. (AAFRC) was founded by 11 firms. In 1966, seven of the original eleven founding firms were still actively involved but its membership had grown to 25 firms. As stated by one of the founders, Carlton Ketchum, "... AAFRC was born in Manhattan, with the help of eight midwives, who tried to soften their glares of suspicion at each other."

On August 12, 1966, at the Union League Club in New York, I met with the Search Committee of the (AAFRC). They were interviewing candidates for a new executive director. Chaired by A. Creed Barnett, President of Tamblyn & Brown, Inc., and staffed by David M. Church, the committee included:

- Edwin Armstrong, Chairman of Ward Dreshman and Rheinhardt, Inc.;

FUND-RAISING INFLUENCES ALL OF PHILANTHROPY

- Lowell H. Brammer, Chairman, and Robert A. Dobbin, President, of American City Bureau/Beaver Associates;
- Donald L. Kersting, President of Kersting and Brown & Co.;
- David S. Ketchum, President of Ketchum, Inc.;
- Austin V. McClain, President of Marts & Lundy; and
- J.O. Newberry, President of Community Service Bureau, Inc.

Six of us had been called for interviews. Church made me welcome as I entered the waiting room. Donald Sheehan, who was also a candidate, rushed over and we each grabbed the other's arms. We hadn't seen each other for several years and this meeting gave us both pleasure. In recent phone conversations, we had talked about how the direction of philanthropy was changing. Key organizations were pushing for more coordinated efforts to increase giving and public understanding of philanthropy. We both felt that the AAFRC should not continue to be as exclusive of these efforts as it has been.

"Jack, it looks like we're in competition today whether we like it or not. But, except for myself, you're my first choice for this job," Sheehan said.

"Don, I hope it'll be you. I've great reservations about even being here. But this is a rare opportunity for one of us to be a factor in some overdue changes in this field."

I was ushered into the private room with the Search Committee seated around a rectangular table covered with a white cloth and coffee settings at each place. The seven company presidents positioned me at the end of the table where all could watch my every move, gave me a cup of coffee, and began the interview. I was expected to be conservative, even deferential, in my answers to this distinguished group. I presumed they would "tell" me what the AAFRC aspired to be and where it should go under the new leadership. The sight of several old friends and the presence of two contemporaries, Ketchum and Kersting, helped make me more relaxed.

"Jack, before we ask you any questions, we'd like you to tell us what you think of the AAFRC, how it can be more effective in this changing society, how it can build more client confidence in our services, and what its plans for the future ought to be," said Barnett.

Since I hadn't yet become very interested in this job and carried great reservations about the traditionally conservative "old guard" mentality of its leadership, my answers were not very deferential. I did my best to describe how the AAFRC was perceived by the field. Except for their wonderful publication, *Giving USA*, the association's efforts had been directed toward building a larger client base rather than on building relationships with other organizations in the field of philanthropy. I stated that:

- This fast-growing field needs more new talent and a better sense of direction.
- There are new and vital organizations which are working together that could use the experience and professionalism of AAFRC members.
- With its resources of practical experience, information gathering capacity, knowledge of proven techniques of fund-raising and the excellent fair practice code that all should emulate, AAFRC could be a catalyst in not only bringing these groups together but helping them develop agendas that will further everyone's interests.
- I would hope that the person you hire for this job would be given an opportunity to branch out and begin to establish closer relationships with such organizations as United Way, American Alumni Council, American College Public Relations Association, the Foundation Center, Council on Foundations, NSFR and the National Association of Hospital Development.

"The opportunity for AAFRC to take this leadership role, in my opinion, has never been greater," I concluded.

This was met by momentary silence. Then everyone began talking. Two points were repeated in several different contexts—How will this affect new business? I was asked. If given a free hand, what would I do to improve relationships with other key organizations?

I said I would try to:

- Gain participation for officers of member firms on the faculty of the many conferences now being held across the country.
- Form and host discussion groups on shared concerns; for example, the need for more trained personnel, the need to build better public understanding of the major accomplishments made possible by the fund-raising profession, the need to open dialogue with donor organizations about the best use of limited resources, and the need to try to develop a party line to lobby for improved federal and state legislation.

I added that, "Regionally, several firms could provide leadership for these measures and any conference on development would gain from a presentation from one of the top association officers."

There was nothing new or startling about these suggestions, but hearing them from an outsider who was in a position to reflect the views of many other professionals seemed to have some impact on these members of the AAFRC board. Before the interview was over, I felt I had accomplished two things: one, paved the way for the man of their choice to initiate change, and two, successfully eliminated myself from consideration for this position.

After some friendly good-byes, I went to Grand Central and called Katy to report. "Never fear," I told her. "I'm not going to leave American Cancer Society in the foreseeable future but I saw some old friends and had an opportunity to get several things off my chest about what this field really needs."

I shared this experience with Speidel at ACS who surprised me by saying that he really hoped I would be selected because the AAFRC's resources, if used well, would provide the best of all vehicles to improve our field. "We need you at ACS, but you've been in the field for over 20 years, know most of the players and are a real student of philanthropy's needs. By far, you are the best candidate," he said.

Whether Speidel's opinion was accurate or not, for the first time my mind started to grasp the long-range implications of obtaining this position. No longer would I be a fund-raiser. From the platform of AAFRC, I could concentrate on planning conference participation, open new doors to work with other groups and use 20 years of active duty to determine priorities for bringing organizations in the field closer together. Yet I knew nothing about running a trade association, and the difficulties of persuading conservative firm heads to try new activities was a formidable barrier. At this point there was nothing further to be done but wait. Of course, while waiting, my desire for this position grew steadily.

On August 16, I received a letter from Church which thanked me for meeting with the Search Committee and noted that they hadn't yet made a decision. I did my best to participate in the Crusade Department's many activities as it geared up for the fall-winter campaign. The annual Crusade Clinic was scheduled for October in Cincinnati and I had to concentrate on preparing my fund-raising courses even though my mind kept jumping to thoughts about AAFRC.

Word came on September 7, 1966 that the AAFRC Executive Committee had agreed to hire me as the Association's Executive Director. The memorandum to member firms by Austin McClain, president read:

> Mr. Schwartz has worked for both John Price Jones and George Brakeley. He is presently Assistant Vice President of the Crusade of the American Cancer Society. He has been active in the Association of Fund-Raising Directors, has served as its president from 1963 to 1965, and is well-known among philanthropic organizations. He is 47 years old and has a good presence. He did not seek the job but was one of those we asked to consider the position. He is now very enthusiastic about it.

"Oh yes!" to that last statement. I couldn't believe my good fortune. And little could I have known that my job changing days were over. I didn't step down until my retirement 22 years later.

On Monday, October 24, I walked into AAFRC's headquarters at 500 Fifth Avenue, on the corner of Fifth Avenue and 42nd Street, in New York City. Marie Medeo, who started as a clerk typist when Church opened the office 11 years earlier, was the acting office manager, greeted me warmly.

Right away, she reminded me that she had told me two weeks before the committee had made their decision that I was a cinch to get the job. A victim of a tragic accident when very young she fell off a swing when it was at the top of its arc and broke her back in several places. She was quite short with a humped back. This may have contributed to her strong and sometimes feisty personality. Always well-groomed, her dark eyes flashed as she approached all problems with a sharp self-confident voice and little tolerance for anyone who didn't see things exactly her way. This was *her* association and she didn't want anyone to forget it. But she seemed genuinely glad to see me. Without her knowledge and insight into the personalities of many of the key officers of the member firms, it would have been much more difficult for me to settle into this job. With boundless energy, she tackled all administrative tasks well and she was invaluable in helping me set up committee and board meetings.

My office was more than I had hoped for. On the corner of the building, it was surrounded on three sides by tall windows. A large new desk was in place with the fourth wall covered by packed book shelves containing virtually every book and pamphlet that was relevant to fund-raising and philanthropy. Waiting for me on the desk was an autographed copy of the just-published *Designs for Fund-Raising* by Harold J. Seymour:

FUND-RAISING INFLUENCES ALL OF PHILANTHROPY

> To Jack Schwartz, veteran of many fronts, whose varied talents and high competence have now marked him for another key role in the leadership of fund-raising. Good luck and best wishes.

This copy remains one of the most cherished books in my library.

Three major tasks needed immediate attention well before the close of the year. First, the fall is traditionally the time for the beginning research for next May's publication of *Giving USA*. Second, the third East-West Conference to be organized by the AAFRC was already scheduled in Chicago in February. Third, as many of the members headquarters as time permitted should have personal visits in order to gauge their needs and desires as well as plant a few seeds of hope for changes in the association's priorities.

Giving USA had become the "classic" for all aspects of the field. A definitive, complete summary of who gave what and to which part of the nonprofit sector, it provided data not available elsewhere. It required thorough and careful research, writing talent, and a well-developed sense of where to go to dig out essential statistics. Some came from the Internal Revenue Service, which made available (always at what seemed the last minute) selected samples of tax returns, some from the Council for Financial Aid to Education (corporate giving totals), some from the Council of Churches, some from the Foundation Center, and more than a little from the imaginative mind of the *Giving USA* editor. All figures were extrapolations. The methodology has since improved but many of the figures cannot be accurately verified. No hard data was, or is, yet available.

David M. Church created *Giving USA*. Reporting to the Association in May 1955, Church was a veteran of the Marine Corps in World War I, a newspaper man with the United Press and later worked with Hearst as Chief of the International News Bureau in London, where he had men like John Gunther and Edward R. Murrow on his staff. He joined the John Price Jones Co. in 1928 as vice president for public relations. He was a revered mentor to all of us trainees right after World War II, and I was humbled to become his successor even once removed.

Church, when he had assumed the job as executive of AAFRC, was described in 1985 by Wolcott Street in "Beacon for Philanthropy," written on the occasion of AAFRC's 50th Anniversary:

> His presence assured the survival of the Association; there now was an able, experienced person on hand to give it full-time direction. Church may well have contributed also to the breadth of view which enabled rival firms to keep working together; the quality of the man,

> his sense of humor, his long experience in working with volunteers and a rather choleric boss (John Price Jones), resulted in an ability to maintain equilibrium....

Although Church was now retired, he had held the AAFRC office together working two days a week while the search was going on for the new executive director. The first thing I did was to go to McClain then acting as president and ask him if we could engage Church to do the 1967 edition of *Giving USA*. I didn't mention my own doubts about my ability to do so even if I had the time. After clearing it with the executive committees McClain agreed. So did Church. I was delighted and relieved. The AAFRC also agreed to my request that we grant $2,500 to NSFR for one year's rental of office space.

Robert F. Duncan, President of Kersting & Brown, asked me to deliver a speech he had prepared on professionalism in the fund-raising field at a scheduled November 1966 meeting of the NSFR. He had a client conflict he couldn't resolve. (Client needs always came first.) It was entitled, "Where is Fund-Raising on the Way to Professionalism?" Following are some excerpts:

> Never in the 333 years of American private philanthropy have so many owed so much to so few as in the past half-century of modern fund-raising. Almost $100 billion has been given by the American public to churches, hospitals, health agencies, welfare agencies, community funds, and education. The application of the techniques of some of the pioneers in this field have made this possible. Men such as Charles Sumner Ward, Lyman L. Pierce, Carlton G. Ketchum, Dr. Arnaud C. Marts, and John Price Jones, along with a few others, have created a whole new vocation which now has some five-thousand men and women busily engaged.
>
> But is fund-raising a profession? The American College Dictionary defines "profession" as "a vocation requiring knowledge of some department of learning or science, especially one of the three vocations of Theology, Law, and Medicine, e.g. the learned professions".
>
> We are not the only one aspiring to the status of learned profession. The January 20, 1965 *New York Times* reported that the presentation of accreditation certificates to 152 members of the Public Relations Society of America.... Let's take a look at the vocation of fund-raising consulting and management. There are shyster lawyers and quack doctors. There are also shoddy, unethical fund-raisers, but one major difference is that the learned professions are respected and well regulated and have taken steps to make sure human weaknesses are curbed. This is a step our vocation has not yet taken. There are two kinds of fund-raising service: 1. individuals and 2. professional firms. Compared to the learned professions, both of these groups are ill-housed, ill-clad and ill-fed.

Duncan's strong prose conveyed a message not only to the NSFR but also to the AAFRC as far as I was concerned. The time was long overdue for all of us to join efforts to establish and enforce ethical standards that would help build public trust in the nonprofit field. I was determined that it would become a key subject for all the boards I was active in including the AAFRC, the New York chapter and the national NSFR.

> **CRITICAL ISSUE #1**
>
> *The ethical standards of conduct and practice established and maintained by the AAFRC, serve as an example for all in the fund-raising field.*

Also my mandate was to gain more respect for the important contribution the member firms made to philanthropy. Their work was little understood by few outside of the firms—even many clients. The firms that formed the association in 1935 knew that it was essential to set ethical standards of conduct and practice in order to gain more public trust and understanding of the fund-raising field. Also this could alert all concerned about the practices they had a right to expect from any fund-raising professional.

Good fund-raising counsel can do certain things for a client but not others. The following things can only be done by an institution:

- Design a program to fulfill the proven needs in a community.
- Enlist and cultivate committed affluent and influential leaders.
- Develop its constituency—both volunteers to work on a campaign and an audience aware of the needs.
- Set a realistic goal that a study determines is feasible.
- Solicit gifts directly. This is a task best done only by volunteers.
- It cannot relieve the top leadership and staff of responsibility for the success of the campaign. Professional counsel will cause them to work harder than ever.
- Since no one, including counsel, can get blood out of a stone these conditions must be in force from the beginning.

There are, however, important things good counsel can provide. Among them:

- Help appraise the potential and sharpen the priorities. If the study shows that only so much can be raised, the client must decide how that money can best be spent for the institution.
- Identify the client's strengths and weaknesses and recommend where possible how to convert the weaknesses into strengths.
- Help set the conditions for action e.g., getting the board and leadership committed to the program and geared to begin key solicitation.
- Provide broad experience drawn from similar campaigns and bring to bear its collective judgment when difficult problems arise.
- Predict costs and maintain strict budget control.
- Provide a program plan that includes schedules, quotas, goals, and deadlines.
- Organize the leadership into the most effective committees for fund-raising.
- Needle and prod the foot-draggers—something that isn't easy for paid staff of an institution to do.
- Finally, an effective professional counseling firm has its own reputation at stake every time it engages in a major program. What former clients say about its professionalism is one of the firm's most important assets. As one college president said, "We must raise money without any regrets."

THE 1967 EAST-WEST CONFERENCE

I began to devote the necessary time to organizing the East-West Conference and the February board meeting. The conference was scheduled for February 15 and 16, 1967. Charles Brecht, vice president of John Price Jones Co., Inc., chaired the program committee. At our first meeting he pointed out that the faculty had to be identified and enlisted and that we needed a keynote speaker. He agreed with me that we should do our best to develop a faculty which represented several areas of philanthropy. In 1964, ACS had a wonderful Crusade Chairman, the Honorable George M. Leader, Governor of Pennsylvania (1955–1959), now an insurance executive. I had gotten to know him well, so I felt free to call him then and there. Leader said yes immediately to our request that he be the keynote speaker, and we were off and running.

> **CRITICAL ISSUES #2**
>
> *Conferences and seminars on any aspect of the philanthropic process gain by having a wide representation of key nonprofit organizations involved in the planning. This can improve both the program and the quality of the attendees.*

In keeping with the goal of bringing together representatives of many branches of the nonprofit sector, this faculty turned out to be a good example of such cooperation. It included:

Dr. William Homer Turner, Vice-President, United States Steel Foundation;
Mrs. John J. Bergan, prominent Chicago volunteer;
John P. Knox, Jr., Director, American Heart Association;
Richard C. Millett, Vice-President, International Paper Foundation;
Edward B. Newhill, President, Indianapolis Hospital Foundation;
Richard F. O'Brien, Vice-President of Development, University of Chicago;
Dr. Manning M. Patillo, Vice-President, Danforth Foundation;
James R. Reynolds, Assistant to the President for Development, Harvard University;
Conrad Teitell, Editor, *Tax-Wise Giving;* and
yours truly.

Four hundred attended despite a Chicago near-blizzard. Speakers were required to prepare papers in advance so that we were able to print and distribute transcripts to several thousand nonattendees two weeks later.

At the reception the first evening, I moved through the crowd with Charles Brecht and Robert Currie, vice president of American City Bureau/Beaver Associates, a Chicago-based member firm. Out of the corner of my eye I realized we were being followed by a pretty, young woman dressed in a skin-tight, very short, sequined dress strumming a guitar suspended on a gold leather strap around her shoulders. She seemed to be singing softly but in that boisterous crowd you couldn't hear a word. Finally, Currie turned to me and said, "This is Elsie, would you please give her 50 dollars?" Raleigh Smith, the AAFRC treasurer had joined us by then; when I looked at him, he gave me a weak smile and shrugged his shoulders. Since it was alright with Raleigh, I complied. Later Brecht told me that he and Currie had been out on the town the night before and found Elsie so entertaining that they thought she would be a nice addition to our reception. Trouble was no one ever heard her. I realized then that my initial assumption of very conservative and proper gentlemen with the member firms needed some revision.

Mrs. John Bergan gave my favorite presentation, "How to Organize and Get the Maximum Mileage Out of Women in Fund-Raising." With wit and charm, she noted that they use the natural advantage of women's intuition in setting the campaign process. She advocated that they made excellent committee chairs. She extolled the proven success of building a solicitation team that includes an enthusiastic woman volunteer along with a man or men with clout and influence.

She left us with a quotation from John Cheever's story, *The Brigadier and the Golf Widow*, as a good caricature of our traditional, narrow outlook on the women's role in fund-raising:

> "I hope it will help put this outlook to rest," she added.
>
> Leaving her house one afternoon, Mrs. Pastern stopped to admire the October light. It was the day to canvass for infectious hepatitis. Mrs. Pastern had been given 16 names, a bundle of literature, and a printed book of receipts. It was her work to go among her neighbors and collect their checks. Her house stood on a rise of ground, and before she got into her car she looked at the houses below. Charity as she knew it was complex and reciprocal, and most every roof she saw signified charity. Mrs. Balcomb worked for the brain. Mrs. Ten Eyke did mental health. Mrs. Trenchard worked for the blind. Mrs. Horowitz was in charge of diseases of the nose and throat. Mrs. Templer was tuberculosis, Mrs. Surcliff was Mother's March of Dimes, Mrs. Graven was cancer, and Mrs. Gilksen did the kidney. Mrs. Hewlitt leads the birth-control league, Mrs. Eyerson was arthritis, and, way in the distance, could be seen the slate roof of Ethel Litteton's house, a roof that signified gout.[1]

KEY FUND-RAISING TIP #26

Effective volunteer leadership depends on individuals who are committed, enthusiastic, and willing to give time and effort to a campaign. No other qualifications such as gender, ethnic background or cultural differences are relevant.

When I returned to New York after the Chicago meetings, I began to take stock of the nuances of this new job. The honeymoon was about

---

1. © 1964 by John Cheever, reprinted with the permission of Wylie, Aitken & Stone, Inc.

over. Already I had learned that an essential step before any meaningful action is first to achieve a consensus of the members involved. The differences in attitudes, desires for new actions, and the need to be part of them was quite varied. As expected, they were preoccupied with running their firms and gave highest priority to gaining and retaining clients. Three board meetings were scheduled each year, with the executive committee on call year-round. To a surprising extent, they expected me to run the association matters while never letting me forget that I would be accountable for balancing the budget, improving our image, making meaningful studies about giving that would help their work with clients, and all activities which would broaden our acceptance and influence.

BRANCHING OUT: THE 501(C)(3) GROUP

From this new platform, before the year was over, I was invited to participate in several organizations devoted to improving the field. One that made the most significant contributions for many years to come was the 501(c)(3) Group. Only organizations that can prove their mission is charitable and nonprofit can receive the 501(c)(3) rating from the Internal Revenue Service. It means that all contributions made to the organization could be deducted from the donor's taxable income. This represents a truly special testimony of the commitment by our democratic government to foster the philanthropic process.

KEY FUND-RAISING TIP #27

Tax incentives are not by themselves the only important incentive to give to charity. Most donors have a menu of reasons for making a gift ranging from:

1. *peer pressure;*
2. *direct personal experience with the program;*
3. *altruism;*
4. *being a fellow-advocate;*
5. *community concerns;*
6. *sharing the desire to further research and increase facilities;*
7. *tax incentives, etc.*

Each individual will put these motivations in a different priority. But tax incentives are important and often provide the means for a donor to maximize the size of a gift.

The 501(c)(3) Group had no charter or constitution or elected officers. It was started in the late Fifties to identify harmful tax measures and agree on the message that should be conveyed to Congress about the effects of passing such legislation. It remained an "informal organization" so as to be less-threatening to people on the "hill." This posture helped relax representatives and encouraged them to be more candid with us.

Our nonmembership represented an impressive array of informed representatives of the philanthropic field including top executives from: national nonprofit organizations for the arts, foreign service, education, religion, social welfare, foundations, United Way, AAFRC, CPAs, and tax lawyers.

Wilbur D. Mills, Democrat congressman from Arkansas, was then the Chairman of the House Ways and Means Committee, through which all tax reforms must pass. In the mid-sixties he was all-powerful and hadn't yet been politically destroyed by his love of alcohol and involvement with Fanne Foxe, a local stripper. Dr. Laurence (Larry) N. Woodward, both lawyer and economist, was the Committee's able and intelligent chief of staff. At least once a year, Larry met with the 501(c)(3) Group to our common gain. He reviewed with us current legislation being considered by congress and the committee. We gave him our reaction and analysis of its potential impact on philanthropy and whether the nonprofit field would back or fight the proposals. He trusted us and we trusted him.

This continuing dialogue not only educated some key congressional staff and us about the subtleties caused by some proposals, but in potentially serious cases (and there was a surprising number—for example, those which surfaced in the 1969 Tax Reform Act) gave us both time and direction in order to prepare rebuttal testimony.

> **CRITICAL ISSUE #3**
>
> *The need to stimulate continuing interest and constant study of proposed changes in tax laws regarding charitable gifts must stay high on the agenda of all key nonprofit organizations. Their future survival can depend, again and again, on being organized to fight bad legislation.*

The 501(c)(3) Group continued its excellent work for nearly 30 years. By mutual consent, its activities were taken over in the early

Eighties by the INDEPENDENT SECTOR'S government relations department which had become very effective.

THE NATIONAL COUNCIL ON PHILANTHROPY

The National Council on Philanthropy (NCOP), as established in 1954, had the primary purpose of advising corporate donors on the merits of the many grant proposals they received from nonprofit organizations. It was closely associated with the National Chamber of Commerce.

Since then, it had broadened its constituency and modified its programs to meet changing conditions. Its annual conference became the principal forum for discussion of issues affecting grantors and grantees. At last there was an organization that brought together two of the major segments of philanthropy—donors and donees. Its impressive board contained corporate and foundation-giving officers from more than a dozen leading corporations ranging from: American Telephone & Telegraph Co., to Sears and Roebuck & Co. The grantees were represented by the Council for Better Business Bureaus, the National Health Council, the National Council of Churches, the National Assembly for Social Policy & Development, AAFRC, and the National Information Bureau.

> **CRITICAL ISSUE #4**
> *The field of philanthropy simply cannot get its act together without identification of shared problems, a full exchange of ideas, and joint participation by both grantors and grantees.*

I accepted an invitation to join the NCOP board in 1967. This board met three times a year. We developed a free and easy exchange with each other and discovered how much we had in common. Building on this, the annual conferences were very popular and attracted a good spectrum of representatives of philanthropic organizations. It became the birthplace of many innovations for the field.

GIVING USA AND AAFRC PUBLIC RELATIONS

Church completed the 1967 edition of *Giving USA* (covering 1966 contributions) in May 1967. It stated that the American public gave $13.939

billion in 1966. This invaluable report was used by virtually every politician, organization, donors and donees, the media, and the general public. It did more to acquaint the government and public about the importance of philanthropy, and it helped make the AAFRC more of a symbol of authority and public service.

Without Church this edition would never have been completed in my first and very busy year. He wanted now to enjoy his well-earned retirement, so I went to the board and obtained permission to hire a (hopefully) permanent assistant to produce the next edition and to help me deal with our growing relations with other organizations. I was very successful in my search. In July 1967, Byrne P. Whalen joined the staff as assistant executive director. Byrne had been the development director for Nazareth Hospital in Pennsylvania, served with the American Cancer Society and a was decorated flyer in World War II. He wrote beautifully, knew how to conduct research, and had direct and useful experience in this field.

With Byrne's strong help, we began to communicate the goals and shared concerns of the Association to the professional staff. In addition to encouraging and maintaining high standards, ethics and professional quality in fund-raising, our programs were directed toward improving public understanding of our services. Statistical analyses of giving to various elements of philanthropy, surveys of campaign results, and costs for major hospitals and institutions of higher education served by member firms, all helped provide yardsticks to measure the efficiency of their work. We produced several pamphlets describing how to engage professional counsel, what they can do, and, very importantly, what they can't do—always with member's participation and final approval. Initial preparation and research for the 1968 edition of *Giving USA* was in progress and Austin V. McClain, the new AAFRC president, spent a great deal of his time on association matters. I discussed every move I made before making it with him.

THE 1968 EAST-WEST CONFERENCE

This was the fourth East-West Conference organized by AAFRC. The first was in San Francisco, February 1965; the second in Boston, February 1966; and the third in Chicago, February 1967. This one was set for May 8 and 9, 1968, at the brand new New York Hilton Hotel. It drew more than 700 individuals representing virtually every segment of philanthropy. The venerable Benjamin J. Buttenwieser, who chaired

Columbia University's $200 million campaign, gave the keynote speech. This time, I followed the suggestion of McClain and other members and confined the rest of the faculty to top officers from each of the 24 member firms. This worked very well because those selected, without exception, were articulate and well-informed. Transcripts of all presentations were printed and over 5,000 were distributed without cost to a wide audience.

McLain wrote in its introduction, "Our speakers represent a wealth of experience in fund-raising for philanthropic causes. We believe that the following transcripts of their presentations will be of interest to all concerned with philanthropy, and a valuable addition to libraries on this subject." This helped to reinforce the recognition of the spirit of public interest contained in the association's programs.

THE PETERSON COMMISSION (THE COMMISSION ON FOUNDATIONS AND PRIVATE PHILANTHROPY)

Claiming that attacks against philanthropic foundations by congressional leaders and others have been becoming increasingly hostile, John D. Rockefeller III invited Peter G. Peterson, Chairman of Bell and Howell, to form a commission to study American philanthropy and foundations in February 1969. Quickly called the "Peterson Commission," Peterson selected 15 private citizens representing education, the arts, legal profession, former government officials, labor, publishing, and corporate executives. All operating funds were raised from private sources to avoid any conflict of interest, no foundations were even approached.

I received a call from Peterson in early August asking if I could meet with him to review the availability of our research and statistical data for the Commission. Just about every professional I knew was excited about the concept of this commission, so with alacrity, I quickly arranged a date to join him in Chicago that week. He picked me up at the Chicago Airport in his private limousine. We chatted and got down to business as we were driven to my hotel in downtown Chicago. My first experience in a real limousine was only outdone by Peterson's magnetic personality and the awesome fact that he had a hand-held telephone whose ring interrupted us several times on the way.

Peter, as I was told to always call him, is a caring, highly intelligent man. Then only 43 years old, he was considered one of the top corporate officers in the country. A handsome, tall man with dark hair and penetrating brown eyes, he was most sophisticated about, and aware of, the issues the Commission would have to face.

One of my first questions was how did they expect to raise the money? He explained that in addition to not approaching foundations for grants, he had decided not to apply for a 501(c)(3) rating from the IRS for the Commission. "No one can accuse us of conflict of interest," he said.

As noble as this was, I couldn't hold back my view that he had missed an opportunity to more fully fund this work. Because no gifts were tax deductible, fund-raising was unnecessarily inhibited and the needed funds for research and programs were always in short supply.

KEY FUND-RAISING TIP #28

As soon as a nonprofit organization is established, it should apply for a 501(c)(3) rating from IRS. This enables donors to deduct their gifts to that cause from their taxable income which provides an important incentive for them to give.

The final report, entitled "Commission Foundations and Private Giving," University of Chicago Press, was issued in 1970. It noted that, among other things, American private foundations had come under heavy siege in recent years, been investigated by four Congressional committees, and analyzed by the Treasury Department. As the House of Representatives moved to enact what would become the 1969 Tax Bill, the following charges against foundations were that:

1. Many or most foundations were nothing but tax dodges for millionaires;
2. Many foundations represented great concentration of money and power, controlled by a self-appointed, self-perpetuating "Ivy League" establishment;
3. Foundations were heavily involved in politics, not charity;
4. Foundations often used their money to further extreme ideologies, whether of the left or the right;
5. Foundations squandered on high salaries and lavish expense accounts money that should go to charity; and
6. Foundations hoarded money as it were their own when, in fact, the money belongs to the public and should be spent on charity.

FUND-RAISING INFLUENCES ALL OF PHILANTHROPY

This description accurately captures the motivations and reasons for forming the commission. The Peterson Commission Report stressed the need for self-regulation by foundations; they needed to do a much better job of policing and wiping out the self-interest and malfeasance of a few "bad apples." According to the Report:

> The aim is to make an objective appraisal of philanthropic foundations in America.... No government agency, however vigorously led, can readily break the crust of bureaucratic habits which can lead to mechanical performance of old things in old ways ... though the old ways may have been rendered obsolete by new conditions.[2]

All this called for a very careful examination by the Commission.... yet when the commission cast about for relevant data, there was very little hard evidence on hand which either refuted or supported the allegations made.

I assured Peterson that the AAFRC would immediately begin to research and share with the Commission early data on 1969 giving, the percentage of the gross national product to annual giving (which we found averaged 1.8 percent), and the trends in corporate giving from 1964 to 1968 (contributions in the Sixties ranged between 0.97 to 1.12 percent of total giving.)

> The Commission began its work when ... Foundations and charitable giving in general were under scrutiny by Congress ... because of the Tax Reform Act of 1969.... In the course of the legislative process, some of the provisions most harmful to philanthropy were eased or eliminated in the final version of the bill.".... Yet the experience as a whole raised an uneasy question: who spoke for philanthropy when the chips were down?[3]

Sad to say, the commission's findings did not create much of a stir. Many copies were read, and then tossed on a bookshelf. But the Report was the basis of Peterson's testimony before the Senate Finance Committee. The Report also forced the field to address the need to establish better relationships with both the government and the public, and to fend off inevitable attacks in the future.

In response, many of us soundly endorsed the Commission's most important recommendation—the establishment of an Advisory Board on Philanthropic Policy. The proposal suggested it be a quasi-governmental board consisting of 10 to 15 outstanding private citizens

---

2. University of Chicago Press. *Foundations, Private Giving and Public Policy* (1970), Preface, pg. XIV.
3. *Ibid.* pg. 5.

through Presidential appointment, with Senate confirmation, and given a specific legislative mandate to advise the Secretary of the Treasury. Its scope included philanthropy as a whole, not just foundations. It was assigned to provide information about philanthropy, continue evaluation of the regulation of charitable organizations, and to continue reviewing the effectiveness and current operation of the tax incentive system.

Operating with the concept that the private sector should set its own agenda and remain above any political considerations, most of us resisted the recommendation that the board be quasi-governmental. This issue would surface again when the Filer Commission's recommendations for a permanent commission on philanthropy were considered five years later.

CRITICAL ISSUE #5

A "private" national nonprofit organization can operate more effectively and more freely if it is not beholden to any political considerations. It should work with the government as an independent "partner."

In late 1970, I agreed to chair a committee to pursue this project and give it collective support. Serving with me were representatives of the Council for Financial Support of Education, the National Society of Fund-Raisers, the Foundation Center, the American Hospital Association, the American Alumni Counsel, and the American Association of College Public Relations. When we informed Peterson about our keen interest we were delighted to learn that he had already made a date to discuss this with President Nixon's top staff, Robert Halderman and John Erlichman. Ironically, Halderman and Erlichman had other concerns on their agenda, and were so impressed with Peterson, that they made a date the same day for him in the Oval Office. After a discussion, Nixon appointed him Assistant to the President for International Economic Affairs. On January 1971, I wrote:

> Dear Peter:
> Congratulations on your prestigious appointment as the Director of the Council on International Economic Policy. My respect in President Nixon's judgment has just increased considerably.
> As you can imagine, I am sad . . . that philanthropy has lost one of its most intelligent, understanding, and articulate spokesmen. However, I am confident that you won't forget how much we need lead-

ership in this area and that if time permits, you will be able to push ... to get the Philanthropic Policy Board established.

Two years later, Peterson was appointed Secretary of Commerce. So much for the Advisory Board on Philanthropic Policy as far as the White House was concerned. But we did not give up, as the next chapter will show.

THE TAX REFORM ACT OF 1969

There was a forest fire of tax proposals raging through congress in 1969 and the emphasis was on creating more government revenue. The integrity and even the need for charities were under review. We were most vulnerable to new taxation. Thanks to the work of the 501(c)(3) Group and the many conferences we had with Dr. Woodworth and John Martin, Counsel for the House Ways and Means Committee, we were pretty well prepared for this fight—and what a fight it was. While we had no mandate to take up the foundations' cause, we caucused to make sure our "party line" and proposed testimony dealt with shared concerns about the whole philanthropic scene. We had to emphasize our position either for or against each major proposal and why.

Tax bills traditionally begin in the House Ways and Means Committee. After this committee hammers out its version, it is sent out to the House. Next, the House votes on it after caucuses, some debates, and amendments. This version is sent to the Senate Finance Committee, which reviews it, conducts hearings and then sends its version to the Senate floor. The Senate floor can amend to its heart's content. Finally, a Senate bill is put in the hopper. Then, both the House and the Senate bills are reviewed by a conference committee comprised of six members of the House Ways and Means committee, and six members of the Senate Finance Committee. Together they come up with a final bill which goes to the White House for the President's signature or veto. Therefore, in addition to approaching members of the two paramount committees, we all did our best to reach and make our case known to as many senators and congressmen as possible by phone, personal visit, or letters signed by an influential volunteer.

The bill on tax reform, H.R. 13270, as passed out by the House Ways and Means Committee to the Senate Finance Committee in the summer of 1969, was, despite our efforts, fraught with passages harmful to philanthropy. Armed with the approach agreed upon at 501(c)(3) briefings on September 17, 1969, a group of us testified on this bill before the Senate Finance Committee. I was given 15 minutes to make my case.

In summary, I identified myself as the Executive Vice President of the AAFRC, an organization with 23 fund-raising counseling firms which serve 1,000 nonprofit organizations annually, on programs that raise $1 billion in contributions. My main points were:

> Partnership with government is mutually advantageous to the public and private sectors; this is readily apparent in health and education; tax advantages have encouraged a dual system of social programs; private giving is a major factor in hospital and educational instruction; tax incentives have encouraged private support which now stands at $15.8 billion annually. Incentives are necessary to continue its advance.

Several sections of the proposed bill will have a drastic effect on contributions:

1. Allocation of deductions;
2. Limitations on tax preferences;
3. 7.5 percent tax on foundations; and
4. Proposed treatment of capital gains in gifts of property to private foundations.

Gifts of appreciated property comprise 48 percent of annual gifts to educational construction, 27 percent of gifts to colleges, 38 percent of gifts to hospital construction and 35 percent of annual gifts to hospitals. The proposed foundation tax would come from funds now available for grants. Foundation grants assume far more importance than their monetary value when they are used as challenge grants. The Ford Foundation made challenge grants to 16 college and university capital fund-raising campaigns, which raised only $35 million in their previous efforts. Thanks to the matching grants, they increased their totals to $118 million—more than three-fold.

Social needs are increasing and projected to double by 1976. We ask that at least these changes be made:

1. Exclude charitable deductions from allocation;
2. Exclude appreciation in charitable gifts from tax preference computation;
3. Delete foundation tax; and

4. Continue present treatment of gifts of appreciated property to all foundations.

John D. Rockefeller III, as the first witness, had made many cogent points. After stressing the importance of philanthropy's many contributions toward solving society's problems, he lauded the success of the partnership between philanthropy and the government to make these programs more effective.

> Our pluralistic system, in which philanthropy is a major element, is the most unique in the world. Instead of all social problems falling to the government, our system makes it possible for private citizens and private organizations to help solve them. With foresight and wisdom, the Congress historically created the conditions for such a system and has consistently maintained them over the years .... The bill now before you would upset the delicate balance of our pluralistic system which has encouraged private initiative to help in a meaningful and constructive way in coping with society's problems .... The basic philosophy of the House bill appears to be that our traditional tax incentives for charitable contributions are in fact tax loopholes .... A number of the provisions would drastically curtail the availability of funds for philanthropic purposes.

Other members of the 501(c)(3) Group elaborated on Mr. Rockefeller's excellent opening statement and joined with me in defending the important role of foundations. In the final version of the passed bill, all our priorities came home except for taxes on foundations. They were hit with a 4.5 percent excise tax ostensibly to provide the Treasury Department funds to audit foundation activity. Within the first year, it became apparent that this tax generated revenue totaled five times the cost of audit activity by Treasury—an inequity that would prevail for several years.

The net result of this fight was that philanthropic organizations learned the importance of joining forces to preserve our capacity in order to serve society's needs. More collaboration was necessary, for real progress, but now we knew each other better and the seeds for mutual trust had been planted.

LESSONS LEARNED

- The improved response by leaders of nonprofit organizations to participate in the planning and execution of seminars and

conferences on philanthropy was essential to progress for the field.
- The nonprofit field began to recognize that it had to give serious attention to proposed tax reforms concerned with charitable gifts in order to organize a fight against those that would hurt charities.
- The NCOP conferences showed that grantors and grantees can communicate, get together, and build improved mutual empathy.
- The Peterson Commission identified many more of philanthropy's problems than its solutions. However, on balance it proved itself to be a seminal influence on future studies embodied by the Filer Commission three years later.
- Drawing on the resources and the professionalism of the AAFRC members, new programs such as expanded East-West conferences, tax-reform testimonies, and working with the Peterson Commission, helped to bring the field closer together.
- The program in the Sixties helped to identify a new generation of leaders in the nonprofit world who would be tried and tested in the developments of the next 20 years.

CHAPTER 5

The Early Seventies— A Time of Burgeoning Efforts to Bring Together Most Elements of Philanthropy

A new awareness overtook the philanthropic community during the early Seventies. The time had come to look inward to identify common concerns and shared goals which could improve the philanthropic process. A combination of factors—the Tax Reform Act of 1969, the findings of the Peterson Commission, the increasing participation of many organizations in philanthropic conferences (including more active roles by the Foundation Center and the Council on Foundations), and the growth of membership and activities of NSFR, AAC, ACPRA— helped everyone get to know each other a little better. With this came a heightened sense of the nonprofit sector as a "community." This community spirit continued to grow. The events which stood as mile markers on the road to improved philanthropic process included:

The AAFRC East-West Conference	May 1970	Peter G. Peterson, keynote speaker, identified the basic problem affecting the field, namely a lack of cooperation and coordination between nonprofit organizations. He urged that steps be taken to ensure such cooperation within the field, and with the federal government.

AAFRC's further involvement with key nonprofit organizations	1970 to 1973	Continued coordination with NCOP, NSFR, 501(C)(3) Group, Campaign for Philanthropy, tax reforms, and Coalition for Public Good.
Personnel changes at the AFFRC	Late 1969 through 1972	Many organizations, like the AAFRC, restructured their top personnel so interaction between organizational peers could be facilitated.
Ford Foundation Seminar for Educational Interns and Institute for Educational Management	June 1969 to March 1972 Late 1969 to 1971	Both of these programs demonstrated that executives of an eclectic group of nonprofit organizations could work together to produce successful and beneficial results.
The Campaign for Philanthropy and The Coalition for Public Good	1971 through 1973	J.O. Newberry's dream of a positive campaign for philanthropy gave birth to the Coalition for Public Good. This Coalition later brought many members of the nonprofit sector together to fight impending tax reforms on charitable deductions.
501(c)(3) Group's study on the effect of taxation on gifts	1971	Dr. Martin S. Feldstein was commissioned by the 501(c)(3) Group to conduct a study which proved that philanthropy would lose more than the government would gain if charitable gifts lost their tax-deductible status. This became a rallying point in the 1973 tax reforms and later led to a more thorough study by the Filer Commission.

1973 Tax Reform Act	Fall of 1972 to Spring of 1973	The Coalition for Public Good armed with the results of the Dr. Feldstein's study helped nonprofit organizations develop a party line in the fight against these new tax reforms. This new sense of cooperation of organizations within the field proved not only beneficial, but absolutely necessary for the continued well-being of the nonprofit sector.
The National Institute of Continuing Education (NICE)	Fall 1793	Under the leadership of its president, Henry Goldstein, NSFR establishes a 501(c)(3) entity NICE to foster programs designed to improve the fund-raising profession.

THE 1970 AAFRC EAST-WEST CONFERENCE

Peter G. Peterson accepted my invitation to be the keynote speaker for the AAFRC's fifth East-West Conference at the New York Hilton on May 13 and 14, 1970. Its theme was "Philanthropy in the Seventies" and its purpose was to "identify, analyze, and discuss solutions to the problems that all facets of philanthropy must face and try to solve in the Seventies." In his presentation, Peter stressed the Commission's frustrations with the lack of available data on foundation activity, as well as the lack of sufficient data on the field of philanthropy as a whole. He graciously praised the work of AAFRC and the ready cooperation the Commission had received from many philanthropic organizations.

"The real battle to build a better partnership with the government is just beginning," he said. His top priority remained the organization of the Advisory Council on Philanthropic Policy. He welcomed all suggestions on its implementation. (As noted in chapter 4, his appointment at the end of 1970 as Assistant to President Nixon for International Economic Affairs unfortunately took him out of this battle.)

> **CRITICAL ISSUE #6**
>
> *Until the late Sixties, very little cooperation existed within the philanthropic community. Insufficient data was kept or released on foundation activities or the field of philanthropy as a whole, as witnessed by the Peterson Commission. Steps had to be taken to ensure better cooperation both within the field and with the federal government.*

I organized a Conference Steering Committee composed of top executives of several key philanthropic organizations including the American Hospital Association, the American Alumni Council, the National Society of Fund-raisers, the Ford Foundation, the National Assembly for Social Policy and Development, the International Paper Company Foundation, the Foundation Center, the American College Public Relations Association, and the United Community Funds and Councils of America (forerunner of the United Way.) We worked together well, agreeing on the faculty, and making sure that the agenda gave adequate representation of each major component of the nonprofit sector. This set a pattern for future cooperative efforts. Over 400 attendees seemed pleased with the conference program and the way it represented so many aspects of philanthropy.

PERSONNEL CHANGES AT THE AAFRC

Late in 1969, Byrne Whalen resigned to relocate in Philadelphia. Harlan F. Lang, formerly with the Young President's Organization, replaced Whalen as director of public relations. Until September 1972, Lang did an excellent job as the editor of *Giving USA* and liaison with key philanthropic organizations. In September 1972, Joan McC. Lundberg from the Council For Financial Aid Education, succeeded Lang. In May 1972, the AAFRC Board changed my title from Executive Vice President to President so "Schwartz could operate on the same level as many of his peers," as they explained. Roger A. Wilson, President of John F. Rich Co. Inc., was elected the association's first chairman of the board. This title, from then on, designated the volunteer head of the association.

> **CRITICAL ISSUE # 7**
>
> *Reorganization began to take place in many key organizations so that peers within those various organizations could interact more freely.*

FORD FOUNDATION SEMINAR FOR EDUCATIONAL FUND-RAISING INTERNS (1969-1972)

James W. Bryant, program advisor for special projects in education for the Ford Foundation, had a BS from Tuskegee Institute, a MBA from the Wharton School of Commerce, and had served as Executive Vice President of the United Negro College Fund. He was highly respected by college educators, especially those from predominantly black colleges.

In 1969, James W. Armsey of the Ford Foundation, Maurice G. Gurin, and Bryant collaborated in designing a new Ford program to train black interns from predominantly black colleges in educational development. Armsey was the Ford Foundation's Program Director who was responsible for the foundation's exciting program that made available matching grants to many colleges and universities, stimulating greatly increased giving to higher education in the late Fifties and early Sixties.

Predominantly black colleges faced two continuing financial crises: one, to make better use of resources they already possessed, and two, to find substantial additional funds for general operations over and above tuition and fees. I was invited to serve on a steering committee of the officers of seven nonprofit organizations. Our task was to conduct a program for black development interns. The presidents of seven predominantly black colleges were asked to choose four to five from their faculty for this program. After screening by the steering committee, 11 interns were selected for a one-year training program in college development.

My assignment was to organize a four-day seminar in New York for initial orientation on the philanthropic field and start-up training on fund-raising for the interns. None of them had any development experience so their minds were open and responsive. As an advocate of the principle that fund-raising skills, once learned, can be applied successfully to a wide variety of causes, my faculty was representative of the field. Over the initial objections of Armsey, and others who would have preferred a faculty of only development officers from higher educational institutions, I enlisted a wide range of development professionals from the Salvation Army, the American Cancer Society, the AAFRC, the United Community Funds and Councils of America, and corporate foundations. We designed a program to give the 11 young and eager black interns, including two women, a broader sense of the field.

Beginning June 16, 1969, for four days at the Roosevelt Hotel, they were taught the fundamentals of fund-raising. Next, each intern relocated for six months to the campus of a major university and worked in the development office under the direct supervision of that school's development officer. This remarkable and inspired move provided the interns with a most useful learning experience. The participating colleges and universities included Amherst, Weslyan, Tulane, Duke, Dartmouth, Emory, Lehigh, New School for Social Research, University of Miami, University of Rochester, and University of Michigan. The participating development officers at these institutions willingly accepted this responsibility in the true spirit of teaching and performing a public service.

Six months into this program, presidents of black colleges were invited to a four-day seminar on important fundamentals of fund-raising and their responsibilities to a fund-raising campaign as the college's chief executive officer. In the final two months, the intern and the supervising development officer returned to the intern's campus to set up a local development program. Even more critical, this gave the intern, with the backing of the senior development officer, the chance to apply newly learned techniques and to acquaint the key faculty and administration of their roles and responsibilities so important to a successful development program.

The first year was so successful that the Ford Foundation repeated the program without change. The final meeting was held at the Essex House in New York on March 21–25, 1971 for the second class of interns and the presidents of their college. In late 1971, Bryant left the Ford Foundation to become vice president of development of Howard University. Samuel N. Gough Jr., one of the original interns, became Bryant's executive assistant. Together they set up a new program for black interns based on the best elements of the earlier project. Ford Foundation made a grant directly to Howard University to fund the program for another four years. Nineteen more interns were trained at Howard for a total of 40 in six years. Communications were kept open between the graduates through the formation of an intern alumni group called AFRO.

The relationships established between the interns, the faculty, and the Steering Committee the first two years were durable in their warmth and friendship. The unique opportunity to have newcomers work along side seasoned veterans had established a real sense of camaraderie. The bulk of the original group, now members of AFRO, invited the Steering Committee to a celebration and reunion in Atlanta two years later. We all attended, including Maury Gurin, who was one of the program's creators. Gurin was about five feet, four inches tall, completely bald with a professorial manner, quite a contrast to my nearly six-feet in height and full head of hair. The "wit" of the interns was a constant source of entertainment for me. I remember one, in particular, by the name of Herman Lunzy. He joined several of us at the opening reception at the Atlanta meeting and said to me, "Hey Maury, how'ya you doing?"

"Herman, I replied, It's good to see you, but I'm not Maury, I'm Jack."

"Well OK. But it's not my fault that all you *honkies* look alike," he said. Everyone within earshot roared with laughter. These interns had a rare opportunity to gain firsthand experience in college development. Without exception each went on to more important assignments. Their rapid upward mobility meant, unfortunately, that none of their original colleges gained from their skills for very long. I remember one vice president for development of a major university commenting " I'd have given anything to have a start like this in my career."

INSTITUTE FOR EDUCATIONAL MANAGEMENT, HARVARD BUSINESS SCHOOL

Robert F. Duncan had a long and distinguished career in the field of philanthropy. A Harvard alumnus, he joined with John Price Jones in running the 1919 Harvard College capital campaign, and was a key member of the group that then formed the John Price Jones Company. He became the firm's president until he and Jones had a falling out during the Fifties when he left JPJ to become president of Kersting & Brown. In 1969, he was 80-years old and was as full of energy, creativity and enthusiasm for the field as ever. His interest in his alma mater, Harvard, never waned. Harvard Business School's Advanced Management Program, using the case method, had been most successful in training corporate executives in strategic planning and management. With this example firmly in mind, Duncan initiated many discussions with the key staff and faculty of the Business School about a management development program for college and university administrators. This resulted in the formation of the Institute of Educational Management (IEM) in 1969.

A grant of $20,000 by the Alfred P. Sloan Foundation helped fund a study to validate the marketability of the course with schools across the country. It was scheduled to run for six weeks each summer. The Sloan Foundation eventually gave $280,000 for the 1970 and 1971 programs and the Ford Foundation contributed $30,000 for minority scholarships. Included in this course was direct instruction in college development techniques.

By 1970, the IEM board had 27 trustees and 10 faculty members. On behalf of the AAFRC, I accepted the invitation to serve on the institute's board of trustees.

Duncan and I taught courses on college development programs and served on this board for several years. We felt good about this program and expected it to produce better, more-enlightened college officials. It was successful and was transferred to the Harvard School of Business a few years later. Its alumni gained important positions in college administration.

Today, IEM has become a permanent part of Harvard's Summer Program. Its curriculum continues to emphasize advanced management for educational institutions and training in education development. Each summer there is a four weeks course with 95 students. More than 2,000 students representing educational institutions from every state and Canada have attended. Similar programs are also established in other colleges including Carnegie-Mellon and Bryn Mawr. Duncan would be very proud of the fruits of his pioneering efforts.

CRITICAL ISSUE #8

Throughout the early Seventies, efforts to get key philanthropic organizations working together to improve their public image and their capacity to serve society's needs continued to grow. Two good examples were that of the Institute for Educational Management and the Campaign for Philanthropy. The campaign for Philanthropy served as the catalyst for the success of subsequent efforts to develop as an effective consortium of organizations.

THE CAMPAIGN FOR PHILANTHROPY, 1971

J. O. Newberry was the next president of the AAFRC. President of Community Service Bureau, Inc.—Dallas, "J. O." (only the very lowly ever called him Mr. Newberry) would have been a casting director's dream if a typical Texan was needed. Along with a perfect Texas drawl and feisty personality, he projected Texas the way he swaggered in his walk and showed less than an abundance of regard for things non-Texan. He started the Community Service Bureau right after World War II and was in absolute and complete charge of everything he touched. Determined, energetic and creative, the field should be ever-grateful that he decided the time had come to really get key philanthropic organizations working together to improve their public image and increase their capacity to serve society's needs.

In 1971, J. O. became the last voluntary President of the AAFRC (my title as the paid executive was Executive Vice-President until 1972). The week after his election by the board, he came to New York to get me and my office cracking on his new project entitled "A Campaign for Philanthropy." Without any doubt, J. O.'s idea was a most important catalyst for the success of subsequent efforts to develop an effective consortium of organizations, such as that which the INDEPENDENT SECTOR was to become 10 years later.

J. O.'s thesis proposed a positive campaign for philanthropy to offset the negative attitudes affecting philanthropic organizations and their effectiveness in serving society. Most of the field's leaders seemed to feel that this kind of program was long overdue. The plan was accepted and applauded by the professional friends we had developed over the last few years.

First, an administrative committee was formed with the objective of including an eclectic group of philanthropic organizations. As an indicator that this was an idea whose time had come, the committee included the top executives from the Boy Scouts of America, the United way of America, the Council on Foundations, the National Assembly for Social Policy and Development, the National Council of Churches, the Committee for Economic Development, the American Council on Education, the University of Pennsylvania and the AAFRC.

> **CRITICAL ISSUE #9**
>
> *The early Seventies also produced a desire for a better understanding of the nonprofit sector by the general public. Key organizations strove to increase the public's awareness of what philanthropy can accomplish through various programs. The Coalition for Public Good broke new ground with the cooperation of 51 top executives from a wide variety of nonprofit organizations.*

An organization meeting on May 11, 1971 at the Mayflower Hotel in Washington D.C. brought together 51 executives and trustees. The meeting broke out into three seminars on the key issues: Program, Communications and Leadership. The purpose of the now named "Program for Philanthropy in America," was defined as follows:

> Although many Americans are giving generously and volunteering their time to nonprofit institutions, the scope and importance of philanthropy are not well known or understood by most persons. To increase public awareness, a Program for Philanthropy is proposed to demonstrate all aspects of philanthropy—colleges, hospitals, health agencies, religious institutions, United Funds, youth agencies, private schools, welfare agencies, etc.

The program's objectives were defined as:

1. To speak with one voice.
2. Develop an information system to determine public attitudes toward philanthropic institutions.
3. Stimulate and assist participating organizations to develop new programs to meet the changing needs of society.
4. Encourage public policies to foster improved tax-incentives and increased giving.
5. Coordinate the public relations policies of participants to unify our voice and strengthen its impact on society.

Six months later, AAFRC hosted a dinner meeting at the Waldorf Astoria in New York City. Thirty-three key philanthropic organizations attended. In addition to agreeing to help achieve the campaign's objectives, they concurred on the next step—gaining the assistance of top volunteer leadership. In these early stages, we were bogged down on enlisting truly committed top leadership. Most influential trustees confined their volunteer duties to the program needs of their nonprofit organization and made little time available for additional responsibil-

THE EARLY SEVENTIES—A TIME OF BURGEONING EFFORTS

ities. But a hard core group of top administrators continued to pursue the program's objectives. The title "coalition" gathered momentum.

United Way of America represented a considerable force for philanthropy. William Aramony, the new chief executive, gave strong support to the program and made the considerable resources of his organization available in many ways. Aramony assigned a UWA vice president, John S. Glaser, to devote whatever time necessary to staff what was now named the "Coalition for Public Good Through Private Initiatives." The effort was boosted considerably by the acceptance of Bayard Ewing, a lawyer from Providence, Rhode Island and recent past president of the United Way of America, as the coalition's chairman.

So an organization was established, but its future development depended upon the enthususiastic participation of many more volunteer leaders like Ewing. They were in very short supply. But this attempt launched an ongoing bonding effort to bring the field closer together. As the group evolved into the Coalition for Public Good many of the same staff leaders who were already comfortable working together, stayed involved. AAFRC and United Way shared the catalytic responsibilities.

In 1971 and 1972, 12 meetings were held by the organization executives in New York and Washington. New leaders actively involved included: Robert Goheen, former President of Princeton University, Chairman of the Council on Foundations; Curtis Frank, President of the Council for Financial Aid to Education; Philip Bernstein, Executive Vice President of the Council of Jewish Federations and Welfare Funds; and Alfred C. Neal, President Committee on Economic Development.

Meetings of the Coalition continued to be scheduled over the next few years and they were well attended by the staff executives. The three priorities were, preparation for more tax reforms, broadening participation in the conferences of the umbrella organizations and trying to enlist the participation of the foundation presidents, corporate executives, and leading volunteer trustees of key philanthropic organizations. We weren't able to get very far with the latter which hampered real progress and frustrated our hopes to bring more of the nonprofit field together.

> **CRITICAL ISSUE #10**
>
> *The newly formed Coalition for Public Good set out three immediate goals:*
>
> *1. Prepare for tax reforms*
> *2. Broaden participation in conferences of the umbrella organizations, and*
> *3. Enlist the participation of foundation presidents, corporate executives, and leading volunteer trustees.*
>
> *All but the third goal was accomplished, which hampered real progress in bringing the nonprofit field closer together.*

THE EFFECT OF TAXES ON CHARITABLE GIVING, 1971–1973

In 1971, the 501(c)(3) Group, at the urging of Hayden Smith from the Council of Financial Aid to Education, engaged Dr. Martin S. Feldstein, Professor of Economics at Harvard University, to do an econometric study on the effect of taxation on gifts. A total of $25,000 had to be raised. Hayden received a $10,000 anonymous grant and the rest came from our respective organizations. The AAFRC donated $2,000.

After a year of intense study and reviewing a 25-year period, working with IRS charitable giving and tax figures, and special surveys, Dr. Feldstein concluded that philanthropy would lose much more than government would gain if charitable gifts were not tax deductible. Every dollar taxed would be worth the equivalent of $1.11 to $1.28 if given to philanthropic purposes. The size of a donor's income accounted for the range; the larger the income, the greater would be the gift equivalent. Most of us had harbored an instinctive feeling that this would be the case, but it was great to have it confirmed by a leading scholar. This study was of great value in making philanthropy's case in future tax reforms and became the basis of an even more thorough study for the Filer Commission in 1974.

> **CRITICAL ISSUE #11**
>
> *The 1971 study by Martin S. Feldstein, Professor of Economics at Harvard University confirmed that philanthropy would lose more than government would gain if charitable gifts were not tax-deductible. This set the stage for a more through study for the Filer Commission.*

THE 1973 TAX REFORM ACT

During the fall of 1972, in the closing days of the 92nd Congress, discussions on the hill about new tax reforms were rampant. Once again, the need for increased tax revenues along with a renewed cry that charitable deductions were a tax loophole, made the tax deductibility of gifts to charities vulnerable. This time, thanks to the Coalition for Public Good, the philanthropic organizations were better organized. All of us from nonprofit organizations who succeeded in being scheduled to appear before the House Ways and Means Committee, submitted our testimony in advance to the Coalition. This helped to establish our party line and to coordinate our efforts. Debriefing sessions were held each day to better orient those scheduled to testify the next day.

On April 12, 1973, I testified before the House Ways and Means Committee on "Philanthropy Today." In summary, I stated that:

- In 1972, Americans contributed $22.68 billion to more than 500,000 nonprofit institutions and agencies. This was possible because the partnership between government and philanthropy resulted in good public policies.
- Most nonprofit organizations felt that the value of charitable programs to our society was not given due credit in the 1969 Tax Act (Public Law No. 91–172). Media coverage of the testimonies given by both volunteers and executive staff of charitable organizations implied that their programs not only fell short of society's needs but most persons only contributed to avoid taxation. A gift to charity is *not* a tax loophole. The donor gives away some assets and reduces his capital. The tax benefits of such a gift are worth less than the gift itself.
- To make philanthropy more effective in the face of growing public need, preservation of the tax benefits passed in 1969 is essential. The following measures should be retained:
  1. The fair market value of gifts of appreciated property and securities is fully deductible with a five-year carry over for any surplus. Nearly 30 percent of gifts to 1,080 colleges and universities in 1970 through 1971 were in gifts of property. Without exception, the results of successful campaigns depend on leadership gifts. In many cases, gifts of appreciated property can be a critical factor in setting the standards for other donors to follow.
  2. Unlimited charitable deduction in estates. In 1971, bequests were $3 billion, 14.2 percent of the total.

3. The 4 percent excise tax on the interest of the capital investments of private foundations be repealed, or at least modified. Ten percent of all giving last year came from foundations. The 4 percent tax reduced their potential total by over $60 million. This tax was imposed to pay to the government the cost of auditing 501(c)(3) organizations. Yet Treasury only budgeted $19 million for this task in 1972.

Without public generosity, stimulated by enlightened public policies, nonprofit organizations cannot provide effective programs for charitable needs.

> **CRITICAL ISSUE #12**
>
> *In the fall of 1972, charitable deductions again came under fire in the 92nd Congress. Many saw these charitable deductions as tax loopholes. Losing the tax deductibility of gifts to charities would have proved disastrous for the nonprofit sector. The Coalition for Public Good brought together all of us who were scheduled to testify before the House Ways and Means Committee. Together, we helped establish a party line and eventually succeeded in all our goals except the reduction of the foundation excise tax.*

THE NATIONAL INSTITUTE OF CONTINUING EDUCATION (NICE)

From 1970 to 1972, Henry "Hank" Goldstein was President of the New York Chapter (AFRD) of the National Society of Fund-Raisers (NSFR). I was serving on the Executive Committee of the NSRF National Board at the time. Hank was quite vocal, analytical, and critical of the tendency of the national board to concentrate on building membership and national issues at the expense of providing more service to the local chapters. I suggested to the Executive Committee that much of Hank's criticism was justified and we would gain if we could have the advantage of his "gadfly" presence on the committee. In 1972, he accepted our invitation to serve on the NSFR Executive Committee. His energy, vision, and innovative approach quickly made him a successful candidate in 1973 for the National NSFR President.

In the President's role, he collaborated with the venerable Bob Duncan to do a prospectus on establishing a 501(c)(30 entity for the NSFR. The National Board chartered the National Institute of Continuing Education (NICE) on September 14, 1973. From then on, the society could raise funds specifically for training programs designed to expand the professional knowledge of NSFR members and to help increase public recognition of the fund-raising field's contributions to American society. Many problems are easier to solve if you invite able critics to join in setting policies.

In 1986, the now called, National Society of Fund-Raising Executives, changed NICE's name to the NSFRE Foundation. Hank's contribution was both important and lasting. Today as president of the Oram Group, Inc., a fund-raising counseling firm, Hank continues his active participation in the NSFRE and the AAFRC.

Of paramount importance, during the early Seventies, we learned not only how to work together with more efficiency, but also that such cooperation was a marvelous path that could be used for future victories. We would never forget that without public generosity, stimulated by enlightened public policies, nonprofit organizations cannot provide effective programs for charitable needs.

LESSONS LEARNED

- Before the Seventies, very little cooperation existed between most organizations in the nonprofit community. Everyone in the field agreed that steps had to be taken to ensure better cooperation both within the field and with the federal government. This was accomplished through programs such as the "Campaign for Philanthropy."
- Reorganization took place within key philanthropic organizations so that peers within those various organizations could interact with one another.
- This new sense of cooperation within the field spawned such successful programs as the Ford Foundation's seminar for Educational Fund-Raising Interns, and the Institute of Educational Management to everyone's benefit.
- J.O. Newberry's Campaign for Philanthropy gave birth to the Coalition for Public Good, a ground-breaking effort in the cooperation of executives from a wide variety of nonprofit organizations. The Coalition for Public Good Earned its stripes when it served as a rallying point during the 1973 Tax Reform hearings. It became apparent that cooperation between organizations in the nonprofit sector was not only beneficial, but necessary to ensure continued survival.

CHAPTER 6

Philanthropy Enters a New Threshold

The Filer Commission set new standards for improving the philanthropic process. The Commission established with the endorsement of key government and private leadership. It provided a vehicle for more intensive research about philanthropy. It disseminated its results and findings to a wide audience. The result was a new perception of the role of philanthropy in American life.

The Evolution of the Filer Commission

November 1973	With the encouragement of several key government officials, John D. Rockefeller III, acting on the overdue need to examine the exact role of philanthropy in American society, established the Commission on Private Philanthropy and Public Needs. JDR III enlisted John H. Filer, Chairman of Aetna Life & Casualty, as the Commission's Chairman. The Commission was then known as the Filer Commission.
December 1973	The Commission's initial budget for research and professional activities was $1,300,000. The importance of the work of the Commission for the future of philanthropy was so well recognized that the AAFRC offered to contribute fund-raising counseling services to help the Commission reach its fund-raising goal.
January 1974	At the Filer Commission's first full meeting in Chicago, it approved of the AAFRC's fund-raising plan as presented by Philip M. Klutznick, the Finance Chairman of the Commission.

March 1974	A survey of 3,000 American contributors had been launched by the Survey Research Center of the University of Michigan which required an immediate payment of $150,000. Since it was too early to approach top prospects (the case statement was not yet completed), the money was obtained as a 90-day loan from the Riggs National Bank. The loan, co-signed by John Filer and C. Douglas Dillon, gave us 12 weeks to get in some key gifts.
June 1974	At a luncheon in New York City for foundation presidents hosted by John D. Rockefeller III and C. Douglas Dillon, $850,000 was raised.
October 1974	By October 1974, the national fund-raising campaign activities had raised $1,365,704 in gifts and pledges from foundations, corporations, and key nonprofit organizations. However, the commission's budget had expanded to $1,900,000.
October 1975	John Filer and John D. Rockefeller III presented the Commission' final report, Giving in America, to officials in Washington, calling for a greater partnership between the federal government and the private sector.
February 1976	By early 1976, over 700 gifts totaling $2,311,584 were raised enabling the Commission to meet all of its financial obligations.

THE ROLE OF JOHN D. ROCKEFELLER III

In addition to his personal generosity to philanthropic causes, the many activities and actions of John D. Rockefeller III (JDR 3rd), showed his dedication to the improvement of both the understanding and effectiveness of philanthropy. As part of his ongoing commitment to philanthropy, JDR 3rd testified before the House Ways and Means Committee for the 1969 Tax Reforms. He stated: "The concept of philanthropy . . . played a central role in American life, but the continuation of this role cannot be taken for granted."

JDR 3rd was also responsible for the organization of the Peterson Commission. In 1973, probably frustrated by little progress, once again, he acted on the overdue need to examine the exact role of philanthropy in American society. With the encouragement of several government officials including Wilbur D. Mills, Chairman of the House Ways and Means Committee; Secretary of the Treasury, George P. Shultz; and Under Secretary, William E. Simon, JDR 3rd started the Commission on Private Philanthropy and Public Needs in November 1973 as a privately initiated, privately funded citizen's panel with two broad objectives:

1. To study the role of both philanthropic giving in the United States and that area through which giving is principally channeled, the voluntary, "third sector" of American society.
2. To make recommendations to the voluntary sector, to Congress and to the American public at large concerning ways in which the sector and the practice of private giving can be strengthened and made more effective. [1]

JDR 3rd enlisted John H. Filer, Chairman of Aetna Life & Casualty, as the Commission's Chairman. Since this appointment, the Commission has been known as the Filer Commission. JDR 3rd also made a grant of $25,000 to help launch the Commission, with the admonition that it must raise the rest of the needed funds on its own. Leonard L. Silverstein, a Washington lawyer knowledgeable on tax legislation agreed to be the full time Executive Director. Gabriel G. Rudney, Assistant Director of the Office of Tax Analysis, the Treasury Department, took a leave of absence to become the Commission's Director of Research. "The Commission's membership included many top national leaders from religion and labor, former cabinet officers, or representatives of minority groups, executives of foundations and corporations (27 members in all). A meeting of tax experts, economists, and sociologists assembled to discuss research needs in August 1973.[2]

CRITICAL ISSUE # 13

The Filer Commission, established with the endorsement of key government and private leadership, set new standards for improving the philanthropic process by providing a vehicle for more intensive and better directed research about philanthropy. Founded by John D. Rockefeller 3rd, and headed by John H. Filer, the Filer Commission succeeded in stirring new life into the philanthropic process.

---

1. Report of the Commission of Private Philanthropy and Public Needs. *Giving in America* "Toward a Stronger Private Sector" (1975) Preface, pg. 1
2. *Ibid*. pg. 2.

FUNDING THE FILER COMMISSION

I was delighted to learn that Leonard L. Silverstein had become the Commission's executive director. I knew him to be an energetic, well-informed advocate of more enlightened tax policies. He approached his commitments with energy and good sense—qualities necessary to deal with what would inevitably be a complicated endeavor. He gave me a call to talk about how we, as publishers of *Giving USA*, could be helpful to the Commission in gathering statistics, data, and facts about the third sector. In early November 1973, we sat in my office and discussed the Commission's plans, needs, and problems. I assured him that AAFRC would turn over to the commission all our historical records and 1973 giving trends as soon as they became available.

"How much money will you need?" I asked.

"Our budget to cover program and research costs is $1,300,000. In addition, law, accounting, and other firms are providing $500,000 in donated study services," he replied.

Remembering all too vividly the Peterson Commission's fund-raising problems, I asked, "I assume you have applied to the IRS for a 501(c)(3) rating and have set up fund-raising plans."

"Oh yes." Leonard replied. "Phil Klutznick has agreed to be our finance chairman and we plan to ask 200 or so foundations and corporations for $25,000 each. Sixty positive responses and we're home free."

As he was saying this, I sat on the other side of the desk, steadily shaking my head.

"What's the matter?" Leonard asked.

"You will be violating one of Si Seymour's seven deadly sins of fund-raising—'raising money by multiplication.' Believe me it doesn't work," I said. "Reaching a goal as large as this can be accomplished only with leadership gifts from individuals, foundations, and corporations—not with many smaller ones. At least 75 percent of the goal must come from the first 20 or so contributors, with gifts ranging from $25,000 to $150,000. This applies to any organization, regardless of the strength of its appeal especially in the short time available."

This must have sounded very difficult to Leonard and he was visibly troubled. Before he had time to react, I added," Like many others in our field whom I've already talked to, I feel that the this Commission could be very important to the future of philanthropy. I'd like to explore the possibility that the AAFRC, with several of its member firms, give you fund-raising counsel as a public service—charging only out-of-pocket costs." Leonard reacted positively to this suggestion, and we both agreed to pursue it, he with John Filer and I with the AAFRC board.

I immediately called the current AAFRC chairman, George A. Brakeley, Jr., and in a short time, the Executive Committee tentatively approved this arrangement, pending full approval by the board. A committee was formed with Brakeley, including Melvin D. Brewer, President of Marts & Lundy Inc., Carl Shaver, President of C. W. Shaver and Co., Charles R. Feldstein, President of Charles R. Feldstein & Co. Inc. and myself, to plan the next steps.

In subsequent sessions with Leonard E. Bert Knauft, Assistant to the Chairman, and Philip Klutznick, we confirmed the AAFRC's willingness to consider donating its fund-raising counsel as a public service. The discussions in these meetings developed into the preparation of a formal campaign plan to be presented to the Commission for approval at its meeting scheduled for January 28, 1974 at the Chicago O'Hare Regency Hyatt. This meeting took place in a beautifully appointed room large enough to seat the Commission members at a rectangular table with flanking seats for the consultants around three walls. A few minutes before it started, Leonard pulled me aside. With some concern he said, "Mr. Filer is not fully convinced that the Commission should become associated with professional fund-raisers."

"Please remind him," I said, "that we will be doing this without charging any professional fees—a fact that should enhance, not tarnish the Commission's reputation."

Having armed Klutznick with the campaign plan to be presented to the Commission, Brakeley, Feldstein, and I took seats along the wall. The Commission's table included John Filer, Leonard and Gabriel Rudney at one end. The entire table was sheathed in strong light brightened further by an ivory table cloth. Those of us along the wall were in semidarkness. Shortly after the meeting began, Paul Ylvisaker, whom I knew from the Harvard Institute of Educational Management program, came in, looked around for a seat, and seemed a little lost. I beckoned him over to an empty seat next to mine. Soon, when a question arose about community development, Leonard said to Filer, "Why don't you ask the expert, Paul Ylvisacker, about that?"

Filer looked over at Paul and said, "Oh, hi Paul. I didn't see you come in. I thought you were one of those fund-raisers."

I remember this with a smile because the Commission's final meeting, 14 months later, was in a very elegant room in the Waldorf Astoria at which John Filer turned to the sidelines and said to me, "I don't know where we would be meeting today without the tremendous help we've gotten from the AAFRC and Jack Schwartz. Probably in a tent someplace." Nothing succeeds like success.

Our campaign plan provided for a qualified campaign director to go on the Commission's payroll but to work in the AAFRC office under the supervision of myself and the committee. The plan proposed:

- Creating small elite groups of leaders who would seek leadership gifts from the top fifty prospects. Using sequential fundraising, large gifts would be sought first from the "family," those members of the Commission who would set an example for the other members.
- Organizing special gifts efforts in several geographic areas where the influence of Commission members could be used. A Chairman should be enlisted for each key city. He, in turn, would enlist three to six community leaders to organize a special gifts luncheon featuring an appropriate speaker to present the Commission's program. Key potential donors would be assigned in advance to the best volunteer.
- Getting assistance, wherever possible, from the officers of a local AAFRC firm in arranging the luncheons.

We set a total campaign budget of $40,500 for travel, office expenses, printing, list building, prospect research, and mailings. The Commission approved our campaign proposal and we got started immediately.

On March 1, 1974, we held our first strategy meeting at 30 Rockefeller Plaza with Leonard, Klutznick, Porter McKeever, representing JDR 3rd, E. B. Knauft representing John Filer, and myself. After amenities, Leonard stated that the Survey Research Center of the University of Michigan, aided by the U.S. Treasury Department and the U.S. Census Bureau, had begun its study of a cross section of 3,000 American contributors. The total cost of this crucial survey was projected at over $400,000. Leonard said, "We need to give them an advance payment of $150,000 in two weeks. Jack, who can we go to for a quick grant?"

"Ouch," I said. "Money like that can't be raised quickly. It needs careful prospect research and cultivation. We don't even have our case statement ready. We could jeopardize the chance to maximize the size of a top prospect's gift by moving in too fast."

Klutznick, always ready with good ideas, said, "Can't we borrow the money?"

"Well, I could try the Riggs National Bank." Leonard said. Encouraged by all present, Leonard picked up the phone and immediately got one of the bank's top officials on the line. After a brief conversation, Leonard confirmed what I'd long suspected—the Riggs National Bank isn't really from this planet. Because of the high caliber of American leadership on the Commission, this bank was willing to make a loan of $150,000, payable in 90 days, provided the application was cosigned by C. Douglas Dillon, former Secretary of the U.S. Treasury, and John Filer. Dillon and Filer, knowing our choices were limited, quickly agreed. We bought time (literally 12 weeks) to corral the first large gifts.

When it became apparent that the campaign director was not moving quickly or efficiently enough, the AAFRC board directed me to give this program as much time as necessary for the next six months even at the expense of slowing down the association's activities.

Alan Pifer, president of the Carnegie Corporation of New York and the only Commission member from a foundation, was unable to attend the Commission meeting in Chicago and, therefore, was unaware of the fund-raising plans. I made a date to see him in April to convince him that Carnegie should make a pace-setting gift for other foundations to follow. He was pleased to learn that the AAFRC was contributing fund-raising counseling and seemed to like the campaign plan. So I asked, "Alan what can Carnegie give?"

"I'm not sure we should give at all. Since I'm on the Commission, it might be construed as a conflict of interest," he replied.

"On the contrary," I replied. "All the other foundations will look to you as an example. And if we don't get several $100,000 gifts from foundations, we'll never reach our goal."

"Well, I'd rather not go to my board, but I can contribute $15,000."

"If that is as much as you can give, please hold any action until we can try to get other foundation grants that will serve as an example. Meanwhile, would you work with us to set up a luncheon to present the case to several top foundation executives?"

"Gladly," he said.

I had no way of knowing then what effect this meeting might have until, with Alan's strong support, we arranged a luncheon for 10 presidents of key foundations at the University Club in New York City, June 19, 1974. None other than JDR 3rd and C. Douglas Dillon, agreed to host it, completely solving the attendance problem. After JDR 3rd's excellent presentation of the commission's objectives, Alan stood up and announced, "The top foundations have so much riding on the outcome of the Commission's work. We need your generous support to make this happen. I'm going to my trustees to ask them to give $100,000."

As a direct result of this luncheon, we raised a total of $800,000 from Ford, Kresge, and Robert Wood Johnson Foundations, Pew Memorial Trust, Rockefeller Brothers Fund, the Rockefeller Foundation and the Carnegie Corporation. All thanks to Alan. He really led the way. The final total from 96 foundations a year later was $1,637,450.

Special gifts luncheons were organized in key cities including New York, Chicago, Detroit, Dallas, St. Paul-Minneapolis, San Francisco, and Los Angeles. Building on their first successful foundation luncheon, JDR 3rd and Dillon agreed to continue their effective roles as hosts. We received important help in organizing these meetings from members of the Commission in each city along with the local AAFRC member firm. For example, working with Klutznick and Lester Crown, both prominent Chicago leaders, Charles Feldstein, and several executives from his Chicago firm put together a superb luncheon. In attendance were many of Chicago's leading citizens. This luncheon served to open up more doors for gaining more financial support for the Commission. It served as an example for the other cities we visited.

The Commission's activities reached a scope never before obtained:

> An Advisory Committee (was formed) of more than 100 experts from the fields of economics, law, sociology, and taxation, plus representatives of many philanthropic and nonprofit areas, from higher education to environmental activism.... It sponsored in the course of its two years of operation no fewer than 85 studies on various aspects of philanthropy and nonprofit activity; extensive analysis of the laws and precedents of philanthropy.[3]

The Commission met, with excellent attendance, seven times in 16 months. Its agenda and progress were always augmented by countless meetings of research groups and task forces, all of whom reported all findings directly to the Commission.

Leonard more than lived up to my high expectations as the administrator. Filer did a superb job of leading the Commission's discussions and keeping them on track. He also showed a remarkable capacity to adjust to new ideas and to help to quell dissent. At the many meetings I attended where I saw him in action, he always had done his homework thoroughly and kept scholars from straying too far off the agenda. He also was deferential to the Commission members without giving up basic control of the meetings.

---

3. *Ibid.* pg. 2.

Officially, Philip M. Klutznick, a successful Chicago lawyer and entrepreneur, was designated as the Commission's finance chairman. Without doubt, he was the best campaign chairman I ever worked with. Because he was so highly regarded by most of the volunteer leadership, he was capable of opening the necessary doors. He attacked his assignments thoughtfully and thoroughly. As a lawyer he was analytical, well-informed, and very creative. Yet, he showed respect for the fund-raising procedures we considered "professional verities."

In his late fifties, he was short but with so much presence you thought him much taller. He had a strong resonant voice that commanded attention. His dedication and enthusiasm to the purpose and programs of the Commission was apparent to all he approached for both support and volunteer time. Nor did he retire from active life for quite a while. He served as Secretary of Commerce under President Carter from 1980 to 1981. This special man not only became a good friend, but did more than anyone else to make our fund-raising success possible. The original fund-raising goal expanded from $1,400,000 to $1,900,000 as research costs grew. In August 1974, gifts and pledges totalled $912,000. By October 1974, the total was $1,365,704. In February 1976, we reached our final total of $2,311,584 from 738 donors at a cost of less than 2 percent. Four hundred and forty-six gifts came from nonprofit institutions and agencies, 122 from corporations, 96 from foundations, and 74 from individuals. The Commission met all of its financial commitments.

THE DONEE GROUP

In late 1974, as word got out about the Commission's progress and initial research findings, several nonprofit organizations representing public interest, social action, and volunteer groups, became concerned about the direction the Commission seemed to be taking. An article in the *Grantsmanship Center News* by Pablo Eisenberg, the highly respected president of the Center for Community Concerns, voiced a worried warning:

> The Commission was stressing the problems and concerns of only one-half of the philanthropic equation—the givers—and had neglected the very real and pressing needs of the recipients or would-be recipients of philanthropic largess. He noted that the questions are: Who gets what? What are the priorities of foundations and voluntary organizations? Do current conditions meet society's changing needs?

PHILANTHROPY ENTERS A NEW THRESHOLD

Have either been played down or completely ignored? . . . . The composition of the Commission and its advisory committee . . . reflected very disproportionately the establishment side of both the voluntary sector and philanthropic organizations.

The Commission responded . . . by asking Mr. Eisenberg to assist them in convening a meeting . . . of this group in Washington on March 6, 1975. At its meeting in the Waldorf Astoria Hotel in New York on April 7, 1975, the Commission approved a proposal by the . . . (now called the Donee Group) to provide additional research and consultation on issues important to recipients of philanthropy.[4]

Most of us working with the Commission were glad for this development. It made possible a more diverse base for our findings and we all agreed that the final report must take into account the needs of the entire field. I was pleased by this turn of events until Leonard told me that another $65,000 was needed to pay for the report.

Now ready for action, the Donee Group included:

- organizations involved in minority rights;
- urban affairs;
- tax reform;
- voluntary action;
- public interest law;
- housing;
- women's rights;
- community organizing;
- service to the handicapped;
- children's rights;
- social service;
- consumer rights; and
- citizen participation activities in addition to scholars.[5]

Considering that most of these organizations often represented unpopular causes, were too newly organized to have built solid giving constituencies, were unable to enlist leadership from the establishment, or were short-staffed and/or struggling for enough funds to meet the needs of their cause, they naturally felt ignored or neglected. And their report reflected this.

We do not believe that philanthropy should have as its primary pur-

---

4. The Donee Group Report & Recommendations, 1975, pgs. II. III.
5. *Ibid., pg. IV.*

pose the support of private institutions performing essential public services that are being delivered by business or government. Higher education, health care, the arts, and other public functions may be performed by public or private institutions. In either case, it is done largely with public rather than private funds. Since the amounts available from philanthropy for support of service organizations will never be equal to the task those organizations must undertake, philanthropy must consider altering its objects of support.... It can do this by applying relatively small amounts of money to social change, monitoring and oversight functions which can have longlasting impact of great significance.... Philanthropy must provide greater access to those new issues and organizations that reflect emerging needs.[6]

Essentially, the Donee Group advocated cutting the philanthropic pie in different proportions with more going to themselves and less to the established philanthropic organizations. Most of us originally involved with the Commission felt strongly that the pie should be made larger, with more for all, not just redistributed.

CRITICAL ISSUE #14

In late 1974, the Donee Group, representing several nonprofit organizations, criticized the Filer Commission's direction. They felt that the Filer Commission was placing too much emphasis on the role of the "givers" and not enough on the needs of the would-be recipients. As a result, at the April 1975 meeting of the Filer Commission, a proposal was approved to provide additional research and consultation on the issues important to the recipients of philanthropy.

Other criticisms of the Commission's perspectives included preserving the status quo, failure to assess public needs, fear of government, and excessive confidence in self-regulation. Also, the Group strongly exhorted:

1. Limiting donor control (of foundations and corporations);
2. Broadening membership of governing boards;
3. Providing sufficient profession staffs;

---

6. *Ibid.* pgs. 9, 10.

4. Expanding public information requirements;
5. Holding annual meetings;
6. Eliminating expenditure responsibility; and
7. Giving nonexclusive access to federated fund-raising.

Not only did the Donee Group criticize the Filer Commission's emphasis, they also developed some controversial recommendations: "The Donee Group believes that the deductibility of gifts of appreciated property without a tax increase on the value constitutes one of the worst examples of inequity in the tax system. We favor taxing all appreciation in appreciated property."[7] (They stressed that this tax change should be phased over a period of several years to minimize its affect on certain nonprofit institutions.)

Their proposal flew in the face of our writings and testimonies before Congressional committees: Pace-setting gifts are a fundamental key to successful fund-raising. If the announcement of a public fund-raising campaign included an impressive total of preliminary gifts (many inevitably obtained through pace-setting gifts), the campaign would usually reach its goal. Gifts of appreciated property account for 20 to 30 percent of most capital campaigns. Since, under the laws then in force, a donor could deduct from his taxable income the fair market value of appreciated property given to a charity (this privilege prevails today in 1993), donors of real means often give in much larger amounts than they otherwise would. Usually, when a potential pace-setting donor decides to make a generous gift to a campaign, he, or she, will consult with a tax expert or financial advisor to determine the best way to give a maximum amount. Possession of property or stocks that have appreciated substantially in value since they were first purchased can provide a generous gift with the added motivation to the donor of a tax deduction of the current market value.

When the Commission's final report was about to be released in Fall of 1975, *The Wall Street Journal* (which jumped the release deadline by two weeks) characterized it as "Two and one half cheers for philanthropy." This article was somewhat critical and concentrated on the report of the Donee Group (which they distributed separately) at the expense of giving the Commission deserved credit. Each member of the Commission had the privilege of dissenting on any of the report's recommendations and of having their views recorded. Most took advantage of it in the final report. In Washington, on November 7, 1975,

---

7. *Ibid.* pgs. 30, 31.

John Filer and JDR 3rd presented the final report to a select group of leaders including George Shultz, Secretary, and William Simon, Assistant Secretary, U.S. Treasury, Wilbur Mills, Chairman of the House Ways and Means Committee, and Russell B. Long, Chairman of the Senate Finance Committee. JDR 3rd's push for increased understanding and further study of the philanthropic process seemed to have been well received.

LESSONS LEARNED: THE MAJOR RECOMMENDATIONS OF THE FILER COMMISSION

I wrote an article, "The Filer Commission: Then Until Now," in the December 1979 issue of *Trusts & Estates*, a magazine published by Communications Channels, Inc., Atlanta, Georgia. The following material identifies the Commission's major recommendations, including those that never got off the ground and those which had stirred new life into the philanthropic process as of 1979.

Proposals That Died Aborning

1. An additional incentive should be given to low and middle-income taxpayers by allowing those with annual incomes of less than $15,000 to take a double-deduction (200 percent) for charitable gifts. Those with incomes of between $15,000 and $30,000 a year to take a 150 percent deduction.
   Update: Since it was estimated that this would cost the U.S. Treasury $7.4 billion even though it would increase charitable giving by $9.8 billion, Congress simply was not interested.
2. Corporations should set aside 2 percent of their pre-tax income as a minimum goal for charitable giving to be reached by 1980.
   Update: Nothing changed. Corporate financial health and the size of giving budgets are determined by profits, not exhortation.
3. The duplication of responsibility for expenditure of foundation grants, now imposed on both the foundations and the recipients, should be eliminated and applied only to recipients.
   Update: There has been no action. Congress' continued prejudice about foundations manifested itself once again.

Proposals Acted Upon

1. Taxpayers who take the standard deduction should be permitted to also deduct their gifts to charity as a separate tax deduction.
   Update: The Fisher/Conable House Bill, H.R. 1785, and the Moynihan/Packwood Senate Bill, S-219, would permit taxpayers who do not itemize and take a standard deduction to list their charitable contributions above the line. (Harvard economist, Dr. Martin Feldstein said that this bill would net philanthropy an additional $4.2 billion a year at a cost to the Treasury of $3.7 billion a year.)
2. Income deducted for charitable giving should be excluded from any minimum tax provision.
   Update: This is now (1979) part of IRS regulation.
3. A tax deduction should be allowed for the fair market value of any gift of appreciated property.
   Update: This is now part of the IRS regulations.
4. The charitable bequest deduction should be retained in its present form.
   Update: The Impressive Filer Commission research conducted by Professor Michael Boskin of Stanford University on the importance of charitable bequests to all nonprofit institutions and agencies, convinced congress to leave this in the IRS regulations. Using figures from past tax returns, Boskin showed that 6 to 7 percent of all giving comes each year from charitable bequests.
5. Larger grant-making organizations should hold annual public meetings to review their programs, priorities, and finances.
   Update: This gave impetus to an already growing trend. More and more foundations had begun to open their meetings to the public and issuing annual reports that include a complete financial report.
6. The 4 percent "audit tax" on private foundations should be repealed and be replaced by a fee to cover only the cost of auditing them.
   Update: This tax has been cut to 2 percent.
7. The Internal Revenue Service should continue to be the government agency which monitors charitable activity.
   Update: Despite many bills introduced to change the government monitoring agency, this responsibility remains with the IRS.

8. All tax-exempt organizations should broaden representation on their boards to account for their constituencies including appropriate consideration of ethnic and minorities groups.
   Update: Progress on this has been recorded since the Filer Commission.
9. All tax-exempt organizations should be required by law to maintain an "arms-length" business relationship between board, staff members, and their relatives with profit-making organizations serving the agency or institution.
   Update: This course is strongly advocated by the Philanthropic Advisory Council of the Better Business Bureau and the National Charities Information Bureau and most organizations comply.
10. To discourage unnecessary accumulation of income, a pay out rate of 5 percent of the principal of grant-giving foundations should be fixed by Congress.
    Update: This started at a higher rate, but by 1979 it was fixed at 5 percent.
11. Nonprofit organizations, other than foundations, should be allowed the same freedom to lobby for legislation pertaining to their programs and interests as business corporations and trade associations. Congress should eliminate the current limitation imposed on such activity by nonprofits.
    Update: Representative Barber Conable introduced a Lobbying by Public Charities Bill which was included in the Tax Reform Act of 1976, Public Law 94–455.
12. The paramount recommendation by the Filer Commission Report, as far as most of us were concerned, was to establish a permanent commission on philanthropy thereby avoiding "reinventing the wheel." This part of the report was written by two eminent tax lawyers, Marion Freemont-Smith and Adam Yarmolinsky. In their report, they stated:

> A new organization of recognized national stature and authority is needed, the Commission believes, to further chart and study, and ultimately to strengthen the nonprofit sector and the practice of private giving for public purpose .... Several major tasks ... already await it. Among these is examining philanthropic priorities in light of America's changing social perceptions, of government's growing role in traditional philanthropic areas, and of the inevitably limited resources of private giving. <u>Also advancing means of insulating voluntary organizations from political and bureaucratic pressures that tend to accompany public funds</u> ... It is proposed that half of the commission's

<u>membership be named by the President, subject to senatorial conformation, the other half by the presidential appointees themselves. Funding would come half from government, half from private sources.</u> (The underlining is mine.)

The Filer Commission report contained shades of the Peterson Commission's recommendation four years earlier. Once again a quasi-governmental entity was proposed and several members dissented. They said it should be established, but it must be beyond, and hopefully above, any of the limitations imposed by political motivations and government bureaucracy. The new commission must be privately supported and its policies determined by private citizens. This conclusion planted the seed for a concerted effort to try to set up a permanent *private* commission on philanthropy.

CHAPTER 7

Post-Filer Commission Activities—A Gathering of Forces

There were many significant developments on the nonprofit scene over the next five years. Among them:

Washington Conference of the National Conference on Philanthropy	*December 1975*	Held immediately after the release of the Filer Commission Report, this conference provided an excellent forum for discussions of the Commission's findings.
Development of a prospectus for a permanent private commission for philanthropy	*Winter and spring of 1976*	After the interest generated by the Filer Commission to establish a permanent commission waned, several nonprofit organizations joined efforts to set up, at least, a coalition.
Establishment of the Coalition of National Voluntary Organizations (CONVO)	*Fall of 1976*	As an outgrowth of the Coalition for Public Good and in response to no further activity by government, the key nonprofit organizations got behind the newly formed Coalition of National Voluntary Organizations (CONVO).

POST-FILER COMMISSION ACTIVITIES—A GATHERING OF FORCES

Disbanding of the federal government Private Advisory Committee on Philanthropy and Public Needs	April 1977	At its first meeting in Washington, C. Douglas Dillon, Chairman of this advisory Committee was informed by Secretary of Treasury, Michael Blumenthal, that President Carter had decided to disband all private advisory committees.
Tax Reform Proposals, 1977	Most of 1977	Tax reforms were high on President Carter's agenda and many being considered would be harmful to charitable giving. Fortunately his other legislative priorities delayed action which gave CONVO members more time to prepare their case.
Congressional efforts to establish federal legislation to regulate charities	1977 to 1978	Lionel VanDeerlin, Congressman from California proposed a bill to require charities to disclose the cost of fund-raising on all their solicitation materials. Congressman Charles Wilson from California proposed a bill to have charitable regulations placed under the U.S. Postal Service instead of IRS.
Establishment of the AAFRC state legislation monitoring program	1967 to 1978	In an effort to reduce the expensive and time-consuming chaos charities must go through to conform to a wide variety of state regulations, the AAFRC set up a system which provided charities with advanced word on pending state bills so that lobbying plans could be made and implemented.
White House Conference on Voluntarism	September 1979	Leaders, staff, trustees, and volunteers attended a seminar and reception hosted by the first lady and joined at the last minute by President Carter. The President gave a warm tribute to American philanthropy.

New efforts to get philanthropy's act together	1977 to 1980	CONVO and the National Conference on Philanthropy began to explore the advantages of merging the two organizations into an organization which would be greater than the sum of its parts.
The Charter meeting of INDEPENDENT SECTOR	March 1980	INDEPENDENT SECTOR was chartered at a meeting in the Mayflower Hotel Washington attended by members of CONVO, NCOP, and Congress. John Gardner assumed the Chairmanship.
J. C. Geever, Inc. becomes a member of the AAFRC	1978	The J. C. Geever, Inc. became the first firm headed by a woman (Jane C. Geever) to join the AAFRC.

NATIONAL COUNCIL ON PHILANTHROPY CONFERENCE, 1975

On December 3, 1975, the day after the Filer Commission's final report was presented to government officials, the National Council of Philanthropy held its annual conference in Washington. There were several key figures from the Commission on the program. John Filer opened the conference with an overview of the Commission's activities and findings. A panel including Leonard Silverstein, Alan Pifer, Bayard Ewing, Congressman Barber Conable, and Herbert E. Longenecker, President of Tulane University, encouraged open discussion. Most of the program was devoted to the Commission's recommendations and reactions to it. The discussion revolved around six basic questions:

1. Isn't there too much emphasis on tax matters?
2. Are current self-regulation efforts sufficient to ward off more government laws and sanctions?
3. Has enough interest been generated to organize a private commission on philanthropy?
4. Wouldn't a quasi-governmental entity have much more influence on public-policies?

5. Were the recommendations of the Donee Group given appropriate attention?
6. Will the leadership interest and participation continue now that the report is completed?

The 635 attendees at this conference represented a wide range of foundation and corporate donors, trustees of nonprofit organizations and top staff of many philanthropic organizations and institutions. Their reactions and views were invaluable in guiding efforts to establish a permanent commission on philanthropy. In general, this group was pleased with most of the Commission's work and their opportunity to express their views to the Commission's leaders. Another result of this open forum was an increased interest in the need to establish both a permanent commission and continuing studies of philanthropy. On a more formal level, the Secretary of the Treasury, William E. Simon, asked C. Douglas Dillon to set up a Presidential Advisory Committee on Philanthropy and Public Needs.

> **CRITICAL ISSUE #15**
>
> In December 1975, following the Filer Commission's Report, the National Council on Philanthropy held its annual conference in Washington. Most of the program was devoted to discussion of the Commission's recommendations and reactions to them.

PROSPECTUS FOR A PRIVATE COMMISSION ON PHILANTHROPY, 1976

In the closing weeks of 1975, I became encouraged by such positive reactions to establish a permanent *private* commission on philanthropy. As soon as I saw the first draft of the Commission's final report, I called Phil Klutznick about the recommendation that it be quasi-governmental. Phil said, "Jack, I'm writing a dissent for the report. While I agree that a permanent commission should be set up, I also believe that the private sector should set its own agenda and be removed from the dangers of political influences."

"That's exactly what I think," I said.

"Why don't you write up a proposal defining the organization of a private commission?"

"I'd be delighted," I said.

I immediately drafted a position paper and proposal for a *private* commission on philanthropy. It was presented first to the 501(c)(3) Group which endorsed it, and then to the Leaders of the Coalition for Public Good—Bayard Ewing, Philip Bernstein, William Aramony, and Kenneth Albrecht, now President of NCOP. After seven rewrites over seven months it was finally accepted by the key organizations involved. The list included the 501(c)(3) Group, the National Health Council, the National Conference on Philanthropy, the National Conference of Catholic Charities, the United Way of America, the Council of Jewish Federations and Welfare Funds, Inc., the National Center for Voluntary Action, and AAFRC.

John S. Glaser, from United Way of America, repeatedly helped me revise the position paper. He is bright, caring, enthusiastic, and visionary about the promise of American philanthropy. As a social worker, he had valuable frontline experience teaching literacy to natives in rural Haiti before he joined the staff of United Way. Because of Aramony's willingness to provide the resources of the United Way to this project we had both John and its former president, Bayard Ewing on our side. In hindsight, not enough credit can be given to the contributions of both of these men.

We were resolved to the fact that most of the leadership of the Filer Commission had moved to other projects, limiting our capacity to organize a permanent commission. But we decided to do what we could. Walter J. McNereney, former member of the Filer Commission and President of Blue Cross Association, was chairing an ad hoc committee to implement the Commission's recommendations. Through Klutznick's continued interest, we stayed in touch with McNerney's committee, but to them, putting together a permanent commission seemed only a future goal.

CRITICAL ISSUE #16

After development of a prospectus for a permanent commission, the Coalition of National Voluntary Organizations (CONVO) was formed in 1976.

COALITION OF NATIONAL VOLUNTARY ORGANIZATIONS, 1976

On July 8, 1976, John Glaser and I presented the seventh draft of our proposal to establish a permanent commission on philanthropy at a meeting hosted by the Council of Foundations. This was an excellent example of many key private organizations banding together. The 501(c)(3) Group, the National Council on Philanthropy, the Council on Foundations, the Coalition for Public Good, the American Hospital Association, the National Health Council, the Council for Aid to Education, United Way of America, and AAFRC were among the organizations represented.

No one questioned the fact that we had met to form a permanent commission, but our prime concern was to combine the professional resources of our organizations to address the shared concerns about the current state and future capacity of American philanthropy. We were well aware of the pitfalls inherent in establishing an organization that would intrude on the autonomy of its members.

We agreed, in advance, that we would form an organization of nonprofit organizations (both grantors and grantees). The appellation "coalition" was already replacing "commission" in most of our minds. The organizational format agreed upon at this meeting essentially strengthened the Coalition for Public Good under the new name of the Coalition of National Voluntary Organizations (CONVO). CONVO's purposes, as developed over the next months, were:

- To maximize the contributions of the voluntary sector in meeting America's human needs and to enrich the quality of American society;
- To increase public understanding of the history, the accomplishments, and the rich capacity of the voluntary sector to improve the quality of American life;
- To gather and disseminate data on the scope and the nature of the philanthropic process;
- To assess current and emerging social needs in order to determine the extent by which these needs are being met or not being met by both voluntary and public efforts;
- To study public policies which impact on the private sector and to recommend appropriate policies which encourage and strengthen a pluralistic society;
- To promote the accountability and accessibility to the public of both donor and donee organizations.

Our resolve was strengthened further by the results of a April 7, 1977 meeting which took place in the U.S. Treasury building. This was the first convening of the private advisory committee on philanthropy and public needs formed by William E. Simon while he was still Secretary of the Treasury. Chairman Douglas Dillon had enlisted 25 members, none of whom were practitioners from any major philanthropic organization. This gave us concern. Nevertheless, many of us who had been involved with the Filer Commission attended.

The new Secretary of the Treasury under President Carter, Michael Blumenthal, strode out on the platform at the front end of the room to open the meeting. He stated that President Carter was working hard to fulfill his campaign promise of cutting down on government bureaucracy and costs. "Thus," Blumenthal said, "he has decided to eliminate all private committees that have been advising the government. In light of this, I regret to inform you that this committee is to be disbanded immediately." Filing out in disgust we were more determined than ever to make CONVO work.

A search committee chaired by Hayden Smith of the Council for Aid to Education was formed to seek an executive director for CONVO. A board with representatives from 12 national umbrella organizations was formed with Bayard Ewing as Chairman, Philip Bernstein as Vice Chairman and myself as Secretary-Treasurer. Operations were to begin in March of 1977.

Funding for the first year's budget came from participating member organizations. The American Cancer Society, the American Heart Association, the U.S. Catholic Conference and the United Way pledged $15,000 each and Council of Jewish Federations and Welfare Funds and the AAFRC pledged $5,000 each. By the end of 1976, a total of $70,000 had been pledged for the first year's operations. In early 1977, we engaged Richard E. Dewey from the Council on the Aging as CONVO's Executive Director. An office was opened at 1214 Sixteenth Street, N.W., Washington D.C.

CRITICAL ISSUE #17

Following the disbanding of the federal government's Private Advisory Committee on Philanthropy and Public Needs in 1977, the need for establishing an organization such as CONVO became more apparent.

CONVO membership was open to national and umbrella organizations. Its functions, as now defined, were:

1. To gather and disseminate statistics and information on both the needs and resources of the voluntary sector;

2. To consider the research needs of the voluntary sector, to identify areas which require further investigation, and to encourage or sponsor such investigation;
3. To monitor activities of government departments in relevant executive and legislative areas with special emphasis on legislation which concerns charitable deductions and the regulation of charities (with the area of state legislation of charity being considered of high priority);
4. To formulate guidelines of accountability and accessibility to the public;
5. To provide the general public with comprehensive information about the impact, the needs, and the achievements of philanthropy.

Dewey dug right in to help raise funds and enlist new members. He also devoted a great deal of time to the identification of potential legislation that concerned the voluntary sector. The board concentrated on membership, fund-raising, and research needs. By the summer of 1977, 37 national and umbrella organizations had joined. Their annual dues were based on each organization's gross salaries, wages, and benefits of the national staff.

Because of the many bills then being reviewed on the hill that might affect charities, CONVO, with cooperation of the 501(c)(3) Group, concentrated on preparing efforts to shoot down the bad ones. This was, at least, a good start. Yet all of us felt frustrated because CONVO could not presume to be a permanent commission on philanthropy. No organization of just nonprofit organizations, without the participation of national leaders, corporate executives and foundation presidents, could be the commission we originally sought to organize. Our dream was still in front of us.

TAX REFORM PROPOSALS, 1977

Senator Russell B. Long, Chairman of the Senate Finance Committee (the committee which reviews all tax changes) gave this definition of tax reforms:

Don't tax you,
don't tax me.
Tax that fellow
under the tree.

The aptness and durability of this ditty was reinforced 16 years later in an article by David E. Rosenbaum in a February 14, 1993 *New York Times* article on the problems facing the new Clinton administration. Rosenbaum's attributed the following comment to former Senator Long:

> *Don't tax him.*
> *Don't tax me.*
> *Tax the man behind the tree.*

Whichever version you prefer, this condition will surely prevail well into the 21st century.

The Carter White House along with the then Secretary of the Treasury Michael Blumenthal, applied strong pressure on the Treasury staff to develop tax reforms. The government then, as now, desperately needed more funds and simplified tax laws. Yet, how can you improve, much less "simplify," the tax system without losing revenue in some areas and increasing the tax burden for others?

In this climate, charitable deductions were particularly vulnerable. The notion of tax credits in lieu of charitable deductions was promoted by the National Committee for Responsive Philanthropy—the organization which grew out of the Donee Group, which was now managed with energy and sharp focus by Robert Bothwell. Professor Martin S. Feldstein had documented for the Filer Commission the fact that the charitable deduction is efficient. For every dollar lost in taxes by the federal government, charities gain from $1.11 to $1.28. Feldstein also showed that while a 30 percent tax credit would increase giving in 1970 dollars by $2.3 billion, it would reduce giving to higher education by 17 percent as well as reduce support for most well-established charities. Such redistribution of the charitable dollar favored new organizations at the great expense of others. Also, the charitable deduction was referred to as a "tax loophole."

Stanley Surrey, a distinguished Professor of Economics from the University of Massachusetts and former Assistant Secretary of the Treasury claimed that charitable deductions were, in truth, a tax expenditure. Therefore, he said, the government had the right to decide how such funds should be spent—an idea that did not appeal to the nonprofit sector.

Another target was the tax law on gifts of appreciated property. Many battles in recent years had successfully preserved the right of a donor to deduct from his taxable income the current fair market value of a gift of appreciated property. What's more, if the value of this gift exceeded the amount he could deduct in one year he could, if necessary, carry portions of the deduction over five years. In simple terms, this meant that a person who gave property or investments that originally cost $10,000 and were now worth $100,000, he could deduct the entire $100,000 from taxable income. If it was sold instead, the tax determined by his particular tax bracket would have to be paid on the appreciated portion or $90,000. Individuals in these circumstances were prime candidates for pace-setting gifts. We never stopped being concerned about the challenges to this wonderful example of our traditional government policy that encourages public support of philanthropy.

Other tax changes under consideration included:

- Reducing the maximum tax credit from 70 percent to 50 percent;
- Placing a 3 percent floor on charitable deductions; and
- Increasing the exemptions for nonitemizers (thereby moving more into the nonitemizing class, all of whom would no longer be able to deduct gifts to charities from their taxable income).

We had gathered plenty of evidence on the damage any of these measures would do to total giving. Also, we had developed a strategy for making our case quickly and efficiently.

President Carter had an energy bill very high on his agenda. The attention given this legislation finally preempted Congressional deliberations on tax reforms for the rest of the year. However, thanks to many meetings of CONVO, in collaboration with the 501(c)(3) Group, we were better prepared for the fight whenever it was needed. And the growing cooperation between nonprofit organizations was being recognized more and more by legislators and their staff.

CONGRESSIONAL EFFORTS TO REGULATE CHARITIES, 1977–1978

In 1977, two congressional bills surfaced for consideration that were designed to increase accountability and disclosure requirements for charities. The first, a bill by Lionel Van Deerlin, Democrat from Southern California, that would require charities to disclose fund-raising costs for the last year in all their solicitations. Van was very open with us and acknowledged from the start that he knew little about the philanthropic process. He was determined that the public receive all pertinent information before being asked to make a contribution.

He called me to his office and listened carefully to my arguments that reporting fund-raising costs alone could distort the real worth of a charity. I explained, "The prospect should always have the right to receive full information upon request, but this should include such material as the history of the charity's programs, the composition of the board, and the total cost of operating and program expenses so that fundraising costs can be judged in proper perspective." I chaired a committee of nonprofit representatives at Van's request to help him explore the implications of a bill. While it never got out of committee, we were able to educate Van and several of his colleagues about the importance of requiring certain reports from charities that gave a broad picture of its administration practices, not just isolated fund-raising costs.

> **CRITICAL ISSUE #18**
>
> *CONVO made preparations to fight the proposed tax reforms of 1997. While many of the new proposals failed to get out of committee, the staff of CONVO learned how to best prepare and research for a fight.*

Also in 1977, a second congressional effort was the introduction of the Wilson bill to the Postal Services Committee by Charles H. Wilson of California. This bill would have required telling the recipient of a mail appeal exactly what it cost to prepare and mail it. Further, it would have the Postal Service take over from the monitoring of the charitable sector from the IRS. This, of course, provoked many comments on how could a government department that screwed up the delivery of mail, ever handle, in addition to its current responsibilities, something as complicated as this?

On March 29, 1977, I testified before the Postal Personnel Subcommittee of the House Post Office and Civil Service Committee. As with the Van Deerlin bill, I explained:

> By asking for ... limited information (the cost of one appeal), the legislation is asking the public to determine whether or not the charitable cause is efficient solely on the basis of fundraising costs ....
> Many factors must be taken into account in judging the effectiveness

of a charity. Fundraising costs are only one of them. We urge that charities be required on request to make full disclosure as in the annual report. Emphasizing fundraising costs at the point of solicitation will inevitably cause some not to contribute—individuals who would give if they knew of the charity's complete financial record, history, and programs. New and lesser programs have high fundraising costs the first year or two. However if properly followed up, seventy percent of last year's donors will renew, driving fundraising costs down considerably by the third year. We also strongly recommend that the IRS, not the Postal Service, continue to monitor charities. Form 990's already have to be filed with IRS by all charities. This would eliminate costly duplication as IRS is already geared up to do a good job.

Several state's attorney generals also testified, emphasizing that they, not the federal government, should monitor charitable activity in their respective states.

Fortunately this bill never got out of committee either. Both bills, however, were symptomatic of the current attitude and concerns of many legislators.

AAFRC STATE LEGISLATIVE MONITORING PROGRAM, 1976–1979

State regulation of charitable activity was a hodgepodge. A few legislators believed that this type of legislation enhanced their political image so they kept introducing more bills. In 1976, there were 31 states with legislation on their books—all different, all requiring the filing of forms, with each form unique to that state. It was confusing and inefficient for hard pressed charities. The board of the AAFRC agreed with my strong recommendation to establish a state legislative program and make it available to the field.

We engaged the Commerce Clearing House in Chicago to send graduate students, many in pre-law, to state capitals and alert us on all bills in committee which could effect charitable activity. Almost daily, during legislative sessions, one state or another was involved with either regulatory changes or statutory amendments. The only good time to head off a bad bill is while it's still in committee where you can present your case before it goes out to the floor. After it reaches the floor, it usually is too late.

In 1977 the Legislative Monitoring Service examined 336 bills which were introduced at the state level and would have had some impact on charitable solicitations. AAFRC service reported in detail and closely tracked 25 of those bills. Each report contained information on:

- The state;
- Regulatory agency;
- Cost limitations;
- Annual financial reporting requirements;
- Monetary exemption ceiling;
- Charitable solicitation disclosure;
- Registration or licensing; and
- Bonding requirements.

Two such bills were passed and signed into law by the governors concerned. The rest of the identified bills either were held over until 1978 or died for lack of action because the about-to-be regulated charities were alerted and fought the provisions. By 1979, the AAFRC had examined 718 bills and established a lasting service to the field.

CRITICAL ISSUE # 19

Before 1976, state regulations of charitable activity was a political and bureaucratic nightmare. Thirty-one states had some sort of charitable activity regulation in the works; each state requiring the filing of forms unique to that state. It was almost impossible to follow. In 1977, the AAFRC set up a state legislation monitoring program which proved to be an invaluable service.

NEW EFFORTS TO GET PHILANTHROPY'S ACT TOGETHER

It was serendipity. In 1977, two important nonprofit groups were suddenly without their chief executive. The National Council on Philanthropy (NCOP) was tightening and improving its organization under the leadership of its new capable president Oscar Carr. Oscar was respected and dedicated to the NCOP mission. Unfortunately, he became ill that summer. It was cancer. It took his life by late fall. Also that fall, Richard Dewey resigned after a little more than a year as executive director of CONVO. As of September 19, John Glaser agreed to give half-time to CONVO and hold down the office until other steps could be taken. Full-time administrative leadership was now sorely lacking in both organizations. CONVO especially needed attention, as its membership had grown to nearly 60 organizations.

As a member of both boards, I was concerned, as were the respective presidents, Bayard Ewing and Kenneth Albrecht. Then, another development helped us make a important decision. Brian O'Connell had been the Executive Director of the National Association for Mental Health for 12 years. Brian knew the field well and was known to be a thoughtful, articulate supporter of efforts to improve the private sector. When he announced that he was resigning at the end of the year, his board members urged him to reconsider because he had done such a superb job as the executive director. Brian stood fast in his belief that it was a good time to make a career change.

> **CRITICAL ISSUE #20**
>
> *In 1979, CONVO and NCOP entered into an experimental, time-limited collaboration which served as a vehicle for planning, organizational cooperation, and a pursuit of common ideas.*

Those of us on the CONVO and NCOP boards agreed to approach Brian to take advantage of his skills. We asked him to do a feasibility study on the possibility of closer collaboration between NCOP and CONVO. In the backs of our minds, we hoped that these two organizations might eventually combine forces, becoming greater than the sum of their two parts.

The voluntary officers of both organizations engaged Brian in the spring of 1978 to do the study. He completed it in September of 1978. He interviewed 25 from both boards and other leaders including several involved with the Filer Commission. Another 15 leaders from the foundation, corporate, educational, and the nonprofit field responded to Brian's invitation to submit their views. One of the most significant results of this study was the "turning on" of two persons:

1. Brian, himself, who made it clear early on that he would like to continue his involvement in any effort to build a better organization; and
2. John W. Gardner, founding chairman of Common Cause, former President of the Carnegie Corporation of New York, and former Secretary of Health Education and Welfare.

The minutes of CONVO's board meeting September 7, 1979 first reported on the just completed study. Chairman Ewing announced:

The feasibility study had recently been completed by Brian O'Connell. The study had been commissioned to determine if a 'critical mass' or central voice for the voluntary sector as a whole could be achieved. The study recommended that both CONVO and NCOP retain their separate structures for the time being, with NCOP emphasizing the conference function and CONVO emphasizing the political function. John Gardner agreed to assume leadership of the interim effort. This had the strong support of Congressman Barber Conable and Landrum Bolling chairman of the Council on Foundations who agreed to chair the fundraising effort. If this is approved by both boards, Mr. O'Connell would be leading the new entity as president (50 percent of his time from October 15 and 100 percent from November 15.) Headquarters will be in Washington, D.C. Estimated budget over three years is $300,000 . . . . All recommendations are subject to approval by the NCOP Board on September 14 and the CONVO membership on October 4.

The main recommendations approved in the feasibility study were:

1. CONVO and NCOP should use the coincidence of their current situations, their similar missions, and their shared convictions for improvements to take the first steps toward creating a vehicle for closer organizational cooperation and for fuller pursuit of common ideals.

    Creating only a secretariat would help the two . . . but it would not offer the prospect of setting into place the larger dimension necessary for the greater good . . . . Merging the two organizations to create a new body might be the answer, but a lot more planning is ncessary.

    What's needed is an entity that can be the secretariat and represent the vehicle for planning and organizing future efforts in order to strengthen the overall worth and impact of the voluntary sector. Such an arrangement must be extremely flexible with a back door for withdrawal and a front door for advance.
2. CONVO and NCOP should enter into an experimental, time-limited collaboration which would serve as a common secretariat for the two and represent a vehicle for planning and organizing for the future.
3. Each organization should retain its name, governance, and program but be served by a common office and staff.
4. This secretariat . . . would have an equal number of representatives from CONVO and NCOP along with members at large who would be approved by the two chief volunteer leaders of the founder organizations.

5. There would be a Management Committee consisting of the two volunteer leaders and persons who serve on the boards of both organizations. Their role would be to handle interorganizational questions.
6. There would be a common chief executive officer for CONVO and NCOP.

Once again, events helped to strengthen our conviction that this was the time to gather our forces together and strengthen CONVO.

JDR 3rd had been killed in a tragic automobile accident on July 10, 1978. The minutes of the September 5th CONVO Board meeting read:

> The Rockefeller interests had indicated a strong interest to continue his work and incorporate a new entity under the leadership of Walter McNerney and Waldemar Nielson, with Bobbie Kilberg as the executive. Funding was to include $25,000 from the JDR fund and $25,000 from the Rockefeller Brother's Fund as a memorial to JDR 3rd. All these groups appeared to be heading in the same direction, but since CONVO and NCOP had broad constituencies, the Rockefeller interests agreed to hold off funding until the new group develops.

Over the next two years, Brian administrated both organizations through two conferences, 10 board meetings and many committee meetings. As chair of the Management Committee during this period, I worked closely with Brian. My respect and admiration for him grew steadily as I observed the excellent job he did to bring together the many diverse interests involved. The original programs of the two organizations were sustained, but much attention and deliberation were given to the next steps.

By common consent, an Organizing Committee chaired by John Gardner for the development of a new organization out of the operating secretariat was formed in late 1978. I had a wonderful experience serving on this committee. There were 26 members from very diverse backgrounds— Congress, labor, education, the arts, minorities, foundations, corporations, umbrella nonprofit organizations, women's and church groups and the law.

Reviewing those days reminds me of an aphorism I heard in England (unfortunately without attribution): *"Hell hath no fury like a vested interest posing as a principle."* Everyone on that committee had an urgent agenda much conditioned by the needs of the organizations they represented. We didn't know each other too well and had yet to learn to trust each other. We remained polite, but "fury" was percolating beneath the surface. Yet we all trusted and respected John Gardner—

thoroughly. He allowed each of us to sound off about our needs, kept us from wandering too far from the agenda, and always brought us back to the larger issues and concerns shared by all of us. Thanks to Gardner's presence, persistence, and caring, we had developed a mutual friendship and respect that abetted many important decisions after only seven meetings.

We ruminated over a name which would truly represent the kind of organization we hoped to form. Hill & Knowlton, an eminent New York public relations firm provided *pro bono* services to the committee and studied several name suggestions. Meanwhile, several of us preferred "Independent Sector." John pointed out that its easy to become overly concerned about the possible impact of a name. He cited "Common Cause" as an example. Its board had a tough time accepting that name, but once established, the organization and its mission—not its name—was all that mattered. Hill & Knowlton reported to the committee that "Independent Sector" was indeed the best choice. That ended that.

The Organizing Committee's final report was completed and approved by the committee on Friday, September 7, 1979. It was immediately sent to the NCOP and CONVO trustees. Entitled, "To Preserve an Independent Sector," it concluded with, "We can't be sure that our model is the best one or even that it will work. But there is a unanimity among us that it has a chance, and the time has come for everyone concerned about this unique aspect of American life to unite and to preserve an independent sector."

The NCOP's board reviewed the feasibility study and its recommendations later that month and termed it "excellent." They asked for some "mild rewriting" particularly on the description of the new board. They desired a balance of corporate executives to ensure the input of the business community. The Organizing Committee continued to consider final revisions as suggested by the CONVO and NCOP boards. At its final meeting on December 18, 1979 they produced the plan to implement the new organization's establishment early in 1980. The uniqueness of the plan is shown by the type of members it contemplated. Voting members included corporations, foundations, and voluntary organizations with national interests or other activity related to the independent pursuit of the educational, health, welfare, cultural, and religious life of the nation—an organization of essentially independent non-governmental institutions.

The board was to number 45 members, many from nonprofit organizations. Also included was a balanced number of volunteer leaders representing many organizations and walks of life but they would not be involved with staffing or administering the organization directly. The Secretariat made considerable effort to raise $676,000 from leading foundations over three years. These funds would permit the organization to move ahead with its projects and programs while providing enough time for the membership fees to build up to cover its annual budget after 1980.

The problems faced by the sector were identified as:

- A relative decline in giving;
- Encroachment on the freedom of citizens to organize;
- Negative impacts of changes in tax policy;
- Greater dependence on tax dollars by independent institutions;
- The limited public understanding of the sector;
- The inadequate recognition of having alternatives and multiple sources of support.

The obstacles identified included:

- The sheer breadth and complexity of this sector;
- The intense desire for independence which exists in so much of this sector;
- The suspicion and actual antipathy which characterizes so many of the relationships in this disparate, quarrelsome, and competing world.

We must serve the constituents well enough to retain their support but carefully avoid representing the lowest denominator, namely the self-interest of the sector. If the INDEPENDENT SECTOR is to serve society well, it must be mobilized for greater cooperation and impact.

The recommended program was to build:

- Public education to improve understanding of the sector's role and function in giving people alternatives, greater opportunities for participation, and for creating a more caring society;
- Communications within the sector so that shared problems and opportunities may be identified and pursued;
- Relationships with government to deal with the infinite interconnections between the two sectors, but particularly to ensure the healthy independence and continued vitality of nongovernmental organizations;

- Research to provide a body of knowledge about the independent sector and about how to make it most useful to society;
- Encouragement of effective operation and management of philanthropic and voluntary organizations to maximize their capacity to serve individuals and society.

CRITICAL ISSUE #21

In March 1980, the INDEPENDENT SECTOR was founded. Its stated goals involved: educating the public; easing communications within the sector; improving relations with the government; providing a body of knowledge about the independent sector and making that research readily available; and encouraging the effective operation and management of philanthropic organizations.

WHITE HOUSE CONFERENCE ON VOLUNTARISM, SEPTEMBER, 1979

President Carter invited more than 200 administrators and key volunteers to honor voluntarism at the White House on September 13, 1979. We held a business meeting of CONVO membership at the Washington Hilton that morning to review progress on forming INDEPENDENT SECTOR.

I arrived at the Hilton where the reception table was already set up with two staff persons. I asked for an attendance list and was handed one off the top of a pile. I looked at it and said to the staff member from CONVO, "Wow! Whatever you do, hide this list and don't hand it out to anyone." You see, in order to get clearance to enter the White House, you must submit your social security number and birth date in advance. The staff had dutifully recorded both for everyone on the list. But there were several, I'm sure, who would not want others to know their age. This could have been an embarrassment. (I kept my copy however.)

CRITICAL ISSUE #22

In the Fall of 1979, President Carter invited more than 200 administrators and key volunteers to honor voluntarism in America. His continued support gave the field a much-needed boost.

We had been told that the President would be too busy to join the reception which was to be hosted by the Rosalynn Carter. So when the President arrived, we were all surprised. He praised the work of CONVO and stressed the importance of voluntarism to the nation. "Organizations providing volunteer service are important to America's well-being," he said. This was a much-needed boost for our efforts at a critical stage.

CHARTER MEETING OF INDEPENDENT SECTOR, MARCH 1980

With agreement achieved on the plan, a charter meeting to launch the INDEPENDENT SECTOR was planned for Wednesday, March 5, 1980. A crowd of 250 leaders from nonprofit organizations, institutions, volunteers, board members, and government officials convened in the ballroom of the Mayflower Hotel in Washington for a luncheon meeting. Papers of incorporation were formally signed by John W. Gardner, Chairman of INDEPENDENT SECTOR, James Lipscomb, president of the Gund Foundation and chairman of NCOP, and Philip Bernstein, chairman of CONVO.

The highlight of this day was the luncheon presentation by Senator Daniel Patrick Moynihan. After extolling the values of America's voluntary efforts for the public good, the Senator took exception to the notion that tax deductions for gifts to charities be termed tax expenditures by the Treasury. He referred to Stanley Surrey, the Treasury official advocating this approach, by quoting Disraeli, "A man distinguished by his ignorance. All his life he had but one idea. And it was wrong."

J. C. GEEVER, INC.

Jane Geever has the distinction of being the first woman to head a company that became a member of the AAFRC. She established her firm in the mid-Seventies by serving the fund-raising needs of start-up and smaller social agencies. Her AAFRC membership application seemed qualified on all counts when she submitted it in 1978. The firm had been in business more than three years, a list of all clients served so far was included with names of the top executives and board chairmen. Most of these were checked as references who attested to the fact that the firm's performance was both satisfactory and professional, its commitments fulfilled, and would be hired again under similar circumstances. The AAFRC membership committee was told by the board to personally check with *all* of her clients (usually only a portion of an applying firm's clients is checked) to insure that her work was so above approach that making her a member would cause no repercussions.

In 1979, Jane's application was accepted. I have strong admiration for the way she conducted her relations with the "male" club. Only in her thirties, with a confident and quiet manner, Jane earned the respect and friendship of her fellow members by her professional performance and cooperative attitude. She always did her homework, gave full attention and effort to her AAFRC committee assignments, and fulfilled them with caring and intelligence. She not only led the way for other women to form and build their own firms, but helped to remind several AAFRC members that the real yardsticks of performance are professionalism, style, results, and lasting good relations.

LESSONS LEARNED

- Most in the field agreed that a private commission on philanthropy which can remain above and beyond political ties and obligations is much preferred to a quasi-governmental entity.
- Nonprofit organizations share many common concerns and goals. This is a strong motivation for the leaders of the field to get together and consider ways to improve the philanthropic process.
- The duplication, confusion, and excessive administrative costs caused by varied state laws regulating charitable activities had been getting out of hand. It was essential that more information about proposed state legislation affecting charitable activity be researched and disseminated. Then the charities could voice their concerns before bad bills came out of committee.
- Once again, committed influential leadership made good things happen. John Gardner, and others on the INDEPENDENT SECTOR Organizing Committee, elevated personal agendas to genuine concerns for the entire philanthropic field. This made the formation of INDEPENDENT SECTOR possible.
- Philanthropy was beginning to get its act together. Key nonprofit organizations were more comfortable in working together.

- The need to closely monitor both state and federal legislation that can affect charitable activities will always be with us. All nonprofit organizations should continue to stay informed and be alert to fight harmful measures.
- More women were assuming key roles in the sector.

CHAPTER 8

Entering The Eighties—Improving Compatibility and Growing Professionalism

Many programs conceived and developed in the Seventies were advancing successfully in the new decade. They achieved a fresh degree of unity and at least a good start in helping philanthropy to "get its act together." The major developments:

Serving on the board of the National Charities Information Bureau (NCIB)	1978	Established in 1918, NCIB is a private agency that sets nine standards to guide charities into conducting ethical and efficient programs and promote informed giving.
The National Center for Charitable Statistics	1980	NCIB set up this center to track financial information on charities by placing on computer their reports to states and the federal government (Form 990).
Serving on the board of the National Institute of Colleges and Universities (NICU)	1979	The program of this privately funded nonprofit organization NICU is to improve the communications, quality, recognition, and funding of private liberal arts colleges and universities. It accomplishes this through research of their needs and trends and disseminating this data.

IMPROVING COMPATIBILITY AND GROWING PROFESSIONALISM

INDEPENDENT SECTOR	1980 to 1981	In its first year of operation, IS gained 133 charter members and raised $817,000 in start-up funds.
United Way Outstanding Agency Professional Award	May 1982	The presentation of this Award was a wonderful highlight of my career. It also highlighted how so much of the nonprofit sector was joining forces.
A study to measure the effect of the Reagan administration cutbacks on funding of programs in the private sector	1982	Commissioned by the 501(c)(3) Group, Lester M. Salamon, of the Urban Institute, did a study that showed that the Reagan administration budget will reduce funding to the nonprofit sector by $25 billion between 1981 and 1984 (compared to the Carter budget of 1980).
The Ditcheley Foundation Conference on Private Giving	December 1982	A three day seminar in England with 34 participants from six nations who examined the cultural differences, varying attitudes, and the effectiveness of philanthropy in the United Kingdom, western Europe, and America.
The CIAO	1982	In order for executives of several key nonprofit organizations to learn more about each other's programs and examine ways to improve both communications and cooperation, CIAO was formed with executives representing six organizations.
The National Society of Fund-Raising Executives	1980 to 1984	Under the leadership of the NSFRE executive vice president, J. Richard Wilson, the Society became an effective catalyst and partner in many programs of other key nonprofit organizations.

Giving USA: 1983 Annual Report	March 1984	In order to improve the methodology of compiling statistics on giving, the AAFRC enlisted nine top statisticians and researchers to form a research advisory group. This improved results, but could not make up for the fact that most hard data doesn't become available until three or four years later.
A Day with John Gardner	April 1984	*This was an opportunity for 12 executives from foundations and nonprofit organizations to learn from John Gardner how to better understand and improve their relations with staff, trustees, other organizations, and society in general.*
The State Model Law Project	Spring 1984 to December 1986	At the invitation of the National Association of Attorney Generals (NAAG), I chaired the Private Sector Advisory Group to work with state charity regulators to develop a model state law to regulate charitable activities.

The broad scope of philanthropy was finally recognized by many practitioners who personally volunteered their time to programs designed to improve professionalism. Many of the various parts of the philanthropic process communicated with each other, identified shared concerns and problems, and often worked together to seek solutions. The organizations representing religion, education, health, human services, arts, culture and humanities, public benefit, environment and international affairs exchanged views. Grantees and grantors met to explore the most effective ways to apportion scarce resources. The maintenance of state and federal legislation which encouraged, not discouraged, more charitable giving also helped bond us together.

Every field has its frauds and philanthropy is no exception. During the Eighties, the media seemed to concentrate more and more on the pejorative stories of malfeasance, and fraudulent behavior of a few. We all knew and respected the fact that since most of the costs of programs, salaries, fundraising, research and endowment building came from donated funds, we were especially accountable to the public and had to be prudent and efficient with all expenditures. We had to be alert and take every opportunity to let the general public know that this is how we feel.

THE NATIONAL CHARITIES INFORMATION BUREAU (NCIB)

It was widely recognized that effective self-regulation not only helped keep government bureaucracy out of our affairs but also provided a set of standards towards which nonprofits should aspire. Two organizations were in the forefront of setting standards for charities, the Philanthropic Advisory Board of the Better Business Bureau (PAS) and the National Information Bureau (NCIB). I knew more about the Philanthropic Advisory Service because its articulate and able Executive Helen O'Rourke, served with me on the board of the National Council on Philanthropy. Both NCIB and PAS competed for attention and funds, but this helped make them more effective.

In May of 1978, I accepted an invitation to serve on the board of the National Charities Information Bureau. NCIB is a voluntary agency formed in 1919 to promote informed giving. Over the years, using the views and input of executives and trustees from a widely representative group of charitable organizations, it developed nine standards designed to guide charities into ethical and efficient, public service programs:

1. *Board governance.* Board members will take no fees, be independent volunteer members, make up a quorum that meets at least twice a year, establish policy guidelines that avoid conflict of interest by board and staff, and promote pluralism and diversity.
2. *Purpose.* The purpose must be appropriately stated.
3. *Programs.* All programs should be consistent with its statement of purpose.
4. *Information.* Its promotion, fund-raising, and public relations should be consistent with its statement of purpose.
5. *Financial support and related activities.* All financial activities are accountable and ethical fund-raising practices without unwarranted pressure must be used.
6. *Use of funds.* The use of funds should reflect consideration of

current and future needs, with at least 60 percent for program activities. Fund-raising costs should be reasonable over a period of time.
7. *Annual reporting.* This should include an explicit description of the organizations major activities, a list of the board, and audited financial statements.
8. *Accountability.* A full disclosure is necessary of economic resources and obligations including transactions with related parties.
9. *Budget.* It should be a detailed annual budget consistent with the major classifications in the audited financial statements.

I served on NCIB's Standards and Practices Committee from the beginning. During that time, I learned about administrative lapses, the transgressions of some charities, and the hard work required to eliminate them. NCIB concerned itself with around 450 charities which, because of their national recognition and importance of their programs, stimulated many inquiries from potential donors. NCIB made available a report on each of these organizations. The report outlined how well each organization met the nine standards. In those cases in which a charity didn't meet all of the standards, the staff of NCIB would work with the charity upon request to help it achieve approval. NCIB standards and approval helped many charities improve their operations and gain increased public support.

> **CRITICAL ISSUE #23**
>
> *The National Charities Information Bureau was founded in 1918 to promote informed giving. Over the years, it has refined nine standards designed to guide charities into ethical and efficient public service programs. The standards covered the topics of board governance, purpose, nature of support, use of funds, annual reporting, accountability, and budgets.*

THE NATIONAL CENTER FOR CHARITABLE STATISTICS, 1980

Wilson C. "Bill" Levis, a dedicated champion of the private sector, a well-trained statistician, computer expert, and creative staff member of NCIB, had developed software for state regulators to facilitate reports

IMPROVING COMPATIBILITY AND GROWING PROFESSIONALISM

by charitable organizations in each state. He started with California and New York. His warm, friendly manner had made a lot of friends for NCIB, but he welcomed help on organizational matters. His ideas were so imaginative and ambitious, I jokingly referred to him as "our unguided missile." Bill, Ellen McGoldrick, Director of Corporate Contributions for Equitable Life Assurance Co., and I agreed that this software program could be expanded to pave the way to secure more and better information on charities. Ellen was ready to contribute $15,000 if the NCIB board would set up a pilot project to explore this concept.

In 1980, the NCIB board appointed me to serve as chairman of a steering committee to set up an organization designed to track financial information on charities from the IRS Form 990 and as many additional states as time and funds permitted. As information was gathered, we planned to store it in a data base of a newly created organization—the National Center for Charitable Statistics (NCCS).

Led by the initial generosity of Equitable Life, I garnered support from IBM, Metropolitan Life, American Telephone & Telegraph, and several foundations to launch it as an NCIB program. The goal was to establish a computerized data base that would include information filed in different states covering 75 to 80 percent of U.S. charitable institutions. For a small fee (designed to cover costs) anyone could have access to this information. By 1982, NCCS' data bank included IRS Form 990s on 120,000 registered charities plus 38,000 state reports from California, 12,000 registered in the State of New York, and 3,000 from New Jersey. The regulators from many states were now meeting face to face (NCCS funds made travel costs available for these public servants—none of whom had state funds for this purpose).

Through this process, we began to attack the serious problem caused by each state requiring a different form for charitable reporting. As a start, they agreed on the same 88-line items for their reports. This breakthrough had a wonderful additional benefit: the IRS announced at a meeting in the appropriately called "Dollar Room" of the Treasury building that it had modified its 990 Form to conform to the new states' report.

People in the field questioned the appropriateness of having this program under the aegis of a private monitoring agency like NCIB. We had formed a board of executives from the Council on Foundations, the INDEPENDENT SECTOR, the Foundation Center, the New York Community Trust, the United Way of America, state regulators, and members of the NCIB board.

As the first elected president, I called a meeting on September 15,

1981 to bring together the INDEPENDENT SECTOR, the Council on Foundations, and the United Way. They all agreed to join in a consortium with NCIB to run NCCS. At this meeting, the United Way made their chief scholar and head of research, Russy Sumariwalla, available to be the executive director. Since then NCCS has been made a program of INDEPENDENT SECTOR, something we all felt was appropriate. Unfortunately, while data is now available for most of the states, the battle to achieve a common reporting form is still going on.

> **CRITICAL ISSUE #24**
>
> *In 1980, the National Center for Charitable Statistics was formed under the aegis of the National Charities Information Bureau. Its goal was to establish a computerized data base that would include information filed in different states covering up to 80 percent of U.S. institutions. For a fee, anyone could gain access to this information. In 1981, a consortium representing the INDEPENDENT SECTOR, the Council on Foundations, the United Way, and the NCIB was established to run NCCS.*

THE NATIONAL SOCIETY OF FUND-RAISING EXECUTIVES (NSFRE)

By the end of the Seventies, NSFRE had engaged J. Richard "Dick" Wilson as its executive vice president. Dick was a breath of fresh air. He almost looked boyish with a slight and small figure, but his capacity to dig right into problems and avoid getting bogged down with unnecessary complications helped him to motivate others in a quiet, but most effective way. He projected integrity and respect for others.

For the first time, he was involved with many aspects of the larger field of philanthropy and allowed to represent the interests of NSFRE—something heretofore reserved for the volunteer head. It was a pleasure to introduce Dick to the 501(c)(3) Group, INDEPENDENT SECTOR, NCCS, among others. He quickly recognized and appreciated the programs of other organizations and worked very hard to relate NSFRE's programs to enhance and compliment those of other leading organizations in the field.

The Society's first priority was to the fund-raising profession, but they made their skills and resources available to many projects designed to improve the philanthropic process. NSFRE has become an

IMPROVING COMPATIBILITY AND GROWING PROFESSIONALISM

important, respected and creative contributor to American philanthropy, as will be documented further on in this chapter.

INDEPENDENT SECTOR: THE EARLY YEARS, 1980–1984

INDEPENDENT SECTOR (IS) was launched in 1980. It had 133 charter members—53 percent were national or umbrella philanthropic organizations and institutions and 47 percent were foundations and corporations with national giving programs. It raised $817,000 in start-up funds. Brian O'Connell quickly built a very effective staff. He enlisted two top executives who he had worked with at the National Association for Mental Health—Robert A. Smucker, who became IS' Vice President for Governmental Relations and John H. Thomas, who became Vice President for Public Relations. Its headquarters were established at 1828 L Street N.W., Washington D.C. Being invited to join its charter board was, for me and others, a great honor. I also served on the management and conference committees and became the assistant treasurer. Its five main programs were:

1. Public education to improve the public's understanding of the independent sector, its contributions and its problems;
2. Communication within the sector to identify shared problems and opportunities;
3. Research to develop a comprehensive store of knowledge about the sector;
4. Encouragement of effective nonprofit operation and management to maximize service to individuals and society;
5. Government relations to coordinate the many interconnections between the sector and national, state, and local governments; open and maintain dialogue on tax policy; protection of guaranteed freedoms; and propose and pursue legislation that preserves and enhances the sector's ability to serve public needs.

While this sounded very similar to the program plans of previous efforts, now the necessary resources, key organizations, and top leadership were involved. I will always be grateful to the officers serving as chair of AAFRC in this period—Edgar D. Powell, Blair Schreyer, and John G. Foerst Jr. They shared my enthusiasm for IS and endorsed the necessity of my devoting time and effort to IS' affairs often at the expense of AAFRC priorities. INDEPENDENT SECTOR didn't profess to be a "private commission on philanthropy," but, as time will show, it was the next-best thing.

Under the leadership of John Gardner as chair, the board meetings were lively, informative, and an impressive display of how so many diverse interests can be brought together to resolve controversial issues. John allowed each of us to express our views but he also kept us on track, and gave everyone a sense of accomplishment.

At one meeting, I remember vividly how he kept the amplitude of negative waves down. We were discussing the current state of society when one of the dedicated board women said, "I've been a social worker all my adult life. Things seem to be worse than ever—and I'm 59 years old." From the head of our long rectangular table, John said in a soft but audible voice, "Oh to be 59 again." Instantly, the room warmed and brightened. She smiled and we all joined her.

> **CRITICAL ISSUE #25**
>
> *INDEPENDENT SECTOR was founded in 1980. Representing 133 charter members, its five main programs covered public education, communications, research, encouragement of effective nonprofit operation and management, and government relations. Although similar to previous efforts, IS had the advantage of obtaining all the necessary resources, and of having both the key organizations and their top leadership to move it along. Although, not a private commission on philanthropy, IS turned out to be the next best thing.*

THE NATIONAL INSTITUTE OF INDEPENDENT COLLEGES AND UNIVERSITIES (NIICU), 1979–1981

In 1979, I accepted an invitation to join the board of this organization whose mission was to improve the intercommunications, quality, recognition, and funding of private American colleges and universities. Virginia Ann Hodgkinson was the very able executive director at the time. Under her leadership, the organization expanded its program and launched a number of research projects that increased the knowledge and understanding of the potential capacities of these schools. It also pointed up weaknesses that needed attention such as:

- *Funding*. Most private schools could not compete with the large universities for leadership and funding sources.
- *Fund-Raising*. With reduced government support under the Reagan administration, private schools had to increase the professional level of their fundraising activities to buck the trend of reduced enrollments and intensifying competition.

The NIICU board and staff worked hard to expand the knowledge about private schools and ways to solve their problems. Virginia motivated them well and the voice of their needs reached many congressmen, trustees and educators. Ironically, she left this post two years after I'd joined this board for an exciting opportunity with another of my favorite organizations.

> **CRITICAL ISSUE #26**
>
> *In the late Seventies, the National Institute of Independent Colleges and Universities launched a number of research projects to document the problems and the potential for growth and more funding for these schools. The NIICU board and staff worked hard to expand the knowledge about private schools, their funding, their enrollment, and ways to solve their problems.*

One day in late 1981, at an INDEPENDENT SECTOR board meeting, Brian mentioned that enough funding was available to engage a director of research in a few months and he would welcome candidates. I corralled him after the meeting and said, "Brian, There's one person so well qualified for that research job that she will instantly end your search."

"Who's that?" Brian asked.

"Virginia Hodgkinson." I said. With a knowing smile, Brian replied, "I've already talked to her, but I feel others should be considered, especially if a board member makes a recommendation." Thus, Brian was one step ahead of me and I had no part in Virginia's hiring.

The research program she has developed for INDEPENDENT SECTOR has stimulated many scholars and practitioners to devote more time and resources to the study of philanthropy. IS' annual Research Forum gives recognition and exposure to these research efforts and contributes to the much needed and now growing body of knowledge of philanthropy. In addition, her office produces valuable papers on the trends and the state of the private sector.

UNITED WAY OUTSTANDING AGENCY PROFESSIONAL AWARD, 1982

As President of AAFRC, it was my responsibility to build the agenda and set the time and place for our board meetings. In 1982, we agreed to go to Chicago for our May meeting, as it was central to the home offices of many member firms. Ten weeks before this meeting, I reminded Marie Medeo, our office manager, to arrange airline and hotel reservations that would bring me into Chicago two days early, as I wanted to spend some time visiting the offices of several Chicago member firms. "Sorry," she said, "But we're going to meet at the Waldorf Astoria in New York, not Chicago." I was startled. After I regained my composure, I tried to find out what was going on. All Marie would admit was that something special was under way and I'd hear about it soon.

The next day I learned that United Way of America was presenting me with the Outstanding Agency Professional Award, an honor given out once in a great while. I would be joining the distinguished company of two previous award winners—Lane W. Adams, Executive Vice-President of the American Cancer Society and Brian O'Connell. Somewhat dizzy and surprised, I did my best to arrange the board meeting around the dinner planned.

There are very few moments in my life that can match the joy, gratitude, warmth, pride and humility I felt on the evening of May 6, 1982. One hundred peers, friends, and professionals attended, along with Katy and my son Kip.

The award read:

> Jack Schwartz' talents have made a special and unique contribution to the voluntary sector. He brings people together. He works through issue after issue with quiet determination. But perhaps his greatest attribute has been his ability to forge the common threads of shared interest and concern which has helped the voluntary sector reach consensus on many vital issues of the day.

Right after dinner, I was roasted by eight of the best in the field. Particularly witty and penetrating, Brian referred to me as "Goldust" Schwartz and noted:

> Jack sure has his board absolutely bamboozled. They really think he's

doing something when he's forming all these organizations or serving on all these commissions and boards. He has them absolutely buffaloed.... I feel sorry for the board but I confess my greatest sympathy goes to Katy. She puts up a good front and I suppose at times could be described as having a good life. But she sure puts up with some strange requirements. Her home is perhaps the only one in America that has pay toilets, which is hard to put up with, even when the proceeds go to your favorite charity.

Helen O'Rourke distributed a BBB Philanthropic Advisory Council Report on my ethics and history and read:

He gained repute as a relentless seeker of evil doers. Was instrumental in bringing to ground unethical fund-raising. It was reported that the subject used ethics to subdue these nefarious hombres.... According to a reliable source, there have not been many complaints received on this organization. Some reducing salons complained because Jack keeps his fine figure.... This report is based on information available to Helen O'Rourke. None of Jack's deviations from CBBB standards are mentionable in this family publication.

I was deeply moved by the respect and affection shown, even in the roasts. I was being rewarded for so many things that others in attendance had earned more than me. In fact, this was a gathering of the real nonprofit sector leaders who were creating a new feeling of togetherness, one that meant we could really get things done.

501 (c)(3) GROUP, 1980–1982

The government affairs activity of INDEPENDENT SECTOR began to gather steam after its first few years, but in the interim the 501(c)(3) Group was kept busy with a full agenda. One matter that concerned us all was the effect that the Reagan Administration's government cutbacks would have on the charitable sector.

Hayden Smith, once again, came up with a valuable suggestion—engage Lester M. Salamon of the Urban Institute to analyze and measure the extent of what will surely be a growing gap between needs and resources. The group agreed to join forces to fund a study and Hayden and I met with Lester. I remember Hayden saying, "Just think Les, the last time the 501(c)(3) Group engaged someone for a study, it was Dr. Martin Feldstein. You probably will become just as famous as he did." (Martin had just been appointed chairman of President Reagan's Economic Advisory Council.)

> **CRITICAL ISSUE #27**
>
> *Early in 1981, the 501(c)(3) Group had its hands full dealing with the newly introduced Reagan Administration's budget cuts. They commissioned Lester M. Salamon of the Urban Institute to investigate the impact this would have on the nonprofit sector. Salamon's study showed that the Reagan budget, as compared to the Carter budget of 1980, reduced federal grants to nonprofit organizations by $25 billion between 1981 and 1984. Indirect cuts, providing funds for related services, would total $115 billion by 1985. This information proved invaluable to future lobbying efforts.*

Salomon's study, entitled "The Federal Budget and the Nonprofit Sector," shook us all up. He showed that the Reagan budget, when compared to the Carter budget of 1980, reduced federal grants to nonprofit institutions and organizations by $25 billion between 1981 and 1984. In addition, indirect cuts, which provide funds for related services, would total $115 billion by 1985. This dramatic and important data became useful ammunition for future lobbying efforts.

DITCHLEY FOUNDATION CONFERENCE ON PRIVATE GIVING, 1982

The Ditchley Foundation was created to promote a joint study of matters of common interests to British and American peoples. The foundation was incorporated in England on February 24, 1958, and is administered by a Council of Management composed of British and American members who reside in England. Only two hours from London and 13 miles from Oxford, Ditchley Park was built in 1720. Beautiful, spacious, and surrounded by pastoral well-groomed grounds, it was used as a conference center many times by Winston Churchill during World War II. Apparently, he preferred it to the other grand mansion, Blenheim.

A conference on philanthropy was scheduled at Ditchley from December 10 & 11, 1982. Along with Brian O'Connell, Lester Salamon, and Hayden Smith, I was invited to participate. There were 11 of us from America, 17 from the United Kingdom, three from France, and one each from Canada, Denmark and Germany, for a total of 34.

Staying in this magnificent mansion for three days provided real insight into the luxurious life of the British upper class. There were servants poised and ready for your slightest command. Katy and I were placed in a huge bedroom on the second floor that had an interesting and disconcerting glass peep hole at one end. We found out that this had been the nursery, but we were assured that there wasn't any nanny now in service to use the peep hole. The first morning we were awakened by a lovely young woman bringing morning tea to our bedside. She asked me what I liked in my tea and I replied, "just plain please." The next morning she was right on time, poured my tea, and kept it plain. I thanked her for remembering how I liked my tea and she said, "It's my job."

I remember this incident only because I feel it is symbolic of a significant cultural difference in our two societies. In America we start out, at least, with the belief in upward mobility. In England, there is an acceptance of remaining in whatever class you are born in.

At breakfast the second morning, Professor Kristof Glamann from Denmark was seated across from Katy and I. Hovering over our table were two of a dozen young women dressed in maid costumes ready to respond to our every breakfast whim. Eggs, scrambled or fried, fruit, all kinds of toast, waffles, honey, maple syrup, coffee, tea, milk, lemon? Just nod. I said, "Dr. Glamann, it wouldn't take long for me to become very used to this." He said. "Yes, but I'd keep looking out the window, expecting the peasant revolution to begin any minute."

The Ditchley conference wasn't all fun. We worked hard. We convened at 4:30 Friday afternoon, remained in session all day Saturday, and reconvened from 9:00 a.m. to 12:30 on Sunday. The conference opened with a plenary session on the current state of philanthropy in Great Britain, Europe, and the United States, with a historic review as well as a review of the present role of the private sector and of governments. Then we broke into three groups; each with a distinct subject matter. The subjects included: the purposes of givers; the needs of recipients; and the relationship between the giver and the state. Some of the differences identified:

1. In the United States, donors contribute to charitable causes as they wish. The government has a "hands-off" attitude as long as the donee is a legitimate charity and there is no direct benefit to the contributor. A tax deduction is gained by the act of giving.
2. In contrast, in both the United Kingdom and Europe, the government is considered the appropriate steward of public wel-

fare. Charitable contributions are encouraged under very tight limits so that they are used only for acceptable public purposes. This reaches its most extreme form in France where all major charitable contributions are subject to approval or rejection by the government.

3. In the United Kingdom, instead of a tax advantage to the donor, there is a repayment system where the charity receives the tax a donor has paid on the amount of the gift provided the donor pays it for four years (the so-called Covenant Law). This, of course, increases the size of a donor's four-year gift by the amount of its tax, but doesn't provide any other advantage to the donor. While many charities welcome the larger gift and can use the four-year commitment for their financial planning, a large potential donor often uses this process to get away with a much smaller gift.

Several representatives of the United Kingdom addressed their doubts about the value of professional fund-raising counsel. While they often do good work, they are very expensive. Any campaign would be better served by allocating the fees to the campaign goal. In the UK, public welfare is assumed to be the responsibility of the government, not the people. Philanthropy is an act by the rich, for the rich. The Americans at the conference agreed that this attitude placed British philanthropy 20 years behind philanthropy in the United States.

This conference did a good job of identifying the differences between the countries but accomplished little in determining what steps could be taken to foster more effective philanthropy without radical changes of attitudes, both by the people and the governments of Great Britain and Europe.

Two weeks after returning to the United States, the American participants received another example of Brian's wit. The following memo was addressed to the "Disadvantaged Ditchley Delegation From the Honors Committee" and read:

> It is obvious that the American delegation to the Ditcheley Conference felt themselves at a disadvantage coming up against such titled English counterparts.... A special committee has been at work to consider (and present) these honors and titles for the American participants. Here is a partial list:
>
> *Sir Knight Lord Lester Salamon, GG.* We should honor Sir Lester for gauging the gap (GG). It is also acknowledged that he came in second place for the honor of Bold Scribe.

Adam Yarmolinsky, Prime Minister. In this egalitarian society, Mr. Yarmolinsky, in essence, is accorded the highest honor. However his position is fragile. Christopher Price (Esq., MP, House of Commons) on the left and Robert Longley on the right are squeezing his support to a splinter.

The Rt. Worthy Sir Honorable Jack Schwartz, CC. As the person most responsible for keeping track of the giving statistics in America, Jack Schwartz is our Count Count (CC). It is euphoniously fortunate that his bride shall be known euphoniously as Countess Katy.

Hayden Smith. Highly deserving, but his dress (particularly that hat!) and the use of the King's English really places him more on their side than ours. Therefore, his fortunes are left up to the other side.

Brian O'Connell. For all the obvious reasons, no title or recognition is given. Should there be a subsequent conference, O'Connell can as usual the American standard of the common man. (Some common man!)

> **CRITICAL ISSUE #28**
>
> *The Ditchley Foundation Conference on Private Giving was held at Ditchley Park in England in December of 1982. On hand were 34 participants from six different nations. Although educational and interesting for the American participants, as well as doing a good job of identifying the differences between fundraising techniques in the various countries, the conference did little to bridge the international gap. Further steps needed to be taken to foster more effective philanthropy without radical changes in international politics and attitudes.*

GIVING USA: 1983 ANNUAL REPORT

Thanks to the excellent writing, research, and editing skills of Fred Schnaue, this publication had more credibility and a wider audience than ever. Fred had joined the AAFRC staff two years earlier and had recently been appointed vice president for public relations. He was a longtime writer for the Hearst newspapers. He was still moonlighting, writing editorials for William Randolph Hearst, Jr. at the time. His desire to make *Giving USA* as good as possible showed in the results.

He and I both felt that more should be done to improve our accuracy in estimating trends and growth in giving. In early 1982, we decided to form an advisory committee of key researchers in the field to review ways to improve our methodology. We found a readiness of key people to take part. They all acknowledged that this publication was the best thing available, but it could be improved. The committee's first meeting was in March 1983. Serving on it were:

- Elizabeth T. Boris, Director for Research, Council on Foundations, Inc.;
- Virginia Ann Hodgkinson, Vice President for Research, INDEPENDENT SECTOR;
- Patricia Read, Director, Editorial Services, the Foundation Center;
- Gabriel Rudney, Senior Research Associate, Yale-PONPO;
- Lester M. Salomon, Director, Center for Management & Economic Development Research, the Urban Institute;
- Hayden W. Smith, Senior Vice President, Council for Financial Aid to Education;
- Nelson Rosenbaum, President, Center for Responsive Governance; and
- Russy Sumariwalla, Senior Fellow, United Way of America.

The next year, at the advice of the committee, we engaged Dr. Ralph Nelson, Professor of Economics at Queens College in New York. As an economist, he worked with the Filer Commission, knew the philanthropic field, and was well-qualified to construct an improved model of methodology. Over the next few years, Fred, with the important help of this committee, expanded our information gathering and enlisted the support and wisdom of each of these organizations. This made it a better publication and increased its credibility.

CRITICAL ISSUE #29

Early in 1982, a committee was formed to improve AAFRC's annual report, Giving USA. *Recruiting some of the top names in philanthropic research, the committee worked diligently over the next few years to expand* Giving USA's *information gathering network. With the backing of such well-qualified individuals,* Giving USA *improved its credibility and became a well-respected publication which reflected the true concerns of the field.*

IMPROVING COMPATIBILITY AND GROWING PROFESSIONALISM

CIAO

Dick Wilson, Bob Harlan, the executive vice president of INDEPENDENT SECTOR and I were concerned about the lack of knowledge we each had about the programs, plans, and priorities of the other key philanthropic organizations. We met in December of 1982, to bring together appropriate representatives to ease this problem. Also in attendance were Richard Strano, Executive Vice President of the National Association of Hospital Development; Thomas Walker, Vice President of the United Way of America; and Richard Edwards, Vice President of CASE. We recognized the value of enlightening each other about our respective organizations and scheduled four meetings a year, rotating the hosting responsibilities.

> **CRITICAL ISSUE #30**
>
> *Late in 1982, the CIAO was formed. This consortium proved to be an important step in bringing different philanthropic organizations together. It became a source of information for planning conferences, setting schedules, and helped to avoid duplication of programs.*

At the first meeting, the name CIAO was agreed upon as a symbol of good friendship. Since our positions kept us in the firing line, we thought we knew a fair amount about each other's operations. After convening at each other's headquarters, meeting the administrative staffs, and touring the facilities, we were surprised to learn how naive we really were.

This "consortium" proved to be an important step in bringing our organizations together. After the first year, we made a point of including several of our key volunteers. CIAO continued to be an on-going source of information that helped in the planning of conferences, schedules, and avoiding duplication of programs.

RICHARD W. LYMAN BECOMES CHAIR OF INDEPENDENT SECTOR

Richard W. "Dick" Lyman, president of the Rockefeller Foundation and former president of Stanford University assumed the chair of INDEPENDENT SECTOR in October 1983. In his acceptance remarks he said:

> Thank you for electing me to take on a fundamentally undoable task: That of taking John Gardner's place . . . . No one can replace John and no one is going to try. And that's too bad, for I often think we could rescue the country and, for that matter this threatened world if there were even a corporal's guard of John Gardners strategically placed around the globe, leading their nations out of their self-regard and the tyranny of their small-mindedness into humane concern for the future of mankind that has always characterized his work.

For the next three years under the leadership of Dick Lyman, INDEPENDENT SECTOR flourished with expanded membership, innovative programs, a vastly improved government relations program that was in the forefront of a steady fight to gain better tax incentives for giving, and the establishment of a task force to examine ways to increase volunteering and giving to American philanthropy. Dick didn't attempt to replace John, but he did a beautiful job of following John's lead in making this organization more effective.

A DAY WITH JOHN GARDNER, 1984

John Gardner's knowledge of how to maintain good relationships between management, staff, board members, organizations, and the general public had become well-recognized. To share his views and broaden the exposure to John's wisdom, Brian scheduled a series of "days with John Gardner." This brought together 10 to 12 heads of foundations, nonprofit organizations, and corporate giving committees to spend a day discussing with John ways they could improve their knowledge and understanding of key relationships.

On April 19, 1984, 12 of us met with John from 9:30 a.m. to 4 p.m. Joanne Hayes, president of Women in Foundations, Corporate Philanthropy, who succeeded me as president of the AAFRC, five years later, was one of the participants.

Since almost 90 percent of all giving in America comes from individuals and successful campaigns are dependent on committed and enthusiastic volunteers and leaders, the field of philanthropy is virtually an unequaled "people" business. Discussion topics lead by John included a session on their motivations, one on what promoted better relationships, one on what improved their performance, and one on how they could help to build better organizations. The following are some of his gems:

> Not long after an organization is formed it begins to defy the creativity

that brought it together in the first place. It begins to build hard lines of organization. It thrusts itself toward separating the "us" from the "non-us."

Creativity is tremendously dependent upon cross-connections and freezing and compartmentalizing activities should be avoided at all costs.

An organization usually starts with a living vibrant purpose. Then the institution moves to slow betrayal of the original purpose. Top executives should be leading, not just managing. One of the biggest obstacles to organizational renewal is the middle manager. They become entrenched. They are in a position of filtering everything that comes up from below, and down from above, and very often stopping things dead at their level.

Any management setting needs to recognize that people need a chance to do more. Everyone has unexplored resources within them. Most operate below their potential. They should be consulted and made to feel that they are a part of organizational decisions.

Knowing yourself is critical. You've got to be interested and capable of being enthusiastic. You need commitment. Your identity is really what you commit yourself to. You should expose yourself to new challenges. An awful lot in life is out of control and you can't do much about those things—just deal with the things you can make a difference with. Also, wherever possible, work with a support group of your peers. This prevents loneliness, broadens your perspective and increases your capacity to deal with your managerial responsibilities.

Everyone gained from this day. It gave me a better perspective on relationships. It helped me to better understand the importance of respecting others and letting others share in developing programs. It remains one of the most enlightening days I can remember.

CRITICAL ISSUE #31

John Gardner retired as chairman of INDEPENDENT SECTOR in October of 1983. His successor was Richard W. Lyman, but his magnificent presence and overflowing knowledge of modern philanthropy could never be replaced. He remains an institution in the field even now.

The State Model Law Project, 1984–1986

In the spring of 1984, the National Association of State Charity Officials (NASCO), who are charged with regulating existing state laws, was asked by the National Association of Attorney Generals (NAAG) to develop a model state law for regulating charities. The need for a model act grew out of the concern that recent U.S. Supreme Court decisions had invalidated parts of many state's statutes. Connecticut's Attorney General, Joseph I. Leiberman, as chair of NAAG's Charitable Trusts and Solicitations Committee organized the effort.

On May 31, 1984, David E. Ormstedt, Connecticut's Assistant Attorney General, invited me, on behalf of Mr. Leiberman, to form and chair a private sector advisory group to work with NASCO in developing a model law. I enlisted 50 representatives of national charities, private umbrella and regulatory groups, constitutional lawyers, and CPAs.

Serving as vice chairs were: James M. Greenfield, Director, Fund Development for the Cleveland Clinic Foundation, and Marion Freemont-Smith, lawyer and board member of INDEPENDENT SECTOR. Chairs of task forces included constitutional lawyer, Adam Yarmolinsky, also a board member of INDEPENDENT SECTOR, an old friend with whom I had worked on many 501(c)(3) projects and a lawyer specializing in representing nonprofit organizations; Bruce R. Hopkins, plus David Ormstedt, and Kevin Suffern, Director, Division of Public Charities, Commonwealth of Massachusetts who represented NASCO and NAAG.

The challenge was to develop a model law that would:

- Be fair to charities;
- Not restrict the climate for charitable giving;
- Be consistent nationwide; and
- Provide the states with enforcement tools to protect the public from fund-raising abuses.

It was a daunting task. Six well-attended plenary sessions and countless subcommittee and task force meetings were held over the next 18 months. We reached advanced agreement with the regulators on all but three major measures:

1. NAAG/NASCO wanted to require "point of solicitation," disclosure of fund-raising costs when a paid solicitor is used (the Supreme Court had already decreed that this violated the first amendment). We didn't agree.
2. The organizations they exempted did not, as we felt they should, include those that confine their solicitations to persons other than the general public.
3. They wanted contracts between charitable organizations and

fund-raising counsel filed prior to the performance of services. This would handicap the fund-raising counsel's effectiveness. Counsel usually presents findings and recommendations of a feasibility study at a special meeting of the charity's board. If the board accepts the recommendations, solicitations and enlistment efforts usually begin right then. The contract is signed and is filed as soon as possible, usually in the next few days.

> **CRITICAL ISSUE #32**
>
> *In the spring of 1984, the National Association of State Charity Officials was asked by the National Association of Attorney Generals to develop a model state law for the regulation of charitable activities. A Private Sector Advisory Group was formed to work with the regulators. In December 1986, the NAAG approved the final version of the law thus bringing together many diverse interests, stimulating discussion, and providing an opportunity for regulators and the private sector to share ideas.*

In December 1986, NAAG approved the regulators' version of the model law, but did not include adjustments for the private sector's concerns. However, this was a most useful exercise. The project brought together many diverse interests, stimulated discussion, and provided an opportunity for regulators and the private sector to share ideas and views. Major unfulfilled needs included a uniform reporting form and a common state law that would allow reciprocity between the states.

Another negative factor was the rapid turnover of key personnel in state regulatory departments. Most able lawyers went into private practice after only a few years of public service. I was scheduled to retire within the year so my agenda became crammed with other priorities. I enlisted a new committee to follow up the effort. Unfortunately, this new effort got bogged down because of personnel changes, and the rapport between the private and public sectors quickly disintegrated.

LESSONS LEARNED

- NCIB, as a private agency, not only helps to guide charities into more ethical and efficient public service programs, but

- helps to promote informed giving and increased accountability.
- Yet to be solved is the problem of the cost in time and administrative resources for charities to fill out and file state reporting forms, as each state has a different form.
- INDEPENDENT SECTOR, with its top leadership and its programs of public education, communications, research, encouragement of effective management of nonprofit organizations, and government relations, has become the next best thing to a private commission on philanthropy.
- The Reagan Administration's cut backs of federal funding of programs of nonprofit organizations has caused shortfalls in their program budgets. But, ironically, it has made them less dependant on government funding and a stronger partner in our pluralistic society of government and the private sector.
- Philanthropy in the United Kingdom and western Europe is about 20 years behind American philanthropy.
- *Giving USA* remains the most effective publication that, each year, measures the amount that Americans give to philanthropy. Its value and credibility have been increased by the high calibre of the members of the Advisory Council. They have helped to improve the methodology of gathering and interpreting giving statistics.
- There were many benefits in bringing together executives of key nonprofit organizations to form the consortium CIAO. We learned more about each other's programs and plans, which helped each of us to plan better, minimize duplication, and give thought to future joint efforts to improve the field.
- The entire field of philanthropy gained and still gains immeasurably from the wisdom and leadership of John Gardner.

CHAPTER 9

Last Half of the Eighties—Nonprofits Learn to Collaborate, Reduce Duplication, and Enhance Programs

The pace of activity and the quality of programs conducted by nonprofit organizations improved for many reasons. They responded well to the fast-changing conditions in our society and identified concerns critical to future growth. One example was their adjustment to the decreased government funding of the third sector. They stopped being so dependent on government grants and worked harder to build private support for their programs. In so doing, they grow into a much stronger force in our pluralisitic society. Much of the "us and them" mentality between the grant-seeking and the grant-giving organizations dissipated. They realized that the lessons learned in building American philanthropy could be shared with European, Asian, and Third World countries for everyone's gain. Our success in working together had built friendships, which made the launching of new programs easier. Some key programs and events included:

The AAFRC Trust for Philanthropy	1985	The AAFRC establishes a 501(c)(3) entity so that it can raise funds to foster programs for more effective philanthropy.
The AAFRC 50th Anniversary	May 1985	A seminar, reception, and dinner held at New York's Waldorf Astoria for top leaders in the philanthropic organizations to celebrate AAFRC's 50 years of service to the field.

Interphil Conference in Venice	*November 1985*	*A conference on international philanthropy with 80 persons from 17 countries provided first hand evidence of how we could learn from each other.*
Indiana University Center on Philanthropy	*1986 to 1990*	*Thanks to a start up grant from Lilly Endowment inc., Indiana University established a Center on Philanthropy to provide training for practitioners, conduct undergraduate courses on philanthropy, become a repository of historical records, and promote more research in the field.*
New plans, new personnel	*1985 to 1987*	*AAFRC began efforts to select a new president and provide a smooth transition as I announced my plan to retire in 1987.*
My retirement dinner at New York's Waldorf Astoria	*May 1987*	*350 top executives in the field of philanthropy attended a seminar, a black-tie reception and dinner for my retirement party. I was toasted, roasted, and overwhelmed.*
The World Fund-Raising Council	*1988*	*As chair of NSFRE International Relations Committee, I arranged a seminar for 27 fund-raising professionals from eight countries to find ways to export our professional knowledge to other parts of the world.*
National Philanthropy Day	*1988 to 1990*	*The NSFRE asked me to serve as president of National Philanthropy Day in February 1988. We expanded the representation of key organizations on the steering committee and encouraged local NSFRE chapters to use this day to honor their philanthropist and fund-raiser of the year.*

Salisbury Cathedral, England	1989	As senior consultant of Community Service Society, I did a Development Planning Study for Salisbury Cathedral to determine how much money could be raised in America toward the $6 million the Cathedral still needed for urgent restoration.
Serving on the Board of the AARP Andrus Foundation	1986 to 1989	The AARP Andrus Foundation gave grants to colleges and universities for geriatric studies.

AAFRC TRUST FOR PHILANTHROPY, 1985

Over the years, many of us with the AAFRC yearned to establish a 501(c)(3) entity in order to raise funds for public service programs designed to improve the philanthropic field. Using the Association's skills and resources for projects that were both above and beyond the self-interest, the members firms (whose top priority always will be servicing clients and seeking new ones) would reinforce what most of us believe—that we should give something back to society and do what we can to make even a small difference in making things better for others.

In 1984, John Grenzebach, the new chairman of AAFRC put this goal high on his agenda. Two young and dynamic heads of member firms—Charles E. "Chuck" Lawson, chair of Brakeley, John Price Jones and Arthur D. Raybin, founder of his own company in 1978—were also steamed up about this concept. Chuck wanted to name it the "AAFRC Trust for Philanthropy." In November 1984, the AAFRC board finally agreed on the name. The plan was to apply immediately to the IRS for a 501(c)(3) rating and begin operation in January 1985. Since Grenzebach, Lawson, and Raybin had put so much into its formation, it was appropriate that they were the three incorporators. The trust's mission was to advance philanthropy through programs of research, education, public information and publication (it took over publishing *Giving USA*). This action was viewed by the members as an extension of the Association's commitment to public service.

To get started, most of the member firms made contributions in three ways—corporate gifts, personal gifts from top officers, and solicitation of their staffs for smaller contributions. A total of $111,051 was raised in the first year. The original board had Lawson as founding chair, Raybin as treasurer, I as president, plus 13 officers of member firms. This was changed very soon to include six outside members representing nonprofit organizations as economists, tax lawyers, scholars, and philanthropists.

The first programs included:

1. A survey of *The 1986 Tax Reform's Impact on Giving* done by the Gallup Organization, which concluded that the effect was minimal.
2. A *Study on Cutting Edge Issues in Philanthropy* under professor Jon Van Til of Rutgers University which brought together the thinking of 14 of the nation's foremost scholars. Funding by the Trust included covering the costs of a seminar for the authors to share their views and publishing the findings.
3. Without doubt, one of the most imaginative and effective programs conceived by the Trust was *Philanthropy in Colleges*. It was the brainchild of Maury Gurin in response to the traditional indifference of academic institutions to philanthropy and its benefits. In 1992, for example, Stanford University had raised $1,200,000,000 in its capital campaign; Yale $618,000,000; Cornell $750,000,000; and the University of Pennsylvania $846,000,000. Obviously, philanthropy is an essential resource to academic excellence. But until 1986, little or no effort was made by academia to understand the philanthropic process, much less include philanthropic studies in curriculum planning.

Gurin went to Dr. John W. Chandler, President of the Association of American Colleges (AAC), and gained AAC's sponsorship of a three-year program to place studies on philanthropy in the undergraduate curriculum at 16 liberal art colleges. Its total cost was over $300,000. The AAFRC Trust gave $50,000 and the Kellogg Foundation $140,000.

Sometimes accompanied by Gurin and sometimes not (despite his creativity, imagination, and innovative ideas, his curmudgeon personality could be an asset with only certain potential donors), I called on the Carnegie Corporation of New York, Lilly Endowment Fund, Dana Foundation, Hearst Foundation, Exxon Educational Foundation, Westinghouse Foundation, the NSFRE, and the Association for Hospital Development. All contributed from $3,000 to $15,000 to this project. Gurin obtained a $25,000 grant from the JDR 3rd Fund making a final total from AAFRC efforts of $176,000 (the Kellogg Foundation grant was obtained by the AAC).

A distinguished Advisory Committee of scholars selected projects for 16 colleges from proposals from 94 colleges. Each was a three-year pilot project examining voluntary service, charitable giving, and nonprofit initiative. The schools selected were a full spectrum of liberal arts colleges, ranging from Tempel and Harvard Universities to Southern University in New Orleans and Randolph-Macon Women's College. Funding provided for a full review after three years and dissemination of the results to other colleges in or outside of AAC.

As another part of the program, Daphne Layton, an expert bibliographer, compiled the first annotated bibliography of studies, publications, and books in the field of philanthropy. The project was an unprecedented example of successful amalgamation of several key elements in the field. They combined their resources and talents for a program that will continue to have positive and long-range effects for the next generations.

CRITICAL ISSUE # 33

In November 1984, the AAFRC Trust for Philanthropy was formed. Founded by John Grenzebach, Charles Lawson, and Arthur Raybin, the Trust's mission was to advance philanthropy through programs of research, education, public information, and publications.

AAFRC 50TH ANNIVERSARY, 1985

Fifty years covered almost two generations and an array of profound social changes, such as the Great Depression, World War II, Korea, Viet Nam, and many shifts in attitudes and culture. The AAFRC continued to grow and expand its services to the nonprofit field throughout these years and, by 1985, it was ready to broaden its scope and services. We planned to celebrate this anniversary with a seminar, reception and dinner on Thursday, May 16, 1985. Dick Lyman accepted my invitation to be the keynote speaker. The 50th Anniversary Committee, under the chairmanship of Charles Feldstein, agreed to organize a seminar that afternoon to explore the problems of managing nonprofit organizations in today's climate. Top executives from CASE, the Girls Scouts of

America, INDEPENDENT SECTOR, NSFRE, NAHD, the United Way, and the Council on Foundations each shared their views with an audience of 350 trustees, foundation and corporate executives, heads of nonprofit organizations, and volunteers.

At the black-tie dinner in the Waldorf Astoria that evening, *A Beacon for Philanthropy*, the 50-year history of the Association written by Wolcott Street, was cited by chairman John Grenzebach. The establishment of the AAFRC Trust for Philanthropy was announced by Lawson. On the dias were the officers of the Council for Advancement of Education, the United Way of America, the Council on Foundations, the National Catholic Development Council, the National Society of Fund-Raising Executives, INDEPENDENT SECTOR, and the National Association for Hospital Development. Each was presented with an AAFRC citation for their contributions to American Philanthropy. Dick Lyman's presentation set the tone for the evening's celebration:

> It's great to have a share in celebrating AAFRC's 50th birthday. It's great to be singing not only for my supper, but also for the significant honor bestowed on INDEPENDENT SECTOR, whose board I have the exhilarating experience to be chairing.
>
> And it's great to be doing all of this in the very same place where, three years ago United Way of America gave your president, Jack Schwartz, its National Executive Award. Jack was a key figure in the founding of INDEPENDENT SECTOR, just as AAFRC was a key mover in the train of events that led to that creation.

The first sentence of "A Program for Philanthropy in America," that effort of the early Seventies that your own J.O. Newberry of Dallas started, from which eventually became the creation of INDEPENDENT SECTOR in 1980, read as follows:

> Private philanthropy is a unique American phenomenon. It is the way each citizen can participate directly in advancing social and educational progress and in alleviating social ills.

CRITICAL ISSUE #34

In May 1985, the AAFRC celebrated its 50th Anniversary. At a black-tie dinner at the Waldorf Astoria in New York, private philanthropy was celebrated and the AAFRC was recognized for the tremendous advances it made in the field over the last 50 years.

INTERPHIL CONFERENCE, 1985

Michael Brophy, as Irish as his name, was in advertising in Britain before he became director of the Charities Aid Foundation. Michael and I were friends from the first day we had met in London several years earlier. The Charities Aid Foundation was established in 1924 to raise and distribute funds to other charities, much like the typical community foundations in America. It is quite predominate in England and has become the major channel for contributed funds to British charities, as well as an advocate for improved tax incentives, and a creator of programs to improve public understanding of British philanthropy.

Michael was also very active with Interphil, a 20-year old organization that strived to bring together worldwide philanthropic efforts. He called me in the spring of 1985 to ask if I would put together a panel on what was going on in American philanthropy for Interphil's fall conference. I asked him when and where, and he came back with the most seductive answer imaginable—Venice, September 26th through 29th.

After a very enthusiastic "yes," I told him that I'd like to show the attendees, who would be from many countries, how important it is that donors and donees get together for good fund-raising results. And for this I'd enlist a panel of fund-raisers and contributors. "Under no circumstances should the term 'fund-raising' be used with this group," Michael said. He explained that most of those attending think that "fund-raising" is beneath them. I smiled to myself as we settled for a panel title of "Synthesizing the Needs of Donors and Recipients."

Because September is just about the best time to be in Venice, all my invitees said yes. I was listed as the workshop chair, and the panel included Sara Engelhardt, Secretary of the Carnegie Corporation of New York; Stephen Halsey, President of the American Express Foundation; Dick Wilson, President, NSFRE; Chuck Lawson, Chair AAFRC Trust for Philanthropy; Arthur Raybin, President, Arthur Raybin Associates; and John G. Foerst Jr., Chairman of Community Counseling Services. We agreed to meet in Venice on September 25, a day before the conference.

As soon as this meeting was set, I accepted an assignment to set up a workshop on "How to Foster the Growth of Professionalism" for the Institute of Charity Fund-Raising Managers (ICFM) in London on September 24th. ICFM was well on its way to becoming the NSFRE of Britain, and we welcomed this opportunity to share some of the experiences we gained in developing AAFRC and NSFRE.

Dick Wilson and Thomas S. Harris joined me for this session. Tom has several distinctions. One, he was the youngest vice president ever in Brakeley John Price Jones; and two, when he decided to leave America and open up his own fund-raising firm in Europe, he sailed his 23-foot sloop across the Atlantic with a friend. Tom's firm, now well-established in Amsterdam, had been doing good work in both Europe and England. Our approach was to share with them the mistakes we had made in America over the years, what we felt our accomplishments were, and the key things their organization should do to foster more fund-raising professionalism in Britain.

We had a warm response from the 60 attendees who surprised us both with evidence that their problems were quite similar to ours and that they were quite sophisticated about fund-raising techniques. This session was the beginning of a continuing interchange between ICFM and NSFRE for mutual benefits that continue to this day.

Michael also invited me to attend a joint symposium set up by the Charities Aid Foundation, Professor J.C. Holt (Master of Fitzwilliams College, Cambridge), and IBM United Kingdom Trust on September 23rd at Cambridge University. Called "Private Funding and the Universities," it was attended by about 100 academic leaders and corporate-giving officers from all over England.

The corporate community agreed to meet with key academicians to discuss ways of increasing private support. The Thatcher administration had made cuts and, in many instances, had frozen its support to higher education in the United Kingdom. The Right Honorable Sir Keith Joseph, Secretary of State for Education and Science, opened the meeting with a warning not to expect any change in government frugality soon. He admonished colleges and universities to work harder to raise private funds.

This seminar was a notable step because never before had the corporate and academic communities (donors and donees) tried to get together on any issue. While Joseph's speech created tension at the start, some synergy was achieved within a few hours. Each side aired long-held grievances—the corporate community complained that college graduates weren't being adequately trained for the business world, and the educators complained that corporations largely ignored the impact caused by growing fiscal problems on the quality of education and the future of the country.

At the end of the morning session, Professor Holt said that he would ask one of the of two Americans there (the other American seated next to me was Kingman Brewster, former Yale University President and former American Ambassador to the Court of St. James) for a reaction to the discussion. After recovering from the shock that Holt was asking me, not Kingman, I said:

> Don't be too hard on yourselves. The fact that you agreed to meet and discuss so many controversial issues is a real step forward. One thing in America that has helped philanthropy so much was the willingness of donors and donees to discuss common concerns which led to a mutual respect and more cooperation in solving unmet needs. For your sake, I hope this is the beginning of many similar meetings.

Eighty persons representing 17 countries attended the Interphil conference in Venice. All of our panel emphasized how the effective partnership between donors and donees has advanced philanthropy and strengthened the private sector in America. This struck a responsive chord with only some of the attendees. Overcoming cultural differences was an almost impossible task. In our country we take for granted that private citizens band together to support programs to help society and the less-fortunate, often consciously keeping government at arms length. As John Gardner says, "With government support comes government forms." And I always remember the apt statement by comedian Will Rogers in the Twenties, "Isn't it great that we don't get all the government we pay for."

In most other countries, people feel that if there is a societal need, let the government take care of it. Charity comes from the church, or is fed primarily by the rich.

This is one reason why so many countries all over the world are decades behind America in the philanthropic process. Exceptions to some degree, are Western Europe, Britain, Canada and Australia. The Interphil Conference was a pleasant and educational experience for our group, but it also was discouraging, because it showed that much must be done to improve the attitudes and politics in many countries before philanthropy can flourish there.

CRITICAL ISSUE # 35

The culture of private enterprise and the tendency of private citizens to band together to solve social problems while keeping government out of the picture, make America quite unique. Our love of freedom of private action is the primary reason why American philanthropy leads the rest of the world.

INDIANA UNIVERSITY CENTER ON PHILANTHROPY, 1986

A news release, dated April 20, 1987 reads:

> Officials of Indiana-Purdue University and Indiana University Foundation announced today that Lilly Endowment Inc. has approved a $4,000,000 grant to the new Center on Philanthropy.

This was exciting news for many. I was asked to visit with some Indiana University officials and Charles A. Johnson, Vice President of Lilly Endowment Inc., in March 1987 to give my thoughts on what kind of a center on philanthropy would be the most helpful to the nonprofit field. I soon learned that several other practitioners had also been asked for similar advice, one at a time.

Henry A. "Hank" Rosso, an old professional friend, had written to me earlier that he had decided to move his very successful Fund-Raising School which he had established in 1974, to the new Center and resolve an old ambition—to incorporate it into a major university. At first, it had been difficult for some of us to accept the fact the Center's plans would not be determined by just academicians. My invitation and Hank's decision helped solve a problem many fellow practitioners and I had—the Center not only was planning courses on the pragmatic phases of philanthropy, but was willing to invite practitioners to participate in its plans. Also, I had a very high regard for Charles Johnson who consistently supported grant proposals designed for programs to improve fund-raising and philanthropy on a national scale.

My first visit left me very impressed. Gerald L. Bepko, Vice President of Indiana University, explained that the plans for the Center on Philanthropy were for a comprehensive, interdisciplinary entity that would conduct research and provide courses on resource development, fund-raising management and the cultural aspects of philanthropy. I learned that Eugene Tempel, Vice President of the IU Foundation had been discussing the establishment of the Center with Hank Rosso, Charles Johnson, and the top IU administrators for quite a while. Now everyone was behind it and they were anxious to solicit the reactions of other scholars and practitioners.

Many questions were posed about the needs and desires of the philanthropic field. Because they were so open and willing to listen, I shared many thoughts such as:

- The field of philanthropy isn't easy to understand and there isn't any learning substitute for direct experience in adminis-

- trating a nonprofit organization and/or running a fund-raising campaign.
- There is a danger in allowing academics without any direct experience in the philanthropic field to dominate planning. To insure both the practical and scholarly qualities, a balance of influence between the practitioners and the academics must be achieved both in the planning and execution.
- This will require diplomacy, for without the involvement and enthusiasm of academic leaders you'll get nowhere.

Sitting around the table with Johnson, Bepko, and Tempel, I was asked, "Jack, what do you think the reaction will be on the two coasts of trying to set up a center with a national program here in Indiana?"

"You'll be without one ingredient—the taint of the Eastern establishment," I replied.

I also met Howard G. Schaller, Executive Dean and Dean of the Faculties, who shortly thereafter became the first Director of the Center. (He insisted that he be called "Acting Director," but we didn't pay any attention to that.) Before I left the next day, Howard and Gene asked me if I would consider doing some consulting for the Center after I retired next fall. I said I'd be delighted.

From the fall of 1987 through 1990, I was one of the Center's two outside consultants. The other was Robert L. Payton, former president of Exxon Educational Foundation and currently Scholar-in-Residence, University of Virginia. I served on the Annual Symposium committee for the first two years. In 1988, I worked with the University's Oral History Department to prepare and implement a study to preserve the wisdom and experience of selected second generation fund-raising managers, 60 years or older. Its object was to help people understand philanthropy's role in American society and the role fund-raising counselors have played.

At the beginning of the 20th century, the first generation fund-raising managers developed the principles and techniques and primary lessons in the field of fund-raising. The second generation worked with these key principles and techniques and expanded fund-raising to meet the needs of a much broader range of people. This second generation is credited with the establishment of fund-raising counseling firms.

The third generation (those primarily in charge today) have built the organizations, newsletters, journals, and conferences which have led to a highly professional structure of fund-raising.

During the first year of the oral history project, 14 managers, all 60 years or older, were interviewed by IU'S very able oral historian, Jeanne Harrah. Seven from the third generation, who, for the most part, now held senior positions with a professional fund-raising counsel firm, were also interviewed. Included among the older respondents were Maury Gurin, George A. Brakeley Jr., and Wolcott Street. In addition to transcripts, most interviews were recorded on videotape thus preserving the views of two generations of fundraising leaders.

The study found some difference between these generations in terms of how they were motivated to enter a field that is noted for its pressures, long hours, and modest paychecks. The second generation motivations included happenstance, commitment to the improvement of the human race, a sense of commitment for an altruistic cause, and aspects of their personal backgrounds. Travel and creating relationships with important people were also factors. The third generation has expanded the professional aspects of fund-raising. They felt that there has been an increased need for professional standards and criteria. By establishing professional ethics, forums which bring professionals together, and improved fund-raising teaching and training programs, they believed that the sense of commitment could be enhanced beyond the income objective.

Armed with this experience, I worked with the University's Oral History Department over the next two years on a similar study to record the views and experiences of two generations of executives of major nonprofit organizations, corporate foundations, private foundations, and volunteer leaders. The original name for this study was "Successor Generation Issues of Philanthropy." More than 40 of the "Who's Who" of the philanthropic field were interviewed by another excellent IU oral historian, Naomi Lichtenberg, with the focus shifting to the current and future roles of American foundations, and how their programs can be adjusted to account for the needs which are increasingly outpacing resources. The great value of recording the opinion of leaders like John Gardner, Alan Pifer, Dick Lyman, and Elizabeth McCormack before its too late, speaks for itself. All of the results are now available to scholars, practitioners, and researchers in the historical archives at Indiana University.

On November 23, 1987, a colloquium inaugurating the Center was held at the new and sumptuous IU Conference Center. It was called "The Challenge of Philanthropy." The panel included Virginia Hodgkinson and Professor James R. Wood with Gene Tempel as moderator. My assignment was to give an address on "Current Trends in Philanthropy." This was a good start and paved the way for both outside and family participation in future meetings.

I was then asked to organize the first annual symposium scheduled for June 8th through 9th, 1988. The keynote speaker was Eugene M. Lang, founder of "I Have a Dream," the program which provided scholarship funds to an entire class of high school students in Lang's alma mater high school in New York City. Thanks to this project, two-thirds of one class went on to college as contrasted to an average dropout rate of over 60 percent. Eugene Dorsey, president of the Gannet Foundation and board chairman of INDEPENDENT SECTOR, also spoke. More than 250 nonprofit and educational leaders from across the country attended and the Center established itself as a national asset for philanthropy.

> **CRITICAL ISSUE #36**
>
> *A new Center on Philanthropy was formed in April 1987 at Indiana University. The Center was designed as a comprehensive, interdisciplinary entity to conduct research and provide courses on resource development, fund-raising management, and the cultural aspects of philanthropy. It was a splendid example of a cooperative effort between academicians and practitioners that succeeded in producing a rich and rewarding program for university students as well as professionals.*

In 1988, I served on the Resource Committee whose role was to identify possible candidates to the Search Committee for the Center's executive director. Schaller was retiring. Payton was just about everyone's first choice but he said he wasn't interested because he and his wife loved Charlottesville, Virginia so much. The search process went on and interested quite a few scholars and practitioners. One day, Payton said he might be interested after all. All search activity came to a screeching halt. Here was a man who had been a foundation and college president, was both a scholar and a practitioner, and was intimate with the Center's program and plans for the future. So Bob took over in the fall of 1988. Under his leadership the Center has become one of the paramount creators of more effective philanthropy in the world.

Other universities also have set up philanthropic centers—Duke, Case-Western, Vanderbilt, City University of New York, and the University of San Francisco among others. The academic world is now actively participating in researching and teaching the new generation about philanthropy. It is adding to the long-neglected body of knowledge so essential to building professionalism.

PERSONNEL CHANGES

Right after my 65th birthday in August 1984, I began to reflect on what I still wanted to do with my life before "beginning to smell the roses." Good health permitting, I set down plans to retire from AAFRC when I reached 68. I looked forward to continuing to work in the field as a volunteer and occasional consultant, unencumbered by the pressures and the tight schedules demanded by running the Association. I shared these thoughts with the current AAFRC Chairman John G. "Jack" Foerst, and he carried my request for three more active years to the board. Many kindly folks said that they never wanted me to retire, but all seemed to appreciate the ample time they'd have to find my successor, and mount the transition. A search committee chaired by James A. Biggins, Chair of American City Bureau, was set up 18 months later.

In 1986, I began a search for a Vice President for Administration in order to tighten up the Association's administration and, hopefully, to provide some continuity during this period of change.

Arthur Raybin had been providing fund-raising counsel to the Seaman's Church Institute and highly recommended Mary B. Rice who had been the Institute's Development Director. Mary B. accepted our offer and proceeded in no time flat to make all our procedures more efficient than they had ever been. More important, as an experienced fund-raiser, she related beautifully to the officers of the member firms, those on the board, and those serving on key Association committees. My last 18 months with the AAFRC were not only smoother because of Mary B.'s skills but gave many of us confidence that the essential things like all arrangements for board and committee meetings, communications, relations with other organizations, and fiscal controls would be well-handled regardless of who became the next president.

I agreed to staff the Search Committee, but under no circumstances would play a part in the final selection. This wouldn't have been fair to my successor or me. We advertised the search for a president in all the professional media plus the newspapers of major cities. I received over 300 resumes which I screened down to 30 for the Search Committee to consider. By the spring of 1987, 12 candidates had been interviewed and the list had been narrowed down to two persons. One was Joanne Hayes, president of Women in Foundations, the other was John N. Bailey an experienced trade association executive. The search committee asked me what I thought about hiring Joanne since she was a *woman*. I said that most in the field would feel that if she were your choice than she must be quite a woman and the Association would be showing welcome maturity. They chose Bailey, who left 10 months later on his own to become the head of America Cancer Society's California Division. The second time around, the members went back to Joanne, who has handled this position with skill and caring for the past five years.

RETIREMENT DINNER FOR AAFRC'S PRESIDENT, 1987

Working with Robert Thompson, current AAFRC chair and chair of Ketchum, Inc., Mary B. organized my retirement dinner in conjunction with the regular fall board meeting. What an event it turned out to be! This celebration was held at the Waldorf Astoria on Thursday, November 12, 1978. It began at 3 p.m. with The Leadership Forum entitled "Philanthropy—The Challenge to Leadership." James T. Morris, President of the Lilly Endowment Fund Inc., addressed foundation leadership:

> Hope to society. Encouragement to the disenfranchised. Foundations are resource institutions. We can give individuals vision and spirit and the time they need to think, study, read, reflect, converse, plan, listen, stretch and share.

John W. Chandler, President, Association of American Colleges, said about education leadership:

> It is ironic that more than half of the colleges and universities are the products of philanthropy and almost all of them are the beneficiaries of philanthropy, yet students and faculty members are generally oblivious to that fact. If today's college students are to assume responsibility for the future of their institutions and the future of our society, then they must have a fuller appreciation of those whose generosity created their opportunities.

Roberta van der Voort, Senior Vice President of the United Way of America, said about organization leadership:

> We cannot achieve our mission alone. America is about wagon trains. About frontier settlements. About corporations. About institutions and associations. Our caring must be driven by a vision as grand as

the problems it addresses. And caring, without action, is a room without air.

Jane C. Geever, President, J. C. Geever, Inc., talked about professional leadership:

> We innovate within our companies. We contribute endlessly to our cause—philanthropy. We have built needed facilities. We have endowed organizations. We have found operating support. We have identified and motivated volunteers.

And then came the dinner. The invitation read:

> It's a long way from navigating the skies of the wartime Pacific to raising funds for some of America's most prominent causes and becoming a respected voice in national philanthropy. Jack Schwartz accomplished this with grace and distinction. On November 12th we will honor his contribution to American philanthropy and offer good wishes for success in his future endeavors.

William Olcott, Editor of *Fund-Raising Management* described it:

> Three hundred and fifty people showed up to honor Jack Schwartz at his retirement dinner at the Waldorf Astoria (Starlight Roof) in New York City. The glittering black-tie testimonial was a joyous occasion, honoring one of the industry's elite, who is retiring as President of the America Association of Fund-Raising Counsel. Several members of the AAFRC, led by George A. Brakeley, Jr., Bob Thompson, Jane Geever, and Maury Gurin took turns praising and roasting Schwartz. Gurin got the biggest laugh when he hailed Schwartz' "imperial presidency."

Dr. Alford H. Taylor Jr., President of the Kresge Foundation, paid tribute to my work with the AAFRC and how much it has helped to improve American philanthropy.

In my comments I said:

> So many of you here tonight are making a measurable difference in the current and future health of our society. There are no words I can muster to completely express my appreciation for your sharing this celebration. And my plans now can best be expressed by the familiar words by Robert Frost about the tired traveler at the end of a long day:
>
>> *The woods are lovely, dark and deep. But I have promises to keep, and miles to go before I sleep, and miles to go before I sleep.*[1]

Brian O'Connell gave the main presentation, stressing the impressive growing cohesion in the nonprofit field. It is no surprise that I had

---

1. Robert Frost. "Stopping by the Woods on a Snowy Evening" (1923).

a wonderful time, but so did everyone else. It will always stand out in my memory as a superb example of how so many diverse elements of the philanthropic field are willing to show mutual appreciation.

My so-called "retirement" lasted less than 12 hours. At breakfast the morning after the party, Jack G. Foerst, chair of the Community Counseling Service, asked me to join the firm as their "ambassador" to several organizations and if I would continue to work with them as a volunteer. Having worked with Jack on many AAFRC projects over the years, I had tremendous respect for him and his firm. I accepted this flattering and generous offer. At CCS, in addition to serving on several nonprofit boards and committees, I wrote some essays on philanthropy and ethics and helped in staff training for CCS.

THE WORLD FUND-RAISING COUNCIL, 1988

I had originally served on the board of the NSFRE for 13 years. In 1988, after a hiatus of seven years, I accepted an invitation to serve a three-year term. I served on the Society's International Affairs Committee. Dick Wilson and I wanted to explore the possibilities of forming an international organization which would expand the knowledge of fund-raising techniques in other countries.

I set up a one-day seminar at the Princeton Club in New York City on June 15, 1988 devoted to an open discussion on how NSFRE can share its experiences and resources to foster more professionalism and public acceptance of the philanthropic process in other countries. Twenty-seven individuals attended representing CASE, Interphil, AAFRC, the United Way, and from Mexico, Great Britain, France, Canada, Australia, and Amsterdam. On the agenda for discussion were such considerations as:

- Shall the Society generate formal agreements with other groups?
- Could this become a program of international affiliates with the Society providing services and information?

The discussions were lively about a number of areas of possible conflict, especially on the fact that anything American is resented by many in England, and even more so in Europe. We must learn to listen and learn from other countries. We should not only be concerned about fund-raising, but about the whole area of financing the voluntary sector. By late afternoon, before the meeting broke up, some agreements were reached:

1. NSFRE is not and should not be an international organization.
2. The United States should be a team player in the group, not necessarily the leader.
3. We would reach for an organization that will relate to fund-raising management, not all aspects of philanthropy.
4. The NSFRE Foundation could help support finding efforts and staffing.
5. It would be called the World Fund-Raising Council.
6. Michael G. Downes, one of the founders of the Australian Institute of Fund-Raisers, was elected chairman.

For the next step, an organizational meeting was set in London on November 6th and 7th, 1988. Fourteen members from eight countries were appointed on the board. I agreed to serve as a member-at-large. The purpose of the Council was to:

- Promote the teaching of the practice of philanthropy and represent the interests of fund-raising professionals and their professional bodies throughout the world.
- Encourage high standards of ethics and practice among persons and organizations raising funds for charitable, religious, educational, and other purposes for the public good.

Its objectives were:

Provide and maintain a medium of exchange among members for information, resources, opinions, and ideas relating to fund-raising.

Promote, develop, and assist in establishing professional associations of persons involved in the profession of fund-raising in any country where such an association does not currently exist.

Today, Tom Harris is the chair. The Council has grown slowly, but despite the great worth of its cause, a viable future will depend on solving three pressing problems:

1. Despite the secretariat services being donated by NSFRE, implementation of its programs is exclusively in the hands of a group of volunteers. They are literally located all over the world with other pressing priorities, so little gets done.

2. To keep action going a full-time executive director with adequate staff support is essential.
3. This requires sufficient funding. Membership fees alone cannot provide the funds for essential ingredients like a good staffing, worldwide travel, conferences, intern and training programs, maintaining a headquarters (WFRC is now incorporated, in Amsterdam), and monitoring and disseminating trends in tax changes country by country.

> **CRITICAL ISSUE #37**
>
> *In 1988, the World Fund-Raising Council was established. This was an international organization designed to expand the knowledge of fund-raising techniques throughout the world.*

NATIONAL PHILANTHROPY DAY, 1988–1990

In January 1988, Dick Wilson asked me if I would be interested in becoming president of National Philanthropy Day (NPD) under the aegis of the NSFRE Foundation. This program was organized in 1985 by Douglas Freeman, a trust lawyer on the West Coast. Most individuals representing nonprofit organizations invited to participate accepted readily, because it made good sense to celebrate philanthropy and its benefits to society. However, the program had apparently begun to bog down after two active years because, taken together, those involved didn't represent a broad enough spectrum of the philanthropic field.

Since we wanted to stimulate interest in philanthropy, both nationally and within active cities and regions all over the country, the original committee set up by Freeman was willing to place it under the aegis of NSFRE which now had 120 chapters from coast to coast. In his letter dated January 8, 1988, Dick said:

> Our vision is to revise and strengthen the management of National Philanthropy Day . . . to make it a role model for all nonprofit organizations. To do this, we need a chairman with strong leadership qualities and impeccable professional credibility. You are our unaminous choice. Several potential funders for NPD have indicated a willingness to make financial contributions contingent upon your acceptance of the chairmanship.

My responsibilities included :

- Organizing and chairing the NPD executive committee.
- Assisting in raising necessary funding.
- Developing and monitoring the budget.
- Appointing committee and task force chairmen.
- Encouraging local-level organizations to participate in NPD activities.
- Serving as spokesman for NPD to press, legislative bodies and the public at large.

This was an exciting challenge. I cleared my acceptance with Jack Foerst, who felt it would be very much in keeping with my CCS activities. This project, along with my voluntary activities and consulting with the Indiana University Center on Philanthropy, filled my days much more than I had planned.

Beside seeking adequate funding, I faced two other challenges; first, to obtain NSFRE board approval for the operating plan and, second, to find the best way to broaden the base of participation. Dick agreed with me that the program should be completely under the aegis of the NSFRE Foundation (a 501(c)(3) entity), but the management and policies would be subject to review and endorsement by a full spectrum of key nonprofit organizations.

All this, as my friend Bob Duncan used to say, "sugared off" to enlisting a good chairman (namely Frank M. Hubbard, who in 1987 had received the NSFRE "Philanthropist of the Year" Award), and enlisting a NPD committee with top executives of American Bar Association, United Way of America, United Negro College Fund, Foundation Center, CASE, NAHD, YMCA of USA, Seventh Day Adventist, Girl Scouts of the USA, INDEPENDENT SECTOR, the Council on Foundations.

The annual budget was set at $120,000. The first year we raised this goal plus nearly $60,000 toward next year's expenses. November 18, 1988 was designated National Philanthropy Day, and we succeeded in getting a bill introduced in both the House and the Senate to obtain a Congressional Resolution for President Reagan's signature. This project truly put to test the grassroots strength of NSFRE. All we had to do was obtain 222 co-sponsors in the House and 52 of the correct political stripe in the Senate. We fell short by only 15 members of Congress the first year, but succeeded in getting resolutions for the next two years. To accomplish this many members of NSFRE, in chapters all over the country, organized letter-writing campaigns to their local member of

Congress and/or arranged visits to their representative on the hill. Chapter presidents were alerted by NSFRE headquarters of those local congress members who had not yet signed on as co-sponsors, whose phone numbers were published in the NSFRE newsletter and a telephone task force was organized in every state. Those in Congress are always more likely to respond to their local constituencies than from any other pressures. This success also helped the entire nonprofit field to realize that of all the organizations, NSFRE has the broadest grass roots reach. Also in the first year, more than 75 NSFRE chapters celebrated NPD usually with a luncheon to honor the local philanthropist, volunteer, and fund-raiser of the year. Invitees included volunteers, campaign leaders, organization executives and fund-raisers, the media, and board members. These numbers would just about double in the next year, helped in no small measure by a public service video featuring George Burns as honorary NPD chair.

THE NEW CLIMATE FOR FUND-RAISING COUNSEL

After 26 years, it was particularly interesting, once again, to become an active staff-member of a fund-raising counseling firm. As a senior consultant, I was spared the vicissitudes of actually conducting a campaign, but I had often daily exchange with those who did. The quality and professionalism of CCS' executives was even higher than I had expected to find. The top officers not only supervised the campaign operations, they provided opportunities to much of the field staff to share their thoughts on management decisions. They also spent a remarkable amount of time helping those out in the field with their problems.

Interstaff communications were excellent. Regular staff conferences for training and reviewing company plans and policies were frequent. CCS had campaigns all over the United States, in England, Ireland, and Europe. I was pleased and proud to be a part of such a distinguished firm, headed by Jack Foerst and Bill Hanrahan, two men I admired and respected. I was expected to assist in firm seminars and recruiting of staff, teach staff about all aspects of the field, represent CCS at key meetings and help to upgrade staff to reflect the latest trends in fundraising and philanthropy. After a year, Jack called me in his office and asked me if I'd be interested in managing a campaign development study for Salisbury Cathedral in England. Was I interested? My strong interest in English affairs had grown substantially while participating in so many conferences there in recent years, and history is one of my favorite subjects. What a wonderful opportunity.

Quoting from the CCS Planning/Action Study completed March 30, 1989, the reason for the study:

> Salisbury Cathedral, Wiltshire, England . . . an historical landmark in the history of christianity . . . is threatened by severe structural problems in its 13th century wooden and stone underpinnings and decay in its outer walls.

It took 95 years to complete Salisbury Cathedral, from 1220 to 1315. It has the tallest spire in England (404 feet) towering over the water meadows beside the Avon River. It is second in height only to Chartres Cathedral in France. A lasting symbol and an historical landmark of christianity, its venerability also puts it in dire need of massive repairs. Once again the British Government had removed itself from any fiscal responsibility. A successful "Spire Appeal" was conducted in England in 1985 and raised about $5.5 million dollars. At least another $6 million was required to complete reconstruction. The study was to determine the degree of American interest as shown by corporations, foundations and affluent Anglophiles in supporting an overseas cause in these days of so many pressing needs at home.

Dean Hugh D. Dickenson and Director General of the Salisbury Spire Trust, Nicolas Tate, provided us with 800 names of potential respondents for interviews in United States. We selected nearly 100 names for interviews, based on geography and their position in society.

In most cases, members of the Spire Committee wrote letters opening doors to the respondents. Then the real work began, colored by an imposing deadline for completion of the study before March 30th. All my memories of studies in the past said that letters like these were all that is necessary for me to get in to see most of the respondents despite their high positions. Not so. Other priorities, the fact that the authors of the introductory letters were living abroad and not in frequent touch, made many completely unavailable.

I soon learned that one change in today's atmosphere for counsel was the necessity of being very aggressive in efforts to see important people. Doors don't become open just by someone else's letter. Without careful cultivation of administrative assistants whose priority is to protect their boss, not much would have happened. We finally managed to interview 67 individuals, friends of the Cathedral, corporate and foundation executives—I conducted over 50 myself. We asked each person about 20 questions such as:

1. Are you familiar with the history of Salisbury Cathedral?
2. Do you think that this cause would be of interest to enough people in the United States?
3. The total projected costs are $12.5 million. Over $5 million has been raised in the United Kingdom. Would seeking one-third, $4 million here over a three- to five-year program be well-received in United States?
4. Where does Salisbury fit into your philanthropic priorities?
5. If a campaign is conducted, would you be willing to give? To work as a volunteer?
6. Who would make an ideal chairman?

When all the interviews were completed, an executive session of top CCS officers correlated the results and formed a plan of action for consideration by The Spire Trust Committee. We were encouraged by the positive response of a few leaders. Special gifts luncheons or dinners organized under the right sponsorship in key cities, should produce good results. However, it was very clear that a successful campaign for $2 to 3 million over a three-year period would depend on strong British leadership efforts to enlist the right American leadership.

In the Summer of 1989, Katy and I had an opportunity to include a visit to Salisbury while in England on other business. The Cathedral Close covers about one-third square mile of a grassy plain bordered by two walls and two rivers. It is entered from a narrow street in the bustling town of Salisbury. The Cathedral, with its imposing tower, is nearly in the center. Along the bordering walls are two- and three-story houses and cottages; a few by their architecture and appearance must have been built in the 16th or 17th centuries.

On our first day we were invited to luncheon by Dean Dickinson and his lovely wife, Jean, at the Deanery. This is a wonderful old English home facing the Cathedral on the front and surrounded by a lovely well-kept garden at the rear. We were served fish caught that morning in the Avon River by the Dean. Although I was not involved in the campaign that had been started in the United States, we discussed at length the difficulties already beginning to show because of the lack of committed leadership. The Dean showed me his determination and desire to improve the condition of his beloved Cathedral. If the right audiences could be formed in America, his sincerity and eloquence should move many into giving financial support.

The next day, the Dean arranged a special tour for us; one that was not available to the tourists who crowded the Cathedral and its grounds. We were placed in the hands of the "Clerk of the Works," Roy Spring. Roy is a fascinating man. He expressed deep love for "his" buildings, had been in charge of reconstruction for a decade, and knew every nook and cranny. We were taken up to the interior of the spire to see the deterioration of the 600-year-old wood beams and the crumbling of the disintegrating stone walls. Roy made note of a set of scrolled initials in one of the stones. "They were just like us," he said. "They wanted to be remembered long after they were gone."

Outside, looking up at the fabulous tower and the intricate bas-relief sculptures of saints, knights and their ladies, gargoyles, and various beasties, we felt overwhelmed by the creativity and engineering skills that made this possible. Yet, the sight of the massive labyrinth of scaffolding covering all sides made us sad because so much needed to be done to preserve this historical treasure.

Next, Roy took us to the main workshop off to one side of the Cathedral. There, a group of British youngsters in their twenties were interning to become masons. They were chipping away at marble slabs using the same tools used by the 13th century craftsmen who built the Cathedral—a mallet and a chisel. Three were women. Otherwise little had changed. Then Roy pointed out a just finished small spire to be mounted on the roof. Perching on its base was a bas-relief of a pretty butterfly put there for posterity by one of the student workers.

For the campaign, the span of the Atlantic seemed to filter out much of the British cooperation. Another factor may be that we're somewhat spoiled in America. Most people here, while hard to commit, take their commitments seriously and keep an eye on the promised deadlines. In any event, after eight months of strong efforts by the campaign director, top leadership resisted involvement and the campaign was expired. This experience showed how difficult it is today to conduct a successful fund-raising campaign for any overseas cause beyond the relief of human suffering. Our American priorities are too pressing.

AARP ANDRUS FOUNDATION, 1986–1990

In 1968, a memorial was established to Ethel Percy Andrus, an educator and founder of the American Association of Retired Persons (AARP). In 1973, it became the Andrus Foundation, a grant-giving organization dedicated to support research in gerontology. I accepted an invitation to serve a four-year term on its board in 1985. Each year, the Foundation granted about $2 million to 35 to 40 colleges and universities for geriatric studies. Funding came from AARP members who were sent appeals each year for all the Association's program. This was a special and enjoyable experience because for the first time I was involved in giving away someone else's money. The projects being funded included research in medicine and health care, in aging, in long-term care, and income problems of the aging.

Two times a year, the nine board members met to identify which projects were to be funded. Several weeks before these meetings, we received about 80 proposals to review in advance. Included with these proposals were the written analyses of the possible worth of each prepared by foundation's highly professional staff. They graded the proposals according to their uniqueness, filling a known need, whether the college or university had a previous or current grant (no school could have two simultaneous grants), the professionalism and track record of the head researcher and the size of the grant request ($50,000 was the maximum allowed).

Each time we began our semiannual sessions, Dr. Kenneth G. Cook, Director, would tell us how much grant money was available. We would review and select grantees all day, adding up the totals until the available funds were used up. In 1988, a total of $1,914,656 was granted to 40 colleges and universities.

This experience of being a grant maker gave me a new respect for foundation program and corporate giving officers. Giving away money wisely is hard work and often leaves you sad, because in the process, you must turn down many worthy projects.

LESSONS LEARNED

- The establishment of the AAFRC Trust for Philanthropy, fulfilled the desire of most of us in the AAFRC to create and fund programs that were designed to improve the philanthropic process and be beyond the self-interest of the member firms.
- A well-documented lesson learned in America is that the more donors and donees collaborate, the better the fund-raisng results. There is resistance to this concept in most other countries.
- AAFRC celebrated its 50th Anniversary proudly because of its many contributions to the philanthropic process over the years.
- The Indiana University Center on Philanthropy was planned with creativity and innovation. Its organization and programs were developed by a balanced partnership of academicians and

practitioners. It now serves as a good example for other schools to follow.
- People in many nations are more aware that private enterprise can accomplish much to improve their society. We should endorse and participate in any effort that will improve fund-raising techniques around the world. The World Fund-Raising Council is a good beginning.
- Serving on a foundation's board showed me how difficult it can be to give money away. There is never enough money available to fund every proposal that is deserving and worthwhile.
- Philanthropy should be both more understood and appreciated by the general public. Toward that end, the NSFRE's National Philanthropy Day program which, each fall, fosters over 100 community Philanthropy Days to honor the local philanthropist, volunteer, and fund-raiser, is beginning to produce measurable results.
- The social, health, and educational needs, along with the problems caused by drugs, violence, the homeless, and the gang wars, are absorbing the interest of most American contributors to charity more than ever. Charities not in the United States are not able to compete for funds and attention.

CHAPTER 10

Is American Philanthropy Ready for the 21st Century?

American philanthropy may be better prepared for the 21st century than many suppose. Reviewing the current state and strategic plans of key nonprofit organizations reinforces this conclusion. Although there are many organizations with programs that are helping to further philanthropy, I have chosen seven in particular, because together, they have a tremendous influence on the philanthropic process. Each is leading the way in an important segment of the field to improve the knowledge and understanding of research, fund-raising, voluntarism, government relations, public education, and grant-giving. Much will depend on how well these organizations can bring together their professionalism and skills to deal with the issues that effect philanthropy's performance. These organizations are:

1. The American Association of Fund-Raising Counsel, Inc. (AAFRC).
2. Association for Healthcare Philanthropy (AHP).
3. Council for Advancement and Support of Education (CASE).
4. Council on Foundations.
5. The Foundation Center.
6. INDEPENDENT SECTOR (IS).
7. National Society of Fund-Raising Executives (NSFRE).

To identify their current position, here is a brief review of their track records, audiences, strategy, and future promise.

AMERICAN ASSOCIATION OF FUND-RAISING COUNSEL, INC. (AAFRC)

The mission of the AAFRC is to:

> Provide leadership in advancing philanthropy, strengthening standards and practices in philanthropic fund-raising, fostering public acceptance of fund-raising counsel, and enhancing the ability of member firms to serve client organizations.

Currently, 24 firms are members of the AAFRC, serving a full spectrum of nonprofit organizations ranging from universities and medical centers to environment and advocacy groups. Usually, these firms apply their experience and professional skills to help the client determine:

- A feasible fund-raising goal (based on the interviews made in advance of the supporters, potential supporters and friends of the organization);
- and the documentation of the needs to be fulfilled, the campaign plan, the fund-raising budget, and the time schedule.

The welfare and the future of the firm is absolutely reflected by how well the client does. Members are acutely aware that the better the state of philanthropy, the better their business. But this is not the only reason why the top officers and staff of the firms go beyond their self-interest to volunteer as a public service a remarkable amount of resources, time, and funds for programs for the benefit of philanthropy. Almost without exception, the able people in this profession have a sense of mission and really want to make a difference for social improvements. If not, they rarely stay in the field very long.

The introduction of the 1992 AAFRC Directory states:

> The American Association of Fund-Raising Counsel was founded 58 years ago to advance the philanthropic cause and ethical approach to fund-raising. Early AAFRC leaders were aware of what philanthropy had accomplished for America ... (they) sought to bring order to a field that was beginning to expand. Their first act was to develop a Fair Practice Code. The Code, now called Standards of Membership and Professional Conduct, is accepted widely as the standard for professional conduct in fund-raising counsel. The Association's 50-year commitment to philanthropy was celebrated in 1985 when it founded the AAFRC Trust for Philanthropy ... whose mission is to advance research, education and public awareness of philanthropy.

Since 1985, more than a million dollars has been contributed by the members firms and their staffs to fund such programs as:

- *The American Association of Colleges/AAFRC Project.* The first comprehensive effort to introduce undergraduate courses in philanthropy into college curriculum.
- *National Philanthropy Day.*
- *John Grenzebach Awards for Outstanding Research in Philanthropy.* Made in cooperation with Counsel for Advancement of Support of Education (CASE), two annual awards have been given to scholars for the past five years.
- *Anthology of Readings in Philanthropy.* This is being compiled and edited by the Program on Nonprofit Organizations at Yale University.
- *The Nonprofit Sector Research Award.* The fund, located at Aspin Institute, awards grants for research in philanthropy. The Trust joined with the Ford Foundation, Rockefeller Brothers Fund, and Charles Stewart Mott Foundation as one of the founding funders.
- *Editing and Publishing Giving USA.* The value of this publication to the entire philanthropic field is unequalled.

AAFRC today represents many from the new generation of leadership in fund-raising counseling. They are following the traditions of their seniors but seem to be even more cognizant of the importance of relating their work and activities to philanthropy's common interests. Setting and enforcing ethical standards which are emulated by other organizations is a tremendous contribution in this time of public skepticism about the nonprofit world. Their contributions to programs designed to help the philanthropic process and the time members devote to recruiting, training and mentoring the new generation will show in many positive ways.

ASSOCIATION FOR HEALTHCARE PHILANTHROPY (AHP)

In 1964, a small group of hospital financial development officers met under the auspices of the Louisiana Hospital Association to discuss aspects of their positions. They met again in larger numbers (51) the next year and established an informal organization called "Developartners." By the fall of 1967, increased interest created the need to set up a more structured organization, and the National Association for Hospital Development was established. In 1990, a mail ballot led to the adoption of a new name, "Association for Healthcare Philanthropy."

In 1992, AHC had 2,427 members; a doubling in membership since 1980. Because its members specialize in financial development for medical institutions, the organization has a narrower focus than some others, but its programs are in the thick of many of our social problems today. The distinction between nonprofit and profit hospitals is becoming harder to maintain in the public and the government minds. According to the AHP Planning Committee report:

> Public exposure of hospital CEO salaries . . . the distinction between nonprofit and for-profit hospitals seems to be blurring as more and more nonprofit organizations enter into for-profit ventures. Hospitals are operating more like businesses—vertical integration, for-profit initiatives, undercutting their philanthropic appeal.

The surge of interest and deliberations on healthcare reform led by Hillary Rodham Clinton and the new administration, place a lot of the AHP concerns on an urgent agenda. The way this organization deals with such issues as preserving the tax-free status of nonprofit hospitals and maintaining tax incentives to giving will be an example for other parts of the nonprofit field.

Fortunately, AHP is motivated by a group of spirited volunteer leaders representing most nonprofit hospitals and medical centers across the country, and an experienced executive staff, ably led by William C McGinly, now in his 10th year as president. They are well organized nationally and have shown their capacity to bring some order out of the chaotic process of obtaining private support for hospitals. As McGinly stated:

> Nonprofits spend far less on achieving results than governments spend on failures they spawn. . . . Unfortunately the value of nonprofits in the healthcare arena seems to be a well-kept secret, which is apparent in the public's . . . negative attitude toward nonprofit hospitals. . . . We cannot shrink from the responsibility and the success of learning to manage ourselves as well as the best managed for-profit institutions. . . . We must learn how to raise money more creatively. . . . Communication of our results is the single strongest tool for making the government and the public aware of the importance of our endeavors and the need for their support.[1]

The Strategic Plan for AHP acknowledges:

> Total quality management will quickly become the watchword in hospitals as it has in industry. . . . There will be growing pressure on hospital development officers to streamline/justify/reorganize their

---

1. Spring 1992 Edition of the Association of Healthcare Philanthropy Journal.

(operations).... Many hospital development officers ... are finding themselves needing to employ the tools and techniques of marketing, public relations, community development, and administration to carry out their primary role as fund-raisers.

AHP efforts to adjust their program emphasis to meet the many changes in health care delivery contributes to making the case for all nonprofit organizations.

COUNCIL FOR ADVANCEMENT AND SUPPORT OF EDUCATION (CASE)

In 1974, after many years of discussions, two rival organizations, the American College Public Relations Association (ACPRA) and the American Alumni Association finally merged into CASE. In 1992, the CASE board approved this mission statement:

> The purpose of CASE is to develop and foster sound relationships between member educational institutions and their constituencies; to provide training programs, products and services in the areas of alumni and constituent relations, communications, and philanthropy; and to provide a strong force for the advancement and support of education worldwide.

Membership totals for 1992 were 3,045 educational institutions; 1,455 four-year institutions, 290 two-year institutions, 889 independent schools, plus 411 others. There are 14,435 individuals representing the institutional memberships. Peter McE. Buchanan, former Vice President for University Development and Alumni Relations for Columbia University, became CASE's president in 1990. Edward G. Call, President of Albert University and Chair of CASE said in the 1991–1992 Annual Report: "Employing a president who was a proven advancement officer enabled CASE to embark quickly on a year-long strategic planning process."

This effort as Peter reports, involved membership as deeply as possible.

> The self-analysis questions posed to the staff, volunteer leaders, and members were: What does CASE do, how well does CASE do it, and how do we know? Those questions were, in turn, driven by overriding commitments to quality, service, access, equity, diversity, and value for our member institutions and their representatives.

The resultant strategic plan takes into account the fact that "Education in general faces daunting philosophical and financial issues and a growing public questioning of education's purposes and practices." To guide planning and action, some of the goals were now set:

- Strengthen advancement professionals at its member institutions.
- Attract and retain a larger, more diverse group of talented people to the practice of institutional advancement.
- Encourage the understanding of advancement as a profession.
- Provide an ethical framework for institutional advancement.
- Influence public policy issues concerning advancement.
- Foster and strengthen the traditions of volunteerism and philanthropy.
- Anticipate changing societal trends.

Thus CASE, like the other leading nonprofit organizations is defining new goals, reaching out to all facets of their membership for their views, adjusting to societal changes and joining a growing chorus on behalf of fostering more effective philanthropy.

COUNCIL ON FOUNDATIONS

Incorporated in 1957 with Wilma Shields Rich as the first executive director, the Council on Foundations is the major philanthropic organization concerned with the grant-making process. Its current membership includes over 1,300 leading foundations and corporate giving programs. Under the leadership of James A. Joseph, president since 1982, it has developed comprehensive programs on:

- Research Projects and Services;
- Communications and Media Relations;
- International Programs;
- Council Task Forces and Study Groups;
- Affinity Groups;
- Religious Philanthropy; and
- Regional Associations of Grant-makers.

Its mission:

> To promote, encourage, and enhance, the contributions and responsiveness of organized grant-making to society, and the public good.

IS AMERICAN PHILANTHROPY READY FOR THE 21ST CENTURY?

In the 1992–1993 Members Guide, Joseph states:

> Organized philanthropy is searching, along with the rest of society, to find new ways of advancing the concept of common ground, both in the larger world and in our own field. Our challenge is to promote pluralism while retaining the coherence needed to act as a single community.... The council's members come from across the country and around the world and represent private, corporate, community, operating and public foundations, and corporate giving programs. Despite your diversity ... you look to the Council for common ground, for information and assistance that enable you to carry on different activities with greater effectiveness and resolve.

The Council's Study Group on the Infrastructure of Philanthropy, established in 1991, has almost completed its deliberations "Critical Issues for the Future." The study areas it is examining are the infrastructure of philanthropy and emerging technology. This serves as an example of the deep interest by the Council in identifying those issues that the field must both recognize and design programs for in the future.

The Council's publication program is most comprehensive including publications on:

Philanthropy
Administration
Communications
Governance/Board of Trustees
Grant-making
Legislation/Regulation
Private Foundations
Community Foundations
Corporate Grant-makers
International Grant-makers

The Council's programs, are truly helping the grant-giving efforts of foundation and corporations achieve more effective philanthropy.

THE FOUNDATION CENTER

Founded in 1956 by F. Emerson Andrews, the Foundation Center plays an unchanging and unique role in the nonprofit field. Its mission is exclusively to provide better and more complete factual information about private grant-making institutions and the grant-seeking process. In addition to a central office in New York City, it has three regional offices, and a network of 191 cooperating libraries. The subjects of its extensive publications program include philanthropy, nonprofit management, fund-raising, private foundation and corporate giving studies, technical assistance books for grant-seekers, and research and scholarly works on the field. Center files are always available to the general public. These materials are in constant use by grant-seekers, grant-makers, researchers, scholars, students and members of the general public who hope to find funding for their special idea or program.

Especially useful to grant-seekers are its complete files of giving policies and giving records of foundations and corporations. These are broken down by:

- Giving interests, from health and environment to social welfare and the homeless;
- Grants to similar projects;
- Geographical location; and
- Nature of grants (for example, some foundations only give to capital improvements and not to annual needs).

The existence of the Center helps to affirm that foundations have become accountable (they must make their policies and grant records available to the public). It also helps the grant-makers by educating the public about the funding research process. Each year, 250,000 people use these services to guide them in fund-raising and also to help them avoid making proposals which cannot be even considered because of the specific, and on record, giving policies of the grant-maker.

Sara L. Engelhardt, whose rich past experience includes being Secretary of the Carnegie Corporation of New York, Chair of the National Charities Information Bureau, and Executive Vice President of the Foundation Center, became the Center's president in 1991. Under her leadership, the Center is constantly refining its services. It now must meet growing needs and have its information available on electronic databases for dissemination nationally and aboard. The contributions to philanthropy of this wonderful service are immeasurable.

INDEPENDENT SECTOR (IS)

INDEPENDENT SECTOR is also unique, as it is the organization that has both grant-makers and grant-seekers in its membership. Now in

IS AMERICAN PHILANTHROPY READY FOR THE 21ST CENTURY?

its thirteenth year it has grown in membership to over 850 organizations. These members include the major foundations and corporations, most all of the leading national nonprofit organizations and a broad representation of the many disciplines of philanthropy. Its mission is:

> To create a national forum capable of encouraging the giving, volunteering and not-for-profit initiative that helps all better serve people, communities and causes.

Blessed with top leadership and a track record of accomplishments it is very satisfying to those of us who were in on its early struggles. One of my treasured mementos is this letter dated September 20, 1983 which I received from the founding chairman John Gardner.

> Dear Jack:
>
> Every once in a while, we're given the chance to have a hand in something important.
>
> At INDEPENDENT SECTOR'S charter meeting I predicted that one day we would all be proud, not only for having been present "at the creation" but for having played a part in the act of creation.
>
> We'll probably forget the long hard hours we all spent, in meetings and on the road—performing the difficult, often frustrating chores of building a new organization. But we won't forget the results: We knew INDEPENDENT SECTOR when it was no more than a promising idea, we knew it when it was a lively infant, and we have seen it mature into a large and important enterprise. I believe that, working together, we have contributed importantly to a valued segment of American life.

The IS board reviews and approves a "Program Plan" every five years. The one for 1991–1995 identifies these important activities for 1993.

- *Government Relations.* To develop and maintain effective relationships with government, based on mutual respect and support for each other's roles ... this includes protection of the freedoms which allow new causes to be created.
- *Research, Including the National Center for Charitable Statistics.* The overall goal is to develop an identifiable and growing research effort that produces the body of knowledge necessary to accurately define, describe, chart, and understand this sector and the ways it can be of greatest service to society.
- *Leadership and Management (Including Values and Ethics).* To enhance the capacity of the independent sector to achieve excel-

lence in the principles and practices of effective leadership and management of philanthropic and voluntary organizations
- *Public Information and Education.* To promote active citizen and community service to achieve increased public awareness of giving, volunteering and the role the nonprofit sector plays in our society.
- *The Give Five Campaign.* To help the American public understand and move toward the standard of "giving five"— five percent of income and five hour a week—to the cause of their choice.
- *The Meeting Ground Program.* To create and maintain a significant sense of community among the organizations of the sector: To provide a 'meeting ground' for cooperation and learning.
- *Membership Retention and Recruitment.* The goals are to recruit at least 50 new members and retain 96 percent of current members.

Brian O'Connell has announced his plans to retire in 1995. He has been at IS's helm since its inception and deserves abundant credit for its many accomplishments. He will be hard to replace but at least the board has sufficient notice to find a qualified successor.

NATIONAL SOCIETY OF FUND-RAISING EXECUTIVES (NSFRE)

On June 21, 1961, in New York City, a small group of volunteers signed the incorporation papers of the National Association of Fund-Raisers (NSFR). Our early meetings were disorganized and full of dreams and speculations. But in 1964, after the New York organization, the Association of Fund-Raising Directors (AFRD), merged into NSFR as its first chapter, the mission and programs became better defined. All involved recognized the need to guide the fund-raising field into more professionalism, to set ethical standards, to build intercommunications, and to help the general public understand the contributions being made by this budding profession. Today, the National Society of Fund-Raising Executives, as it has been called since 1978, has over 14,000 members in 143 chapters in all but two states—plus Mexico and Canada.

It began to accelerate its growth and join forces with other organizations to improve philanthropy under President J. Richard Wilson. In August 1988, the NSFRE Board appointed Gale Clarke Senior Vice President and Chief Operating Officer. Sadly, Dick died suddenly in

December 1988. Gale became responsible for a holding action to give the board time to search for a new president. She did an excellent job of refining staff, cutting costs, moving the programs along, and responding to Board demands.

The search process went painfully slow and was protracted even further because the first appointee resigned after 6 months. Finally in March 1991, more than two years after Dick's untimely death, the board appointed Patricia F. Lewis as president. Under her leadership, NSFRE is really making its mark again in the field. Pat has gained respect for her administrative ability, her articulateness, her knowledge of the field and its most pressing needs, and for her integrity and caring. The central purpose of NSFRE is:

> To advance the profession of fund-raising and the institution of philanthropy throughout North America.

Its eight objectives are to:

1. Serve the interests and concerns of fund-raising executives.
2. Foster the development and growth of professional fund-raising executives committed to the preservation and enhancement of philanthropy in our society.
3. Establish and promote a professional code of ethical standards and practices for fund-raising executives.
4. Provide opportunities for professional education and certification to all fund-raising executives.
5. Research, collect, analyze, publish and disseminate information about the historical management and technical aspects of philanthropy and fund-raising.
6. To promote public understanding of fund-raising and philanthropy.
7. To support legislation favorable to the fund-raising profession.
8. To enlist, organize, and support members for the achievement of these purposes.

Two years ago, the board, fortunately, took it upon itself to reorganize the policy process of the Society. There had been an unwieldy and inefficient 147 members on this board. Now it is kept at a manageable 35, accompanied by a national assembly to provide a membership voice for all the chapters. These activities are not only lifting the professional level of philanthropic fund-raising, they are opening a much wider path to attract and train the next generation. There are many who say that fund-raising still has a long way to go to become a real profession. I disagree. We are almost there.

LESSONS LEARNED

Separately, the programs and policies of all seven of these organizations contribute a lion's share toward American philanthropy's growth and effectiveness. If they would combine forces to attack some of philanthropy's problems the effect would be tremendous. "No man is an island, entire of itself."[2] Neither is any organization.

---

2. John Donne (1572–1630).

EPILOGUE

Dealing With Philanthropy's Critical Issues

Reflecting on nearly 50 years in the field of philanthropy brings to mind the story of a TV interview with a Cape Cod senior citizen. The commentator asked him,

"Have you lived here very long?"

"Yup. All my life."

"Oh. How old are you?"

"Just reached 83."

"Wow, I'll bet you've seen a lot of changes."

"Yup. And, I've been against every damned one of them."

No, I'm not against all the changes since my first fund-raising campaign back at the Metropolitan Museum of Art in 1946. In fact, I feel we all should both approve and be deeply proud of the changes that make today's American philanthropy so great.

As I have believed for so long, this has become a wonderful field for women. It is no longer a "male" bastion. Sixty percent of the members of National Society of Fund-Raising Executives are women. The fact that the presidents of NSFRE, the Foundation Center, the John D. & Catherine T. MacArthur Foundation, the New York Community Trust, the Commonwealth Fund, the United Way of America, and the AAFRC are all women show that any "glass ceiling" that still exists has become pretty lofty (unfortunately, salary differential is still far from resolution). The field is much better for the changes and I don't mind at all being a member of a growing minority which feels that way.

The fund-raising profession (many might disagree, but I feel, we have almost become a profession) is now respected by most. I can still remember the wife of one of my John Price Jones Colleagues in 1949 saying to several of us, "At last, I've found a way to avoid generating anguished and disapproving looks when I answer the question 'What does your husband do?' I no longer say he's a fund-raiser, I just say that he plays piano in a bordello. This doesn't create nearly as much fuss." Now, all components of the field talk to each other formally in seminars and informally during constant joint efforts to improve the field. There is growing recognition by most that we are part of an interconnected initiative and it requires individual and collective cooperation to make things work well.

The greed and self-interest so widespread in the Eighties is subsiding, but Americans must be convinced to give more. The gap between needs and resources steadily grows wider. Most leaders in the field agree that more must be done to make the philanthropic process more effective.

The number of philanthropic centers and studies of philanthropy in colleges and universities is growing. This is proving to be a very effective way to expand both the knowledge and understanding of the next generation about the important role philanthropy is playing in improving our society. Inevitably, this will help to attract more young people into careers in the nonprofit sector. I am against the exponential growth of techniques that commercialize the solicitation of charitable gifts through phone-mail, telemarketing, and massive repetitive direct mail. They are impersonal and not cost-effective. Because there is so much of this, the public is becoming skeptical about all charities at a time when we must do more to foster the voluntary spirit.

I take comfort in the fact that those in the philanthropic field have always been aware that funds for programs must come from voluntary giving. This leads to high ethical standards and practices which are respected and followed by all but a very few. To paraphrase John D. McDonald:

> Integrity is not a conditional word. It doesn't blow in the wind or change with the weather. It is your inner image of yourself, and if you look in there and see a (person) who won't cheat, then you know (you) never will. Integrity is not a search for the rewards of integrity. Maybe all you'll ever get for it is the largest kick in the ass the world can provide. It is not supposed to be a productive asset. Crime pays a *lot* better.[1]

Philanthropy's critical issues remain many and complex. To help

---

1. McDonald, John D. *The Turquoise Lament*, J. P. Lippencott Company (1973).

EPILOGUE

it reach the new level of effectiveness required by the times, we need to develop more effective ways to:

- Reduce parochialism and open up wider communications between donors and donees, and the varied philanthropic causes.
- Set and adopt a universal code of ethics.
- Persuade more able young people to make philanthropy their careers.
- Apply the principles of our pluralistic society to improve the partnership between the private and the public sectors.
- Educate state and federal legislators and their administrative staffs on the importance of making philanthropy more effective—which cannot be accomplished with punitive legislation and reduced tax incentives.
- Help board members and trustees accept increased responsibility for their stewardship.
- Increase the interest in and development of philanthropic studies at *all* levels of education.
- Establish a single generic certification process for all professionals.
- Increase the level of professionalism of fund-raisers, foundation and corporate program officers, and trustees.
- Increase the public's understanding of philanthropy and fund-raising.
- Attract, train and retain more minorities.
- Identify and train leaders in the new generation.
- Preserve for posterity the wisdom and experience of the older generation.
- Increase accountability.
- Establish guidelines and ranges for executive salaries and benefits to ensure the principle that the mission of all philanthropic organizations is never secondary to personal gain.
- Compensate all staff on the basis of skill, responsibilities and seniority, regardless of gender or ethnic background.
- Reduce the commercialization of the field and strengthen the essential values of voluntarism.

Marshaling the combined forces of key nonprofit organizations to address these issues can make a substantial difference. Provided the key nonprofit organizations would agree to participate, two steps could well mark our future path: One, design and distribute a survey questionnaire to representative members of key organizations to obtain consensus on which issues are the most critical. And two, using the survey results as an agenda, schedule a two-day retreat for the top officers and board members of the organizations to discuss and plan how they can combine forces to deal with the most pressing problems.

The programs of organizations such as the American Association of Fund-Raising Counsel (AAFRC), the Council on Foundations, the Council for Advancement and Support of Education (CASE), the Association for Healthcare Philanthropy (AHP), the Foundation Center, the National Society of Fund-Raising Executives (NSFRE), and the INDEPENDENT SECTOR are accomplishing a great deal. But as individual organizations, their programs are less efficient and inevitably duplicate others directed at improving philanthropy. They need to work together with a common agenda addressing shared concerns.

I've seen lots of changes, but much stays the same. The philanthropic process, I repeat, still thrives best only if it has all five essential ingredients:

1. A strong case;
2. Top and committed leadership;
3. Cultivated and enthusiastic volunteers;
4. Enablers (good fund-raising managers);
5. And, the most important of all, the voluntary spirit.

As I near the half-century mark in the field, I hope I will still see the day when the key organizations really get together and prove how much more effective they can make philanthropy for our society. What a wonderful harvest this would be.

John J. Schwartz
Westport, Connecticut, April 20, 1993

APPENDICES

APPENDIX A

Peterson Commission 1968:

Peter G. Peterson
  Chairman of the Commission and Chairman, Bell and Howell
J. Paul Austin
  Chairman, The Coca-Cola Company
Daniel Bell
  Professor of Sociology, Harvard University
Daniel P. Bryant
  Chairman, Bekins Van and Storage Company
James Chambers
  President and Publisher, *Dallas Times-Herald*
Sheldon S. Cohen
  Former Commissioner of Internal Revenue, U.S. Treasury Department
Thomas B. Curtis
  Former U.S. Representative
Paul A. Freund
  Professor, Harvard University Law School
Martin Friedman
  Director, Walker Art Center
Patricia Roberts Harris
  Former Dean and Professor, Howard University Law School
A. Leon Higginbotham, Jr.
  U.S. District Court Judge

Lane Kirkland
   Secretary Treasurer, AFL-CIO
Philip R. Lee, M.D.
   Chancellor, University of California
Edward H. Levi
   President, University of Chicago
Franklin A. Long
   Director for Program on Science, Technology and Society, Cornell University
A. S. Mike Monroney
   Former U.S. Senator

APPENDIX B

National Council on Philanthropy (NCOP) 1979:

Kenneth L. Albrecht
   Chairman of the Executive Committee and Vice President Corporate Affairs, The Equitable Life Assurance Society of the United States
James S. Lipscomb
   Chairman of the Board and Executive Director, The George Gund Foundation
Rosemary Higgins Cass
   Vice Chairman of the Board and Attorney at Law
Robert W. Thill
   Vice Chairman of the Board and Public Relations Manager, American Telephone & Telegraph
L. Philip Ewald
   Treasurer of the Board and Vice President, National Executive Service Corps
Ruth J. Abram
   Executive Director, Women's Action Alliance
William Aramony
   National Executive, United Way of America
Fred G. Armstong
   Chairman, Arctic Environmental Council
Judy Barker
   Executive Director, Borden Foundation Inc.
Joseph M. Bertotti

APPENDICES

    Manager, Corporate Educational Relations, General Electric Company
William L. Bondurant
    Executive Director, Mary Reynolds Babcock Foundation, Inc.
Leo J. Brennan, Jr.
    Associate Director, Ford Motor Company Fund
Henry R. Brett
    Corporate Contributions Counselor, Standard Oil Company of CA
Jonathan B. Cook
    Executive Director, The Support Center
Walter D. Eichner
    Executive Director, Atlantic Richfield Foundation
Samuel Goddard
    Goddard and Ahern
John R. Haire
    President, Council for Financial Aid to Education
Thomas R. Horton
    IBM, Director of University Relations
Franklyn A. Johnson
    Assistant to the President, Barry College
Robert C. Lauppe
    Vice President, St. Paul Companies, Inc.
Warren R. Lewis
    Secretary, Financial Aid Committee-Corporate Relations
Carlos W. Luis
    Vice President, Public Affairs
John R. Meekin
    Director of Philanthropic Activities, The Chase Manhattan Bank
Charles M. Menagh
    Consultant
Alfred C. Neal
    Economist
Patrick F. Noonan
    President, The Nature Conservancy
Brian O'Connell
    President, National Council on Philanthropy
Doris O'Connor
    Senior Vice President, Shell Companies Foundation
Michael J. O'Connor
    The Lubrizol Foundation
Helen L. O'Rourke
    Vice President, Philanthropic Advisory Service Division

Manning M. Pattillo, Jr.
    President, Oglethorpe University
Ormsbee W. Robinson
    Director, International Program, National Council on Philanthropy
John J. Schwartz
    President, American Association of Fund-Raising Counsel
Gene L. Schwilck
    President, The Danforth Foundation
John L. Sundheimer
    Director, Corporate Contributions, Republic Steel Corporation
W. Homer Turner
    Consultant, Academy for Educational Development
Edward H. Van Ness
    Executive Vice President, National Health Council
Homer C. Wadsworth
    Director, The Cleveland Foundation
Edward T. Weaver
    Executive Director, American Public Welfare Association
Bevery With
    Secretary to the Board, National Council on Philanthropy

APPENDIX C

Filer Commission 1974

John H. Filer
    Chairman of the Board and Chairman, Aetna Life & Casualty
Leonard L. Silverstein
    Executive Director of the Board
James W. Abernathy
    Director of Research, Grantsmanship Center
William H. Bowen
    President, Commerical National Bank
Lester Crown
    President, Material Service Corporation
C. Douglas Dillon
    Chairman, U.S. & Foreign Securities Corporation
Edwin D. Etherington
    Former President, Wesleyan University

Bayard Ewing
    Tillinghast, Collins & Graham
Frances Tarlton Farenthold
    Past Chairperson, National Women's Polical Caucus
Max M. Fisher
    Chairman, United Brands Company
The Most Rev. Raymond J. Gallagher
    Bishop of Lafayette-in-Indiana
Earl G. Graves
    Publisher, Black Enterprise
Paul R. Haas
    President and Chairman, Corpus Christi Oil & Gas Company
Walter A. Haas, Jr.
    Chairman, Levi Strauss & Company
Philip M. Klutznick
    Klutznick Investments
Ralph Lazarus
    Chairman, Federated Department Stores, Inc.
Herbert E. Longenecker
    President Emeritus, Tulane University
Elizabeth J. McCormack
    Special Assistant to the President, Rockefeller Brothers Fund, Inc.
Walter J. McNerney
    President, Blue Cross Association
William H. Morton
    Trustee, Dartmouth College
John M. Musser
    President and Director, General Service Foundation
Jon O. Newman
    Judge, U.S. District Court
Graciela Olivarez
    State Planning Officer
Alan Pifer
    President, Carnegie Corporation of New York
George Romney
    Chairman, National Center for Voluntary Action
William Matson Roth
    Regent, University of California
Althea T. L. Simmons
    Director for Education Programs, NAACP Specoal Contribution Fund

The Rev. Leon H. Sullivan
: Pastor, Zion Baptist Church

David B. Truman
: President, Mount Holyoke College

Special Consultants to The Filer Commission:

Howard A. Bolton
: Milbank,Tweed, Hadley & McCloy

Martin S. Feldstein
: Professor of Economics, Harvard University

Wade Greene
: Writer and Editor

Theodore J. Jacobs
: Former Director, Center for Study of Responsive Law

Porter McKeever
: Associate, John D. Rockefeller 3rd

Ralph L. Nelson
: Professor of Economics, Queens College, City University of NY

Waldemar A. Nielsen
: Director of Program on Problems of American Pluralism, Aspent Instiute for Humanistic Studies

John J. Schwartz
: President, American Association of Fund-Raising Counsel

Sally J. Shroyer
: New York

Carlton E. Spitzer
: Vice President, T. J. Ross & Associates

Stanley S. Surrey
: Jeremiah Smith Professor of Law

Adam Yarmolinsky
: Ralph Waldo Emerson University Professor, University of Massachusetts

Paul N. Ylviasaker
: Dean, Graduate School of Education, Harvard University

APPENDIX D

Coalition of National Voluntary Organization (CONVO) 1978:

Bayard Ewing
: Chairman of the Board and President, National Information Bureau

Philip Bernstein
  Vice Chairman of the Board and Executive Vice President, Council of Jewish Federations and Welfare Funds
John J. Schwartz
  Secretary Treasurer of the Board and President, American Association of Fund-Raising Counsel, Inc.
William Aramony
  National Executive, United Way of America
Rev. Msgr. Lawrence J. Corcoran
  Executive Director, National Conference of Catholic Charities
Dr. Luther Foster
  President, Tuskegee Institute
David Freeman
  President, Council on Foundations, Inc.
Dr. Claire Fulcher
  First Vice President, American Association of University Women
Carl Holman
  President, National Urban Coalition
Pauline Miles
  Assistant Vice President, National Health Council
Gov. George Romney
  Chairman, National Center for Voluntery Action
Hope Skillman Schary
  President, National Council of Women in the U.S.
Wesley Uhlman
  Trustee, American Council for the Arts
Cynthia Wedel
  Director of Volunteers, American National Red Cross

APPENDIX E

The 501 (C) (3) Group 1986:

Rev. Charles V. Bergstrom
  Executive Director, Office of Government Affairs
Robert O. Bothwell
  Executive Director, National Committee for Responsive Philathropy
Alan C. Davis

Chairperson and Vice President, Govenment Relations, American Cancer Society
Ms. Deirdre Dessingue
   Assistant General Counsel, United States Catholic Conference
John Edie
   General Counsel, Council on Foundations
Dr. Aaron E. Gast
   President, United Presbyterian Foundation
Jack Herman
   Secretary and Director of Development, Hospital for Joint Diseases Orthopedic Institute
Walter A. Jensen
   Director, Business & Finance, Lutheran Council in the USA
Kenneth H. Liles
   Counsel, Sutherland, Asbill & Brennan
Gordon Manser
Leon O. Marion
   Tolstoy Foundation
Dr. Roland C. Matthies
   Committee on Gift Annuities
Jack Moskowitz
   Treasurer and Senior Vice President, Federal Government Relations
Nordan C. Murphy
   Assistant General Secretary for Stewardship, National Council of the Church of Christ in the USA
John Holt Myers
   Williams, Myers & Quiggle
George E. Reed
   Office of General Counsel, United States Catholic Conference
James R. Reed
   President, Christian Church Foundation
John J. Schwartz
   President, American Association of Fund-Raising Counsel, Inc.
George L. Shearin
   Ray, Trotti, Hemphill, Shearin & Finfrock, PC
Hayden W. Smith
   Senior Vice President, Council for Financial Aid to Education
Robert M. Smucker
   Vice President, Government Relations, Independent Sector

APPENDICES 209

Dr. Elvis Stahr
    Atorney-at-Law, Chickering & Gregory
Sheldon E. Steinbach
    General Counsel, Division of Governmental Relations, American Council on Education
Leonard W. Stern
    Executive Director, The National Assembly
Conrad Teitell
    Prerau and Teitell
Dr. W. Homer Turner
    Attorney-at-Law and Consultant, Academy for Financial Development
Stanley S. Weithorn
    Baer, Marks & Upham
J. Richard Wilson
    President, National Society of Fund-Raising Executives

APPENDIX F

Independent Sector Organizing Committee 1978–1979:

Ruth Abram
    Executive Director, Women's Action Alliance
Kenneth L. Albrecht
    Vice President, Corporate Affairs, The Equitable Life Assurance Society of the United States
Philip Bernstein
    Executive Vice President, Counsil of Jewish Federations and Welfare Funds
Landrum Bolling
    Chairman, Council on Foundations
Leo J. Brennan, Jr.
    Associate Director, Ford Motor Company Fund
Rosemary Higgins Cass
    Attorney-at-Law
Barber Conable
Jack Conway
    Senior Vice President, United Way of America

Bayard Ewing
   President, National Information Bureau
Joseph Fisher
John Gardner
   Chairman and Founder Chairman, Common Cause
Carl Holman
   President, National Urban Coalition
James P. Hosey
   Vice President and Executive Director, U.S. Steel Foundation
Thomas Leavitt
   Director, Herbert F. Johnson Museum of Art, Cornell University
James S. Lipscomb
   Executive Director, The George Gund Foundation
Waldemar Nielsen
   Waldemar Nielsen, Inc.
Brian O'Connell
   Staff Director of the Organizing Committee
Manning M. Pattillo, Jr.
   President, Oglethorpe University
Alan Pifer
   President, Carnegie Corporation
David Ramage
   President, The New World Foundation
John J. Schwartz
   President, American Association of Fund-Raising Counsel
Eleanor Sheldon
   President, Social Science Research Council
Robert W. Thill
   Public Relations Manager, American Telephone & Telegraph
Glenn Watts
   President, Communication Workers of America
Cynthia Wedel
   Director of Volunteers, American Red Cross
Sara-Alyce Wright
   Executive Director, YWCA of the USA
Raul Yzaguirre
   National Director, National Council of LaRaza

APPENDIX G

Independent Sector Charter Board 1980:

John Gardner
    Chairperson of the Board and Founding Chairman, Common Cause
Landrum Bolling
    Vice Chairperson of the Board and Chairman and Chief Executive Officer, Council on Foundations
Kenneth H. Dayton
    Vice Chairman of the Board and Chairman of the Board of Directors and Chief Executive Officer, Dayton Hudson Corporation
Vera Foster
    Vice Chairperson of the Board and VOLUNTEER (Formally Center for Voluntary Action)
Raul Yzaguirre
    Vice Chairperson of the Board and President, National Council of LaRaza
Kennth Albrecht
    Secretary of the Board and Vice President, The Equitable Life Assurance Society of the USA
Mary Ripley
    Treasurer of the Board and President, VOLUNTEER
Luis Alvarez
    President, National Urban Fellows
William Aramony
    National Executive, United Way of America
Judy Barker
    Director, Civic Affairs and Executive Director, Borden Foundation, Inc.
Philip Bernstein
    Executive Vice President, Council of Jewish Federations
Janet Brown
    Executive Director, Environmental Defense Fund
Frank T. Cary
    Chairman of the Board and Chief Executive Officer, IBM
Rosemary Higgins Cass
    Practicing Attorney and Member of the Bar of New York and New Jersey
Carolyn Sue Chin
    Marketing Manager, AT&T

Linda Hawes Clever
: Chairman, Department of Occupational Health, Presbyterian Hospital of Pacific Medical Center

Msgr. Lawrence J. Corcoran
: Executive Director, National Conference of Catholic Charities

Ada Deer
: The Native American Rights Fund

Walter D. Eichner
: Executive Director, Atlantic Richfield Foundation

Bayard Ewing
: Partner, Tillinghast, Collins, and Graham

John Filer
: Chairman of the Board, Aetna Life and Casualty

Samuel Goddard
: Former Governor of Arizona

Nancy Hanks
: Vice Chairperson, Rockefeller Brothers Fund and Former Director, National Endowment of the Arts

Andrew Heiskeli
: Chairman of the Board and Chief Executive Officer, Time Inc.

Carl Holman
: President, The National Urban Coalition

Boisfeuillet Jones
: Managing Director, Lettie Pate Evans Foundation and President, Emily and Ernest Woodruff Foundation

Juanita Morris Kreps
: Former Secretary, Department of Commerce

Thomas Leavitt
: Director, Herbert F. Johnson Museum of Art

James Lipscomb
: Executive Director, George Gund Foundation

Richard Lyman
: President, Stanford University

Leon A. Marion
: Executive Director, American Council of Voluntary Agencies for Foreign Service

Walter V. McNerney
: National President, Blue Cross-Blue Shield

Steven Muller
: President, The Johns Hopkins University and The Johns Hopkins Hospital

Waldemar A. Nielsen
   Waldemar A. Nielsen Associates
Martin Paley
   Executive Director, San Francisco Foundation
Antonia Pantoja
   President, Graduate School for Urban Resources & Social Policy, University of San Diego
David Ramage, Jr.
   Executive Director, The New World Foundation
John J. Schwartz
   President, American Association of Fund-Raising Counsel, Inc.
Janet C. Taylor
   Executive Director, Associated Foundations of Greater Boston
Christine Topping
   Vice President and General Counsel, National Association of Independent Colleges and Universities
Edward H. Van Ness
   Executive Vice President, National Health Council
Faye Wattleton
   President, Planned Parenthood Federation
Cynthia C. Wedel
   President, World Council of Churches
Harold H. Wilke
   Board, Goodwill Industries and Board, First National Easter Seals and President's Commission on Employing the Handicapped Rehabilitation International
Sara-Alyce Wright
   Executive Director, YWCA of the USA
Adam Yarmolinsky
   Practicing Attorney, Kominers, Fort, Schlefer & Boyer

INDEX

501(C)(3) Group, 71–73, 79, 81, 118, 121, 147–48
  members of, 207–9
Acheson, Barclay, 34
Adams, Lane W., 52, 146
Advisory Board on Philanthropic Policy, 77–79, 85, 117, 120
Albrecht, Kenneth, 118, 127
American Alumni Council (AAC), 42
American Association of Fund-Raising Counsel, Inc. (AAFRC), 40–41, 54–55, 56, 60–68, 85
  fiftieth anniversary of, 163–64
  future of, 186–87
  state legislative monitoring program, 125–26
  Trust for Philanthropy, 161–63
  See also East-West conferences
American Cancer Society, 51–54, 55, 63
American College Public Relations Association (ACPRA), 42
Andrews, F. Emerson, 42, 191
Andrus, Ethel Percy, 182–83
Aramony, William, 93, 118
Armsey, James W., 87
Armstrong, Edwin, 60
Association for Healthcare Philanthropy (AHP), 187–89
Association of Fund-Raising Directors (AFRD), 41, 50

Badeau, John S., 31–32, 33, 34–37, 43
Bailey, John N., 173
Barnett, A. Creed, 60
Bepko, Gerald L., 168–69
Bergan, Mrs. John J., 69, 70
Bergstrom, Edwin, 53
Bernstein, Philip, 93, 118, 120, 133
Biggins, James A., 172
Black colleges, 87–89
Blumenthal, Michael, 120, 122
Board of directors
  responsibilities of, xv–xvi
Bolling, Landrum, 128
Boris, Elizabeth T., 152
Boskin, Michael, 111
Bothwell, Robert, 122
Brakeley & Co., Inc., G. A., 42–43
Brakeley, George A., Jr., xiv, 42–43, 44, 48, 102, 170
Brammer, Lowell H., 61
Brecht, Charles, 68, 69
Brewer, Melvin D., 102
Brewster, Kingman, 166–67

Bright, Sallie, 27, 28, 30
Brophy, Michael, 165, 166
Brosnan, Cyril, 49
Bryant, James W., 87, 88
Buchanan, Peter McE., 189
Buttenweiser, Benjamin J., 74–75

Call, Edward G., 189
Cameron, Carlton, 28, 30, 31
Campaign for Philanthropy, 90–94
Carr, Oscar, 126
Carter, Jimmy, 120, 122, 132, 148
Chandler, John W., 162, 173
Charities Aid Foundation, 165
Cheever, John, 70
Church, David M., 40–41, 54, 55, 60, 63, 65–66, 73–74
CIAO, 153
Clarke, Gale, 194–95
Clee, Gilbert, 29
Clinton, Hillary Rodham, 188
Coalition for Public Good Through Private Initiatives, 92, 93, 94, 95, 96, 97, 118, 119
Coalition of National Voluntary Organizations (CONVO), 118–21, 126–33
  members of, 206–7
Commerce and industry effort (C&I), 10–11
Commission on Private Philanthropy and Public Needs, 100
Community Service Society, 10–12, 27–30
Conable, Barber, 116, 128
Conferences and seminars, 69, 81–82
  See also East-West Conference
Congress, U.S.
  efforts to control charities, 123–25
  See also Taxes; Tax reform acts
Cook, Kenneth G., 183
Cooperation in philanthropic community, xv, 86, 92–94
Council for Advancement and Support of Education (CASE), 42, 189–90
Council of Foundations, 41–42, 190–91
Crown, Lester, 105
Currie, Robert, 69

Davis, Stanley P., 10, 12, 27–28, 32
Dewey, Richard E., 120, 121, 126
Dickenson, Hugh D., 180–82
Dillon, C. Douglas, 104, 117, 120
Dilworth, J. Richardson, 27–29
Ditchley Foundation Conference on Private Giving (1982), 148–51
Dodge, Cleveland E., 33

Donee Group, 106–10, 117
Donors
  anniversary of gifts from, 10
  increasing gifts from, 29
  with large gifts, 47
  reasons for giving, 71
Dorsey, Eugene, 171
Downes, Michael G., 176
Duncan, Robert F., 6, 7, 66–67, 89–90, 96, 178

East-West conferences
  (1967), 68–71
  (1968), 74–75
  (1970), 85–86
Economic climate, 6
Edwards, Richard, 153
Eighties, The, 136–84
Eisenberg, Pablo, 106–7
Engelhardt, Sara L., 165, 192
Enthusiasm, 27, 37–38, 70
Ethics, xvi, 67, 112, 139–40, 190, 195
Ewing, Bayard, 93, 116, 118, 120, 127, 127–28
Executives
  responsibilities of, xv-xvi
  See also Ethics

Feasibility studies, 8, 16, 45
Feldstein, Charles R., 102, 105, 163
Feldstein, Martin S., 94, 111, 122, 147
Fifties, The, 18–38
Filer, John H., 99–106, 110, 116
Filer Commission, 78, 98, 99–106, 108, 110–13
  members of, 204–6
Foerst, John G., Jr. (Jack), 143, 165, 172, 175, 178, 179
Ford Foundation, 44, 87–89, 97
Foreign Policy Association (FPA), 48–51
Forquer, Gus, 13
Foundation Center, The, 41–42, 191–92
Foundations
  charges against, 76
  See also Peterson Commission
Frank, Curtis, 93
Frantzreb, Arthur C., 43, 44, 45
Freeman, Douglas, 177
Freemont-Smith, Marion, 112–13, 156
Fuller, Bill, 36
Fund-raising, 59–82
  professionalism in, 66, 138
  reasons for giving, 71
  responsibilities of consultants, 24, 67–68

G. A. Brakeley & Co., Inc., 42–43
Gallup, George, 8
Gardner, John W., xv, 127, 128, 129–30, 134, 144, 154, 154–55, 167, 170, 193
Geever, Inc., J. C., 133–34
Geever, Jane C., 133–34, 174
Gemmel, Edgar M., 52
Gifford, Walter S., 10

Giving USA, 41, 62, 65, 66, 73–74, 86, 101, 151–53, 158, 161
Glamann, Kristof, 149
Glaser, John S., 93, 118, 126
Goheen, Robert, 93
Goldstein, Henry (Hank), 96–97
Gough, Samuel N., Jr., 88
Government
  and partnership with philanthropy, xv, 77–78, 80, 95
Greenfield, James M., 156
Grenzebach, John, 161, 164
Grove City College (Pa.), 12–15
Gumbrecht, Albert C. (Gummie), 10, 11
Gurin, Maurice G., 87, 89, 162–63, 170

Halsey, Stephen, 165
Halsey, William F., 8–9
Hanrahan, Bill, 179
Hanson, Abel, 41
Harlan, Bob, 153
Harrah, Jeanne, 170
Harris, Thomas S., 166, 176
Harvard Business School, 89–90
Hawkins, Roger, 26
Hayes, Joanne, 154, 173
Hayes, Samuel P., 49
Haynes, David W., 23–24, 26, 27
Hertel, Frank, 12
Hill & Knowlton, 130
Hiller, Eldridge, 54
Hodgkinson, Virginia Ann, 144–45, 152, 170
Holt, J. C., 166
Hopkins, Bruce R., 156
Horowitz, Samuel, 43
Howard University, 8
Hubbard, Frank M., 178
Hubbard, Fred P., 44, 45

INDEPENDENT SECTOR, 73, 91, 130, 131, 132, 133, 134, 141–42, 143–44, 147, 158, 164, 192–94
  members of charter board of, 211–13
  members of organizing committee, 209–10
Indiana University Center on Philanthropy, 168–72
Internal Revenue Service, 76, 111
  See 501(c)(3) Group; Taxes; Tax reform acts
International Schools Foundation, 43–44
Interphil Conference (1985), 165–67

Jackson, Andrew, 46–47
John Price Jones Co., Inc., 4, 6–8, 11, 16
Johnson, Charles A., 168–69
Jones, John Price, 6–8, 66
Joseph, James A., 190–91
Joseph, Keith, 166

Kersting, Donald L., 61
Kersting & Brown Co., 28
Ketchum, Carlton G., 16, 60, 66

INDEX

Ketchum, David S., 61
Ketler, Weir C., 13
Khouri, Hannah, 35–36, 36
Kilberg, Bobbie, 129
Klutznick, Philip M., 101, 102, 103, 105, 106, 117, 118
Knauft, Edwin B., 102, 103
Knox, John P., Jr., 69

Lang, Currier, 21
Lang, Eugene M., 171
Lang, Harlan F., 86
Lansing, Ambrose, 5
Lawson, Charles E. (Chuck), 161, 162, 165
Layton, Daphne, 163
Leader, George M., 68
Leadership
  importance of, 5, 9, 16, 33, 38, 67, 68, 70, 103
Leiberman, Joseph I., 156
Levis, Wilson C. (Bill), 140–41
Lewis, Patricia F., 195
Lipscomb, James, 133
Logue, Emily, 10
Long, Russell B., 110, 121–22
Longenecker, Herbert E., 116
Lundberg, Joan McC., 86
Lunzy, Herman, 89
Lyman, Richard W. (Dick), 153, 154, 163, 164, 170

McClain, Austin V., 61, 64, 66, 74, 75
McCormack, Elizabeth, 170
MacDonald, Charlotte, 25
McDonald, John D., 198
McGee, George C., 33
McGinly, William C., 188
McGoldrick, Ellen, 141
McKeever, Porter, 103
McNereney, Walter J., 118, 129
Martin, John, 79
Marts, Arnaud C., 16, 66
Matching funds, 13, 14, 44, 87
Maul, Baldwin, 25
Medeo, Marie, 64, 146
Medical and Surgical Relief Committee, 8–9
Metropolitan Museum of Art, 4–5
Millett, Richard C., 69
Mills, Wilbur D., 72, 100, 110
Minorities, xiv
Montgomery, Robert, 8
Moran, Alfred, 30, 32
Morris, James T., 173
Moynihan, Daniel Patrick, 133
Muir, Malcolm, 8

Nason, John W., 48, 49
National Association of Attorneys General (NAAG), 155–56
National Association of State Charity Officials (NASCO), 155–57

National Center for Charitable Statistics (NCCS), 140–42
National Charities Information Bureau (NCIB), 139–40
National Committee for Responsive Philanthropy, 122
National Council on Philanthropy (NCOP), 73, 82, 126–30
  conference (1975), 116–17
  members of, 202–4
National Institute of Continuing Education (NICE), 96–97
National Institute of Independent Colleges and Universities (NIICU), 144–46
National Philanthropy Day, 177–79
National Society of Fund-Raisers (NSFR), 41, 50
National Society of Fund-Raising Executives (NSFRE), 142–43, 194–96
Neal, Alfred C., 93
Near East Foundation, 31–37
Nelson, Ralph, 152
Newberry, J. O., 61, 91, 97, 164
Newhill, Edward B., 69
Newhouse, Samuel I., 45, 47
Nielsen, Waldemar, 129
Nixon, Richard M., 78–79
Norwalk Hospital (Conn.), 20–23

O'Brien, Richard F., 69
O'Connell, Brian, 127, 128, 143, 145, 146, 148, 150, 151, 174, 194
Olcott, William, 174
Ormstedt, David E., 156
O'Rourke, Helen, 139, 147

Pace-setting gifts, 48, 109
Parochialism, xv
  See also Cooperation in philanthropic community
Patillo, Manning M., 69
Payton, Robert L., 169, 171
Peace Corps, 48
Personality clashes, 21
Peterson Commission, 75–79, 82, 85, 99, 113
  members of, 201–2
Peterson, Peter G., 75–79, 85
Pew, J. Howard, 12, 13, 14
Philanthropy
  cooperation in community of, xv, 86, 92–94
  definition of, xiii
  future of, xvii, 185–96
  and government in partnership, xv, 77–78, 80, 95
  international, xvi
  lessons learned, 16–17, 37–38, 55–56, 81–82, 97, 134–35, 157–58, 183–84, 196
  minority involvement in, xiv
  post World War II, 3–17
  public image of, 90, 92
  reasons for giving, 71

Philanthropy *(Continued)*
  training for, xiv-xv
  women in, 22, 25, 34, 70, 135, 197
  See also Fund-raising
Pierce, Lyman L., 66
Pifer, Alan, 104–5, 116, 170
Pope, Bayard, 10
Powell, Edgar D., 143
Powell-Tuck, James B. (PT), 20–23
Public image, 90, 92

Quotas in fund-raising, 22–23

Raybin, Arthur D., 161, 162, 165, 172
Read, Patricia, 152
Reagan, Ronald, 145, 147, 148, 158
Reed, Ed, 14, 15
Reynolds, James R., 69
Rice, Mary B., 172, 173
Rich, Wilma Shields, 41–42
Rockefeller, David, xiii
Rockefeller, John D. 3RD, 43, 75, 81, 99–100, 104, 110, 129
Rosenbaum, David E., 122
Rosenbaum, Nelson, 152
Rossman, Newell, 46
Rosso, Henry A. (Hank), 168
Rudney, Gabriel G., 100, 102, 152

Salamon, Lester M., 147, 148, 150, 152
Schaller, Howard G., 169, 171
Schnaue, Fred, 151, 152
Schreyer, Blair, 143
Schwartz, John J.
  receives United Way award, 146
Scott, S. Spencer, 11–12
Seventies, The, 83–135
Seymour, Harold J. (Si), xiv, xvii, 51–52, 53, 64–65, 101
Sheehan, Betty, 13, 14
Sheehan, Donald T., 13, 14
Shriver, Sargeant, 48
Shultz, George P., 100, 110
Silverstein, Leonard L., 100–105, 116
Simon, William E., 100, 110, 117, 120
Sixties, The, 39–56, 59–82
Sloan Foundation, Alfred P., 90
Smith, Hayden, 94, 147, 148, 151, 152
Smith, Raleigh, 69
Smucker, Robert A., 143
Social attitudes, 6
Speidel, Jess, 50, 51–54, 63
Staff meetings, 30
Stettinius, Edwin R., 8
Stevens, Harley C., 33
Strano, Richard, 153
Street, Wolcott, 65–66, 170
Suffern, Kevin, 156

Sumariwalla, Russy, 142, 152
Surrey, Stanley, 122, 133
Swanson, Victor, 53
Syracuse University, 44–48

Taxes, 71–73, 76, 82, 93, 94–96, 109, 110, 111, 149
Tax reform acts
  (1969), 77, 79–81
  (1973), 95–96
  proposals for (1977), 121–23
Taylor, Alford H., 174
Teitell, Conrad, 69
Tempel, Eugene, 168–69, 170
Thomas, John H., 143
Thompson, Robert, 173
Tolley, William P., 44, 45, 46
Tousley, Claire M., 10, 12, 27
Traveler's Aid Society, 23–27
Turner, William Homer, 69
Tuthill, Erwin D. (Tut), 54–55

United Kingdom, 149–50, 179–82
United Way of America, 93
  gives award to John Schwartz, 146
  scandal at, xiv, xv

Van Deerlin, Lionel, 123–25
van der Voort, Roberta, 173–74
Van Til, Jon, 162
Voluntarism, xvi-xvii
  motivation for, 27
  reenlistment of, 29
  White House conference on (1979), 132–33
  women as, 22, 34

Walker, Thomas, 153
Wallace, Lila Acheson, 34
Ward, Charles Sumner, 16, 66
Watson, Thomas J., 5
Weeks, Carnes (Piggy), 8–9
Whalen, Byrne P., 74, 86
Wilson, Charles H., 124
Wilson, J. Richard (Dick), 142, 153, 166, 175, 177–78, 194–95
Wilson, Roger A., 86
Winternitz, Emanuel, 4–5
Women, 25
  discrimination against, 22, 197
  as fund-raisers, 70, 135
  as volunteers, 22, 34
Wood, James R., 170
Woodward, Laurence N. (Larry), 72, 79
World Fund-raising Conference (1988), 175–77

Yarmolinsky, Adam, 112–13, 151, 156
Ylvisaker, Paul, 102